AMERICAN EXPLORATION AND TRAVEL

Indian Sketches

Indian Sketches

TAKEN DURING AN EXPEDITION TO THE

Pawnee Tribes

[1833]

BY JOHN TREAT IRVING, JR.

EDITED AND ANNOTATED BY

JOHN FRANCIS McDERMOTT

UNIVERSITY OF OKLAHOMA PRESS

NORMAN

Edited by John Francis McDermott
Published by the University of Oklahoma Press

Indian Sketches, 1955
Up the Missouri with Audubon, The Journal of Edward Harris, 1951
The Western Journals of Washington Irving, 1944
Tixier's Travels on the Osage Prairies
(translated by Albert J. Salvan), 1940

Library of Congress Catalog Card Number: 55-6365

New edition copyright 1955 by the University of Oklahoma Press
Publishing Division of the University
Composed and printed at Norman, Oklahoma, u.s.a.
by the University of Oklahoma Press
First printing

To the Memory of
ALICE IRWIN KENDRICK
My Mother-in-law

Editor's Preface

In June, 1835, John Treat Irving, Jr.'s *Indian Sketches, Taken during an Expedition to the Pawnee Tribes* came off the press in Philadelphia. Before this time, proof sheets had been sent to London for the English edition, which appeared in the same year. In 1888 Irving published a revised version of his work in one volume; here he added introductory material and inserted further details and anecdotes. The present edition is a faithful reprinting of the first American edition with the new matter of 1888 acknowledged where pertinent.

For special courtesies I wish to thank, first of all, Messrs. Walter V. and Harold Irving, grandsons of the author, for the opportunity to examine closely the manuscript of the 1888 edition, for the photograph of the 1836 miniature of Irving, and for many interesting and useful suggestions in relation to this project. Professor Nelson F. Adkins of New York University aided in my search for material. Dean Leonard B. Beach of Vanderbilt University sent me two letters by Edward A. Ellsworth. The Yale University Library, the Henry E. Huntington Library and Museum, the New-York Historical Society, and the New York Public Library kindly permitted me to use the Ellsworth and Washington Irving letters. The Presbyterian Historical Society (Philadelphia) and the National Archives have provided important manuscript material. The Kansas, Nebraska, and Wisconsin state historical societies, as well as the Missouri Historical Society, have aided me. To the St. Louis Mercantile Library and Clarence E. Miller, its librarian, I am particularly indebted for special courtesies. M. Knoedler and Company was kind enough to give me a photograph of the Charles Bird King portrait of Ietan, the Otoe chief. As always, I close these acknowledgments with thanks to Mary Stephanie McDermott, my wife, who shares fully the burden of all my work.

The dedication of this volume to Mrs. R. M. Kendrick, my mother-in-law, was intended to be a little surprise, for the manuscript was completed months before her death. It can now be only a memorial. I shall miss the affectionate and flattering comments with which she would have greeted its publication.

JOHN FRANCIS McDERMOTT

St. Louis, Missouri
January 9, 1955

Contents

CONTENTS

[*x i i i*]

Illustrations

Editor's Introduction

It may have been any boy's longing for adventure among the wild Indians beyond the frontier that sent John Treat Irving, Jr., to the Pawnee country in 1833, but it is likely enough that his enthusiasm was fired by his uncle Washington Irving's excitement about the new world he had explored the previous year. The famous writer, returned from a seventeen-year visit to Europe determined to live out his life in his own land, saw the Far West with Indian Treaty Commissioner Henry L. Ellsworth and grew more enthusiastic the farther his travels carried him from home. When he reached Fort Gibson in October, he wrote with real satisfaction to his sister, Mrs. Paris, that he was now "completely launched in savage life. . . . I am tremendously excited and interested by this wild country, and the wild scenes and people by which I am surrounded." His delight did not abate even when the travel became strenuous. Nine days later, after he had crossed the Arkansas in a bullboat, he declared to her again: "We are now on the border of the Pawnee country, a region untraversed by white men, except by solitary trappers. . . . [I] never . . . enjoyed myself more, and the idea of exploring a wild country of this magnificent character is very exciting."[1]

No doubt in this close-knit family the letters sent to his aunt were read by the nephew. And that famous excursion was surely talked about frequently by uncle and nephew when Washington took young Treat with him on a trip south as far as Charlottes-

[1] Pierre M. Irving, *Life and Letters of Washington Irving*, III, 23, 24.

ville, Virginia, in April and May, 1833.[2] Possibly it was at Washington, D. C., that Treat was introduced to Ellsworth and the first exciting talk arose of a trip to the Far West. Uncle Wash (as his nephews called him) interceded with his brother, Judge John Treat Irving, to let the twenty-year-old youth accompany the commissioner on his second expedition "to visit the wild tribes of the Prairies."[3] Thus Treat was launched on his first great adventure, one never forgotten during his ninety-four years, for he still loved to talk about it in his old age.

The preamble to Treat's adventure had opened a year earlier when Congress authorized a commission to "visit and examine the country set apart for the emigrating Indians," to adjust difficulties between tribes, and to make necessary treaties.[4] Accepting an appointment to the commission in August and setting out for the West almost immediately, Ellsworth had met Washington Irving, with his companions, Charles Joseph Latrobe and the young Count Albert-Alexandre de Pourtalès, on a Lake Erie steamer and had invited them to go with him to the buffalo range. Arrived at Fort Gibson, the military outpost, with Irving as secretary pro tem (without pay), they had made a tour on the prairies as far southwest as present-day Norman, Oklahoma. In December the board of commissioners was officially organized, councils were held with various tribes in that neighborhood, and treaties made with them. When spring came, the board decided that Ellsworth should carry the treaties to Wash-

---

[2] *Ibid.,* III, 32.

[3] Washington Irving to Thomas Aspinwall, New York, May 31, 1835. John Treat Irving, Jr. (December 2, 1812–February 27, 1906) was the son of Judge J. T. and Abby Spicer Furman Irving. He graduated from Columbia at sixteen. On his return from the West he studied law and was admitted to the New York bar in 1834. In addition to the *Indian Sketches* and the novel, *The Hunters of the Prairie, or The Hawk Chief* (1837), which he laid in the Pawnee country, he was the author of two other novels, *The Attorney* (1842) and *Harry Hanson or the Benevolent Bachelor* (1844?), both of which had appeared serially in the *Knickerbocker* as the "Quod Correspondence," and of *The Van Gelder Papers and Other Sketches* (1887, 1895). In the family he was commonly known as Treat. For him, consult *Dictionary of American Biography* (hereafter cited as *DAB*), IX, 503.

[4] 23 Cong., 1 sess., *Sen. Doc. 512,* II, 870–75

ington and make a personal report. On the last day of April he was in Cincinnati and expected shortly to be in Washington.[5]

When Ellsworth set out from Washington early in July for Fort Leavenworth, Treat Irving went with him, as did his son, Edward A. Ellsworth (who was the secretary pro tem of this expedition), and John Dunlop, a Scottish gentleman "travelling for information and amusement."[6] From the capital they went by stagecoach as far as Guyandotte (where the Guyandot River meets the Ohio) and thence by steamboat to St. Louis. "This road via Guyandotte was very bad," Ellsworth wrote to Elbert Herring, commissioner of Indian affairs, "and we found Cholera 60 miles East of the Ohio river & have been travelling amongst it ever since."[7] At Cincinnati he consulted with physicians about this dreaded disease and the precautions to be taken against it.[8] When they arrived in St. Louis on July 11, the commissioner found cholera rather bad; in this town of six or seven thousand people ten or twelve a day were dying. The medication advised sounds almost as bad as the disease: "the most celebrated & successful remedy is the following taken in powders once in 2 hours

> viz 5 grains of Calomel
> 3 grains of African cayenne
> ½ grain of opium—

[5] *Sen. Doc. 512*, IV, 193. A summary of the organization and activities of this commission, especially for 1833, will be found in Grant Foreman, "The Life of Montfort Stokes in the Indian Territory," *North Carolina Historical Review*, Vol. XVI (October, 1939), 373–80. The full history of this incompatible group (Governor Stokes, Henry L. Ellsworth, the Reverend John F. Schermerhorn, and Colonel Samuel C. Stambaugh) remains to be written. The fullest accounts of Ellsworth (1791–1858), of Hartford, Connecticut, are those of Stanley T. Williams and Barbara D. Simison (eds.), in their introduction to *Washington Irving on the Prairie, or a Narrative of a Tour of the Southwest in the Year 1832 by Henry Leavitt Ellsworth*, and of Williams in *DAB*, VI, 110–11. Consult also John Francis McDermott (ed.), *The Western Journals of Washington Irving*.

[6] John Treat Irving, *Indian Sketches* (1888), 4.

[7] St. Louis, July 14, 1833. The letters from Henry Ellsworth to Elbert Herring and Lewis Cass, the letters from Montfort Stokes to Lewis Cass, and the official documents relating to this expedition are among the records of the Office of Indian Affairs in the National Archives.

[8] *Indian Sketches* (1888), 37–38.

It is said by physicians that the character of the disease is changed this year in some respects—Calomel so efficacious alone, last year, is not administered this season, without being combined with opium—"[9]

At St. Louis, Ellsworth found Governor Montfort Stokes of North Carolina waiting (the Rev. John F. Schermerhorn, another member of the commission, had returned home to New York State on a visit), and they planned to leave shortly for Fort Leavenworth to "complete the arrangements for meeting the tribes of the Missouri in conformity with their instructions."[10] Their immediate concern was making outfit for the expedition. "In this we were aided," Treat Irving added in the revised edition of his *Indian Sketches* (1888), "by General Clarke ... [who] had much to tell of the wild regions into which we were to penetrate, and of the more wild people we were to encounter there. ... The General was a fine soldierlike-looking man, tall and thin. His hair was white; but he seemed to be as hardy and vigorous as ever, and spoke of the exposures and hardships of his campaign [that is, the Lewis and Clark expedition] with a zest which showed that the spirit of the old explorer was unquenched, and that he still hankered after fresh adventures in the saddle and on the prairie."[11] Now, too, they hired servants for the journey: Joseph Deshetres, son of Uncle Wash's Tonish, and Mordecai, half-Creek and half-Negro.[12]

Toward the end of July they rode out of St. Louis on horseback[13] with the hired men driving two dearborns laden with

[9] Ellsworth to Herring, St. Louis, July 14, 1833. For some notes about cholera and its remedies in Missouri in 1833, see "Cholera Epidemics in St. Louis," *Glimpses of the Past* (Missouri Historical Society), Vol. III (March, 1936), 51–56.

[10] Ellsworth to Lewis Cass, St. Louis, July 13, 1833. Specific written instructions have not been found.

[11] Pp. 5–6.

[12] All facts in this introduction not otherwise accounted for are drawn from the original (1835) edition of the *Indian Sketches* here reproduced.

[13] Stokes, who had cholera in St. Louis, had remained behind; he did not reach the Shawnee Agency until mid-September and then only to find that Ellsworth had left Fort Leavenworth two weeks earlier (Stokes to Cass, Fort Gibson, October 27, 1833).

"flour, sugar, ham and various other articles necessary for the camp life which we expected to lead . . . between St. Louis and Fort Leavenworth." Their first stopping place was at St. Charles. As companion and guide to Independence, the author added half a century later, they had with them "Mr. R., the Agent for the Osage Indians . . . [who] had lived for many years in the wilds of Arkansas, and was a thorough backwoodsman who knew every hole and corner of his own State, and looked upon every settler within a hundred miles of his dwelling as a near neighbor." He entertained the travelers with tales of frontier life— and Methodist hymns. Sometimes they found lodgings for the night in the cabin of a settler; sometimes they encamped in the woods.[14]

The last halting place before crossing the frontier was Independence, a town of "twenty or thirty houses, a court-house, and a nondescript population of trappers, Indian traders and frontiersmen . . . the starting place for all kinds of adventurers, who intended to cut adrift from civilization, and to seek their fortunes upon the prairies and in the mountains beyond them."[15]

A digression is necessary. Treat had no wish or intention to be a historian or to tell a personal story. His *Sketches,* he emphasized in the preface to the 1888 edition, "were not intended to form a continuous narrative, but to give an idea of the habits and customs of the Indian tribes whom the author visited, and, who, at that time, lived in their pristine simplicity." He was concerned not with a day-to-day record of observations but a series of sketches of aboriginal life. Consequently, except for indicating the members of the party and describing the servants

14 *Indian Sketches* (1888), 7, 9. The identity of this "Mr. R." cannot be determined. The Osage agent at this time was Paul Liguest Chouteau of St. Louis, whom Irving met in that city (E. A. Ellsworth to Irving, Fort Gibson, January 7, 1834). One subagent was Alexander McNair, son of the first governor of Missouri; the other was Thomas Anthony.

15 *Indian Sketches* (1888), 11–12. For some account of this route across Missouri the year before, see Charles Joseph Latrobe, *The Rambler in North America,* I, 118–26.

hired, he gave in 1835 no information about the organization of the expedition or its movement from Washington to the frontier. The stagecoach and steamboat trip from the capital to St. Louis, the horseback journey to Independence, and the frontier towns were passed over entirely. Interested only in Indian life, he began his narrative when they left the frontier settlements, and even then he chose to omit a description of the Shawnee Agency and set down almost nothing by way of picturing Fort Leavenworth—those places still had something of the aura of civilization about them. In his revision, fifty-five years later, he saw the desirability of more introductory matter and from his notes or his memory drew forth details which, with the commissioner's official correspondence and young Ellsworth's letters, enable us, in spite of his original intentions, to fill in the story and to see some of the frontier scenes that passed before his eyes.

The stay at Independence was brief. The commissioner rode over to Westport on July 31 to talk with Isaac McCoy, Baptist missionary and frontier surveyor.[16] Edward Ellsworth gathered up a few hasty impressions of life in western Missouri: "There are no Churches west of Sᵗ Louis [he wrote with some exaggeration from Fort Leavenworth] & indeed after passing the Mountains the only indications of its being Sunday is the unusual Gambling & noise, & assemblies around taverns—we have so traveled that except at Washington & Sᵗ Louis once in each we have not been able to go to church a single time. Farming & every thing goes on as usual between here & Sᵗ Louis in many places indeed there was an altercation between some persons as we came along whether it was Sunday or not." Edward rather sympathized with the Mormons and disapproved the general reaction against them. "In the upper part of Missouri Clay county the mob govern every thing they got together and said they would knock down any man that bid upon certain sections of land but themselves and they bought the whole at a shocking low price they have also driven off the poor mormons who are

16 Journal of Isaac McCoy, August (i.e., July) 30, 1833.

perfectly inoffensive people having their religion to themselves But the mob will govern." The young man from Connecticut also noted with satisfaction that the farmers who had emigrated from Ohio were removing to Illinois. All emigration from the East, he reported, had changed from Missouri to Illinois "*merely and on no other account than one is a slave state and the other is not.* . . . There is no enterprise in Missouri. Slaves do all the work and of course it is done poorly."[17]

At Independence they met an officer from Fort Leavenworth who had brought to the civilian courts "two rough-looking fellows captured in attempting to smuggle whiskey into Indian territory." Though, said Irving, there was clear evidence of their guilt, the men were freed by a jury of sympathizing frontiersmen. Lieutenant John Nicholls, released from prison escort duty, offered to guide the travelers to the fort. "We found him to be a very pleasant, genial fellow, who, being a dead shot with the pistol, was much respected on the frontier."[18]

Now at last they were over the frontier. Irving saw his first Indian, a Shawnee, and he lamented what white civilization had done to the red men. That night they stopped at the house of the blacksmith to the Shawnee. The next day (they were still south of the Kansas River) they met a company of mounted rangers returning from escorting the spring caravan over the Santa Fé Trail to Mexico. Presently they crossed the Kansas in a ferry operated by a Delaware and stopped briefly at the cabin of the Delaware blacksmith, the last building they would see on the road to the fort.

17 E. A. Ellsworth to Chauncey Goodrich, Jr., Fort Leavenworth, August 8, 1833.

18 *Indian Sketches* (1888), 12. John Nicholls, cadet from Connecticut at the U. S. M. A., 1818-23, had been promoted to first lieutenant on October 31, 1827. An officer of the Sixth Infantry, he was stationed at Jefferson Barracks, 1832-34. At this time he was detached for service at Fort Leavenworth (see George W. Cullum, *Biographical Register of the Officers and Graduates of the U. S. Military Academy at West Point*, I, 253; 23 Cong., 1 sess., *H. Rep. 474,* [where Ellsworth refers to this specific episode]; and various pay vouchers in the Richard Graham Papers).

Midday on August 3 brought them within distant sight of Fort Leavenworth, "a snowy speck resting upon the distant green." But many miles intervened, and it was sunset when they rode into the post. They were quartered in the same building with the family of the ranger officer they had met near the Kansas, a "frankhearted soldier, full of anecdotes of his adventures in Indian warfare and in the hunt."[19]

Treat was a bit disgusted to find the fort a "speck of civilization dropped into the heart of the wilderness."[20] Edward Ellsworth too found that it failed to come up to his expectations of a frontier fortress: "If you have never been to a Fort," he told his cousin, Chauncey Goodrich, Jr., "I assure you it is quite a different thing from what you suppose—I thought it a dirty [?] sort of a Castle with Cannon protruding from each loop hole but on the contrary there is not a house in the whole better fortified than our own in N. Haven that is by any thing more than the mere arms of the soldiers there are 4 large buildings for the soldiers barracks and about a dozen most [?] elegant houses for the officers. . . ." Life in such quarters was comfortable and pleasant. "We have as fine and I hesitate not to say finer provisions of all sorts & lodging than we have had at any hotel on our road. . . . there is a fine library of one or two hundred novels here also other books we all eat together that is Officers & us excepting those who have families for there are but 3 wives belonging to one Company allowed to come into the garrison." Twenty ladies gave the cantonment an air of so-

19 *Indian Sketches* (1888), 25.

20 In *The Hunters of the Prairie* he described the fort as follows: "Upon a high bluff, commanding a fine view of the Missouri, stood Wolf Hill cantonment, one of the pioneer garrisons scattered along the whole Indian frontier. About a dozen houses of various styles of architecture composed the barracks, which were surrounded by no walls. Upon the highest peak of the hill stood a block-house, strongly built of rough timber. In front of the cantonment a fence enclosed an open square of greensward, here and there shaded by tall trees, the remnant of the forest. Behind it rose a dense wood of dark timber.

"The appearance of the whole place was that of a border settlement; and but for sentinels at their posts, and here and there a soldier in his undress, lounging lazily in the sunshine, there was nothing of a military nature" (I, 119–20).

ciety; eight or ten of them were officers' wives, "all well edu-
cated [and] some from Connecticut." Duties of the officers were
not strenuous, Ellsworth observed. "I do not wonder why it is
the Officers of the U. S. Army are so corpulent for they do not
get up till 7 or 8 oclock and then with the exception of an hour
or two of commanding or reviewing the troops they do nothing
all day but eat & sleep   The more active can hunt or fish but
do little at the latter for fear of musquitoes which would almost
kill a man." A night deer hunt on the Missouri was soon in prospect: "We [shall] take some soldiers to row us that is 4 or 5 of the
Officers & Irving, Dunlop & myself." After four days' residence,
during which time he visited all the officers' quarters and saw
their families, he declared: "I admire this place exceedingly if
it were not for the musquitoes which I assure you are very
troublesome."[21]

There was more to interest and entertain the travelers than
the military. A band of Sacs visited the fort on August 7. Major
Riley asked them to dance for the ladies and the visitors, and
Edward paid particular attention to their painting of their bodies
in preparation for the dance:

They retired & stripped naked except for a cloth tied around
their middle & painting themselves with vermilion & black soot all
over in alternate streaks were nearly redy for the dance   they had
emblems on which consisted as follows   around the knees of those
who had killed an enemy was a pole cat skin or a fox skin tied and
arround no others for they would severely punish any attempt at
deception   for those who had not killed an enemy but were desirous
of so doing the skins were tied to their ankles   On the body & arms
& limbs of those who had killed enemies the number of those killed
was designated in the following manner   they take some black stuff
resembling black soot and extending the fingers of their hands put
the palm & bottom part of fingers in it then taking it away they

21 E. A. Ellsworth to Chauncey Goodrich, Jr., Fort Leavenworth, August 8,
1833. The ranger quarters were half a mile from the barracks (H. L. Ellsworth to
Herring, Fort Leavenworth, August 23, 1833).

press their hand on their breast or cheek or wherever they please and it leaves the impression of a hand and as many hands as they are about an Indian so many enemies he has killed   there was one indian there the strongest and most athletic looking fellow I ever saw who had killed 9 & 4 white men   he was one of Black Hawks tribe. . . .

In painting I notice the following to be the general course pursued   they paint for an inch arround the eyes vermilion then they streak their faces—but in the first of all they paint all over excepting the little that is covered up by the braguet with vermilion   they then draw a black streak around one eye then streak their faces some horrisontal & some perpendicular & no one is allowed to paint like another   sometimes they paint a streak up ½ of their face & body one arm & one leg and all the ways immaginable.

Finally, the twenty warriors were ready to demonstrate their war dance, which Edward watched intently:

The manner of their dance is beyond description but I will try my best at it   in the first place after dressing up so they took an little cask about the size of a common drum & taking a soaked deer skin they strained it over the top in the same manner as our drums are tightened   they then pass a strap over the shoulders of a small sized indian & to it affix the drum   they had previously whittled out a stick like to an arrow to beat upon [it]   now they are ready they all set up the most diabolical yell you can immagine and walk off to the place they intend as their dancing ground   they now mix up together in a mass and one of them taking the drum stick goes to the drum & beginning a love [?] song or grunt as it were beats slowly on the drum   soon he becomes animated and as he gives a loud yell another indian repeats it and begins to jump up & down raising both feet from the ground but setting one down after the other a little   then they continue yelling and one after another all the Indians fall in   they have their tomahawks in one hand & their spears in their other and it seems most wonderful to me they dont kill each other they flourish them around so   All of them then jump up and down trying to make their heels strike their seat   this

they continue for some time then they all give a tremendous yell
& stop 1 then steps out & raising himself on tip toe stretches out
his arm to its utmost length his hand holding a spear in a horrisontal
direction he then calls out in Indian for some thing to cut & reviles
his enemy in a short speech the drum all the while continuing to
beat When he is through they all yell and go on as before when
another does the same thing In dancing they have no regularity
but run around among each other stricking their tomahawks & kicking like fury at each other as it seems[22]

Life was by no means dull or uniform for the travelers. Miss
Livermore's listening to God's voice among the Kickapoos made
some stir around the cantonment. To the commissioner she
meant only trouble:

On my arrival here, I found a female preacher who claims to
have received a communication from Heaven, to dwell among the
Kickapoo Indians. Her name is Miss *Livermore*. She is the same person, who last year, thought she was directed to sojourn with the
Osages, and consequently we met her at Fort Gibson. She now evidently appears more deranged, and I was sorry to find her thus far
among the Indian tribes N.West. It is true, her visit to the Kickapoos
is by the consent of the Superintendent of Indian affairs at St Louis.
But I do not believe, Genl Clark is acquainted with her present
principles. With the kindest feelings as a Gentleman, to a Lady, I
am decidedly of opinion that her residence among the Indians can
do no good and may do much harm. Such is the concurrent opinion
of Mr Cummings the agent, Mr Alley the disbursing agent, Major
Riley and all the officers of this post. Miss Livermore is in correspondence (*she* says) with the President Mr Barry & others, all of
whom have urged her to visit the Indians. I doubt the fact. But lest
she might deem my opinion, a matter of persecution I beg to mention
what she publicly professes to believe & teaches here

1 That Bonaparte is *not* dead but will soon reign as antichrist
   and rule over the white man & Indian.
2 She pretends to receive direct communications from Heaven,

22 E. A. Ellsworth to Goodrich, August 8, 1833.

and believes that the Kickapoo prophet receives communications also from Heaven in an *audible* voice. This she has told the prophet on a visit to her at this post.

3 That immediately after the reign of *this* President a military despotism will be established in this country.

4 She believes that she is to be translated by Elijah to Heaven from Kickapoo ground and that all the Kickapoos are going up with her, and she is very anxious to get settled on Kickapoo ground, before the 4 of Sept when some great event is to occur, and she has informed a few Kickapoos of their speedy translation in company with herself.

She requested an interview with me yesterday. I stated to her what I heard as to her belief or expressions—she admitted all—I then told her I thought her residence among the Indians would be *injurious.* The Gov^t did not want to have the Indians believe that God communicated in an audible voice to their prophet—The last [Black Hawk] War showed the bad influence of Indian dreamers—Nor did the Gov^t wish the Indians to believe that they were to be carried to heaven in a short time and neglect to raise provisions for their families who would probably remain on earth sometime. I told Miss Livermore that while as commissioner I was opposed to her residence among the Kickapoos or even visiting them as a preacher, I would do what I could as a gentleman to make her departure agreeable. I added also that as the family in whose quarters she got permission to stay a "few days" found it inconvenient to accommodate her longer, I would recommend it to her as a friend, not to declare any more that God had forbid her recrossing the Indian line and she would only go in irons; but that she would as a lady of delicacy accept of the most easy conveyance that could be procured for her.[23]

The commissioner waited somewhat impatiently for Governor Stokes to arrive from St. Louis, but it was not the old man's

[23] Ellsworth to Herring, Fort Leavenworth, August 19, 1833. By way of explanation of this curious letter, he pointed out that "Miss Livermore has preached frequently in Washington & elsewhere. She has some friends who urge her residence among the Indians, and many highly respectable citizens who feel interested in her welfare. She has lately through Mr. Barry, transmitted a new revelation, which she told me, she hoped the President would have published in the [Congressional] Globe. . . ."

absence that held up the expedition.[24] Edward Ellsworth was down with a fever for some time, and even when the young man wrote to his uncle, Chauncey Goodrich, on August 28, he was still so weak that he could walk only "80 or 90 feet from the house." The commissioner had found Fort Leavenworth healthy when he reached the place, but four days later the alarming news came from upriver that Major Dougherty's agency at Belle Vue had been devastated. "The subagent Major Beacham [Beauchamps]—2 blacksmiths, a wife of one of the blacksmiths & one or two more dead—Mr Dougherty was taken with the same disease but is recovering." By August 23 the cholera had hit the post: "One ranger died day before yesterday—a soldier was taken last evening—is now a little better—his countenance when taken to the hospital was very blue—his spasms soon commenced—his tongue & extremities cold & great evacuations like [illegible] water—he may recover—a woman was taken about the same time & lies low."[25]

A threatened epidemic of cholera was by no means entertaining, but an amusing episode developed which found a place in the 1888 revision. Among the recommendations for cholera medicines made to the commissioner at Cincinnati had been a mixture known as "Preparation No. 6"; if the patient swallowed this, it was urged, the cholera was "bound to quit." It was made by "putting about half a pint of [cayenne] pepper

24 In fact, his correspondence shows that Stokes had no thought of going to the Pawnee country; he had expected only to attend councils at the fort.

25 Ellsworth to Herring, Fort Leavenworth, August 4, August 8, August 23, 1833. In the last letter Ellsworth called attention to the lack of medicines and the importance of having a second physician at Fort Leavenworth. The post surgeon at this time was Dr. Fellows, whom Ellsworth thought "a skillful man and well qualified for the situation." The doctor had traveled up the Missouri with Prince Maximilian of Wied in the *Yellowstone* in April, 1833; on his return trip a year later, the Prince noted that Fellows said he had lost only one cholera patient (*Travels in the Interior of North America, 1832-1834*, in Reuben Gold Thwaites [ed.], *Early Western Travels*, XXII, 252; XXIV, 114-15). The ranger Ellsworth referred to was probably Samuel Carey, who died August 20; two others, John K. Green and Benjamin F. Phelps, died on August 28 (Muster Roll, Captain Matthew Duncan's Company F, Mounted Rangers, June 30-August 31, 1833, Richard Graham Papers).

into a a quart bottle, and filling up the bottle with brandy, and was to be administered a teaspoonful at a time in half a tumbler of water." The party had reached Fort Leavenworth without having had need for this pungent medicine, but at the post they kept the bottle ready for an emergency. One afternoon Dunlop was lying half asleep when several Kansa Indians entered the room. "A great swarthy fellow skulked stealthily to the mantel-piece, took up the bottle, drew out the cork, smelt at the mouth of the bottle, then took a long draught, containing about twenty doses. Few Indians have ever replaced a bottle more quickly than he did. A sound between a hiccup and a yell burst from him as he rushed from the room." Most of the other Indians followed him, but one other "seized the flask and took a huge swallow" and ran for the river in his turn. No other member of this band of Indians came into their rooms during their stay.[26]

Treat was impatient. He longed to be out deep in the Indian country. But he found some bits of savage life to interest him. A Sac warrior was indeed the picture of the noble savage:

Never had I beheld such a princely fellow. He stood unmoved as we came up, viewing us with a calm, cold, but unwavering gaze. His eyelid never drooped; nor was the eye averted for an instant as it met our look. A large blanket, here and there streaked with vermilion, and ornamented with hawks bells, was so disposed around his folded arms, that it left bare his finely formed shoulder and half his high and sinewy chest. A bright, steel headed tomahawk peeped from beneath its folds, and a quiver of arrows hung at his back. His legs were cased in leggings of dressed deer skin, with the edges cut into a rough fringe. He wore a pair of moccasins of dressed buffalo hide. The top of his head was closely shaven, and covered with vermilion; but his face was free from any colouring whatever, with the exception of a ring of black paint, which was carefully drawn around each eye.

As we approached he drew himself up, and threw his head slight-ly backward with an air of haughtiness which well became his high

26 *Indian Sketches* (1888), 37–40.

stern features. He seemed to feel like a proud but desolate being. Upon his head was bound an eagle's plume, but it was crushed and broken. . . . his stern features told that he asked no pity, and would brook no insult.

For some time he stood in front of us returning gaze for gaze, and for a moment a smile played over his features; then drawing up his tinkling blanket, he wrapped it closely around him, and walked off.

Treat, whose genre sketches are as good as those of his uncle, was provided with his first view of Indian domestic life by the band of Kansas who wandered into the post. "Give the Indian a fire, and you give him a home." Here were forty of them gathered around a small fire under a great oak in front of the quarters. Most of the men were lounging about. "Several were leaning listlessly upon their hunting spears, too indolent to bear even their own weight. Some were resting against the tree; and a band of five or six were lying upon their backs, with their feet to the fire, drumming with their fists upon their breasts, and chanting out a sleepy ditty, the chorus of which was filled up by a loud yell from every throat in the band." With an artist's eye he noted among these Kansas a little squaw with a "most peppery tongue" and "an acidity in her black glittering eye" which added zest to remarks directed at one of the Indians. Soon she turned her wit (in her own tongue, of course) against the young white men and raised "loud bursts of merriment" from most of her audience. This continued until one old Indian, quite unamused, finally shut her up.

So many Kickapoos came to the fort that Irving and his friends one day rode over to visit their village, some four or five miles away. As they drew near, they stopped to watch a horse race. At the town of thirty flimsily-constructed bark houses, the young man's attention was caught by a domestic scene: a "diminutive, spider-legged Indian, who looked as if he had withered away under the gall of his own disposition," flourishing a stick at a "fat blowzy squaw" who rushed shrieking from one of the huts.

[*x x x i*]

Nearly four weeks had passed during which the commissioner had been concerned with straightening out Kickapoo objections to the lands assigned them and pondering on the problems of the Delaware, who "have lately been out on a war party and burnt the houses or huts of the Pawnees which will exasperate the latter very much."[27] But at last he had had enough talks with the Indians of the neighborhood and had consulted the Indian agents. His son had recovered, and Major Dougherty, agent for the Otoes and Pawnees, had arrived from Belle Vue to guide them on their visit to those tribes. To his party he added Dougherty, Dr. William S. May (later he wrote to Lewis Cass, secretary of war: "He was much needed, for all were sick more or less during the tour"[28]), and a Negro cook. Seven men of the Sixth Infantry were taken for escort (the commissioner had planned to use twenty-five rangers, but they had been unexpectedly ordered to Jefferson Barracks[29]). Two heavy wagons loaded with presents and supplies and the two dearborns made up the small wagon train.

Now at last they are launched "in savage life" and Treat is in his element. Not from him are we to learn how such a party moved over the prairies, crossed the creeks, made camp, or any of the other commonplaces of travel. From his pen came only descriptions of Indian life. And in that concentration lies the value of his *Indian Sketches*. Many another has told of the hazards and difficulties of pioneer travel, but none before John Treat Irving has looked at the Otoes and Pawnees with his fresh, eagerly interested eyes, and has seen them not as a soldier sees a potential enemy, a trader a business operation, a missionary his converts to God, or a scientist the specimens whose habits and customs are to be collected, but as living, human beings, handsome and ugly, brave, boastful, accomplished, worthy of pity and admiration, a bit ludicrous, but always fascinating.

---

[27] Ellsworth to Herring, Fort Leavenworth, August 4, 1833.
[28] Ellsworth to Cass, Fort Leavenworth, November 4, 1833.
[29] *Ibid.*

What happened on the journey can be summed up briefly. Heading north and keeping some 20 or 30 miles west of the Missouri, the expedition in about two weeks reached the Otoe village overlooking the Platte some dozen miles beyond Saline Creek and about 180 miles from the fort. There they pitched camp on September 17. A council was held on September 20 and 21 and a treaty was signed. For reasons not given (possibly sickness), they remained at the Otoe village for more than two weeks. On October 3, Ellsworth received a delegation of Omahas headed by Big Elk (Ongpatonga).[30] The next day they must have started west along the south bank of the Platte, escorted by some twenty Otoes, for the Grand Pawnee village about 80 miles away. A council was held and a treaty made with the four Pawnee tribes on October 9 and 10. Following a distribution of presents to the Grand Pawnees, the expedition set out to visit briefly and distribute presents to the three Pawnee villages on the Loup Fork about 30 miles to the northwest. The return trip must have begun in mid-October, their party now augmented by sixteen official Pawnee representatives, with wives and volunteer delegates bringing the Pawnee strength up to eighty. Probably the expedition headed as directly across country for the fort as possible—Treat is no help to us topographically. In the last stretch —somewhere near the Big Nemaha—the author managed to lose himself and spent several days and nights alone on the prairie, eventually to make his way to the Kansa Agency. Thence he rode with Marston G. Clark to the fort. The last chapters are devoted to Ellsworth's council for a peace treaty between the tribes of the West. That signed, Irving said farewell and headed east.[31]

[30] Ellsworth to Herring, Otoe village on the Platte, October 4, 1833, with enclosed address of the Omaha chiefs, dated October 3.

[31] Ellsworth's movements and the business of the commission can be traced through various documents in *Sen. Doc. 512*, Vol. IV; see also *H. Rep. 474*, pp. 78ff., for the report of the commissioners to the Secretary of War, Fort Gibson, February 10, 1834. According to Edward Ellsworth, the commissioner, his son, and Mr. Dunlop, with Major Dougherty and the Otoe and Pawnee chiefs, left Fort Leavenworth on November 20, stopped to treat with the Piankashaws at the

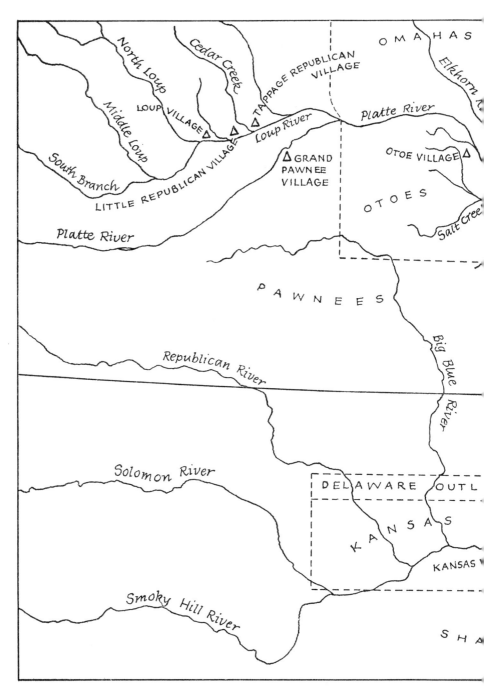

The Pawnee Country

1833

O	25	50	100

MILES

BELLE VUE

BEAR River

naha R.

maha R.

M I S S O U R I

Charitan River

40°

Grand River

KICKAPOOS

Delaware River

KICKAPOO VILLAGE

△ FORT LEAVENWORTH

○ DELAWARE VILLAGE

Missouri River

ELAWARES

LA PLUME △

Stranger Cr.

△ DELAWARE VILLAGE

○ INDEPENDENCE

as River

□ SHAWNEE AGENCY

△ SHAWNEE VILLAGE

KANSAS AGENCY

E S

Osage River

95°

Irving's *Indian Sketches* has documentary interest as the description of a detail in the complex subject of the relations of the white man and his government with the Indians. But he lives and is remembered because he devoted himself to the picture of Indian life, because he captured on his canvas the dignity and the humanity of the Indian in his native country. How vividly and with what freshness of view, what effectiveness of detail he has done this!

The tremendous excitement that must have seized the newcomer to the Plains when he first experienced an Indian welcome is caught up dramatically. The Otoe chief had met the travelers, greeted them cordially, and was riding with them to his village. Suddenly, he galloped a few yards ahead, waved his arms, and broke into a shrill yell.

A loud roar rose from behind the bluff, and a dark troop of wild horsemen burst round its base, and came pouring down upon us. There must have been several hundred of them. Every man was naked, but glaring with paint. They flooded onward, pealing out scream after scream, brandishing their spears, and whirling their tomahawks around their heads. . . . Still they came on, and the din increased. The old chief was unmoved and sat like a statue upon his horse. I looked around upon our little band, there were several lowering brows and tightly compressed lips, and the fingers of two or three were on their gun triggers. They were not accustomed to the Indian welcome; and to them, all this long parade of yelling warriors wore a menacing appearance. The band had now approached within a hundred yards. We could perceive the flashing eyes of the straining horses, the bare teeth, scowling brows and starting muscles of the riders. Bow clattered against bow; tomahawk clashed against tomahawk, and voice was blended with voice, until the whole din

---

Shawnee Agency, arrived at Independence three days later, re-outfitted, and traveled by way of Harmony Mission to arrive at Fort Gibson on December 8. The young man continued to act as secretary pro tem for some weeks; Dunlop apparently struck off for New Orleans (Ellsworth to Irving, Fort Gibson, Arkansaw, January 7, 1833 [i.e. 1834]).

rose in the air, like the wild tumultuous roar of a raging sea. They were close upon us;—another moment—and we were lost. The eyes of the soldiers began to flash fire, their teeth were clenched, and there was an expression about their faces, which told, that in spite of numbers, their resistance would be bloody. At that moment, at a signal of the Iotan, the wild horde separated, and whirled around, enveloped in a cloud of dust.

The old chief smiled with an air of grim satisfaction, as he observed the effect produced upon us by his warriors; then raising his voice, he joined in the wild melée around us. . . .

After this scene of hubbub and confusion had continued for about fifteen minutes, the crowd gradually ceased its clamor, and formed a large circle round us, with their horses' heads towards the party. Presently the ring broke and was extended in two lines, through which a band of about thirty warriors slowly advanced, to a long solemn chant, sung by the whole troop, and accompanied by a kind of drum. This band was formed of the flower of the Indian village. None were admitted except those who could boast of having taken a certain number of scalps, or of having performed an equally honourable service, in stealing a large number of horses. These warriors were highly ornamented; paint of every hue was laid upon their bodies. Their heads were decorated with feathers and the variegated plumage of the gaudy birds of the Platte islands. Long strings of wampum hung from their necks and ears. Each bore a calumet adorned with feathers and tinkling bells. Some wore glittering armlets and collars of tin. Their heads were shaven, and covered with vermilion, and from the top of each hung the chivalrous scalp lock, generally adorned with an eagle's plume.

But now we notice another characteristic of Irving: he is filled with admiration for these bold, magnificent warriors, but he always has an eye for what his uncle called the comic and grotesque. While this proud mass of braves was moving into the village, an old Indian, showing off for more than he was worth, took a spill. A shout of laughter rose. "Laugh on! I am old and feeble now; but there was a time when you would not have dared to have done this." When the Grand Pawnees staged a like welcome, Irving saw not only military show but also "a withered, gray-headed squaw . . . mounted on a little, wall-eyed, cream-coloured pony . . . a lurking devil looking out of his half-closed eye, the very antipodes of his rider, who sat upon his back like the picture of Patience." She had four children in her charge, one astride the neck of the horse, one dozing in her arms, a third clinging to her back, and the fourth "peering from the mouth of a leather bag, fastened between her shoulders." The horse capered on its hind legs, balked, kicked its heels in the air to shake off the load, but, finally convinced, set off at full gallop for the village.

His portraits of chiefs and warriors make a gallery of noble figures. The Sac warrior at Fort Leavenworth he painted with vivid and dramatic understanding. The young "Kioway" living with the Grand Pawnees was, Irving wrote, "slight and beautifully formed . . . a fire in his eye; a swell of the nostril; and a proud curve of the lip . . . showed a spirit that brooked no opposition, shunned no danger. . . . His long black hair, which trailed behind him on the ground, was plaited together and ornamented with about twenty plates of massive silver. A band of silver was fastened round his throat, and several large medals of the same metal hung upon his breast. Upon his arms were several bands of silver, and rings of the same upon his fingers. His leggings, though more finely wrought, like those of the chiefs, were fringed with scalps. A scalp consisting of the entire upper part of a human head, hung from the bit of his fiery horse. . . ." Souwahnock of the Delawares, who had "first kindled the torch of war, between his own tribe and the Pawnees, and led the expedition that sacked the Pawnee village . . . was without ornament, except a heavy silver plate, resting upon his calico hunting-shirt. He was not tall, but muscular, and his eye was as searching as an eagle's. There was a proud curl upon his lip, and withal, an iron firmness marked his whole deportment. He seemed to think that the whole weight of the anger of the Pawnee nation, was about to descend upon himself, but was ready to meet it. He did not deny that he had incited his nation to the outrage, upon the Pawnee nation. Nay, he gloried in it; and was now ready to meet them in friendship or as enemies." These are portraits as dignified, as romantically impressive, as any done by Charles Bird King or the other artists whose paintings were being lithographed at this time for McKenney and Hall's great work, *History of the Indian Tribes of North America*.

Something more of humanity, however, finds its way into Irving's portraits than is commonly seen in the "noble Roman" tone of the lithographs. There was a "look of comic slyness . . . an irascible twinkle" in the eye of the Ietan. Big Kaw was "rather good natured, but gifted with a large supply of mulish obstinacy, and a temper like gunpowder." In the manners of Blue Coat there was "an ease . . . which almost made his guests forget that they were conversing with a wild, untutored savage." Long Hair was a "stern, gloomy looking man, with an anxious, wrinkled brow, a mouth like iron, and an eye like fire. He evidently made efforts to be sociable; but it was not in his nature; and during the whole feast, the stern, unbending character of the Indian warrior, was continually peering out from beneath the show of hospitality. He urged us to eat, and he even attempted to smile; but it more resembled the angry snarl of a wildcat, than the evidence of any pleasurable emotion." An unnamed Indian was "tall, thin . . . with a wrinkled, hard-looking face, and a head covered with profusion of long, knotty hair, which he occasionally combed, by raking it with his fingers. He seemed as if smoke-dried for a century. . . . He had a very small, busy eye, which twinkled with an incessant play of humour. It overcame even the grave disposition of the oldest warriors, and surprised them into [broad laughter]."

There is much more in Irving's book than portraits of warriors, noble or humorous. The familiar life, the domestic scene is an area peculiarly his own. In his pages an Indian village is not a pastel exotic to be sighed over; it is not a contemptible place to be sketched in harsh strokes of uncomprehending realism. His Indian town is alive. Real people go about their ordinary, everyday business in it.

We had been a week in the village, and had become familiar with all the antiquated gossips of the place. The old warriors would stop us as we lounged around, to listen to some sly joke, which as in duty bound, we relished most highly; though the wit of it was for the most part beyond our fathom, as it lay hid in the arcana of their language. The old squaws would hold us by the button, and whine into our ears some lugubrious tale of misery, equally unintelligible. The children soon lost the shyness, which had at first marked their conduct; they were continually hanging around the tents, teasing the black cook, or frightening the oxen. When not thus engaged, they were scampering like deer across the prairie, in the enjoyment of their wild games. Here and there, too, a knot were busily engaged in gambling away arrows, which they had received from their parents; discussing with the most earnest eagerness, the fairness and unfairness of each toss of their competitor.

With Irving we go into a chief's lodge and are immediately at home. We find the chief seated on a leather mat:

Around him were lounging about a dozen Indians. Some, reclining with their backs against the pillars supporting the roof, with their eyes half closed, were smoking their stone pipes. Some were lying half asleep upon the clay floor, with their feet within a few inches of the fire; and others were keeping up a sleepy song.

At a short distance from the fire, half a dozen squaws were pounding corn, in large mortars, and chattering vociferously at the same time. In the farther part of the building, about a dozen naked children, with faces almost hid by their bushy, tangled hair, were rolling and wrestling upon the floor, occasionally causing the lodge to echo to their childish glee. In the back ground we could perceive some half a dozen shaggy, thievish-looking wolf-dogs, skulking among the hides and bundles in search of food, and gliding about with the air of dogs, who knew that they had no business there.

Upon our entering, the lounging Indians roused themselves

from the floor; the smokers woke from their reveries, and the dogs slunk out of sight. The women and children, however, went on as before, the former pounding and chattering, and the latter frolicking over the floor. When we had seated ourselves, a large bowl of boiled buffalo flesh was placed before us, and signs made for us to fall to. The chief himself acted as master of ceremonies. He thrust his hands into the bowl, and turned over and over the heap of smoking meat, selecting the best morsels [for us], and welcoming us with warmest words of friendship. Several times, appearing to be annoyed by the noise and clamour of his wives, he turned round, and let out a volley of angry words, which, however, they treated with no attention.

The Ietan, great chief, mighty warrior, and skilled politician, let the young travelers into the miseries he was subjected to by the caprices of his five wives and the difficulties which he found in maintaining proper discipline "where there were so many mistresses and but one master." When the visitors went feasting among the Otoes, Big Kaw took them to his lodge, but "the lady of the house had not expected company, and was unprepared for visiters. There was evidently a storm gathering, I read it in her lowering eyes, and in the uneasy, stealthy look of the Indian. He made no parade, but glided across the building, and motioned us to a seat, with a guilty air; then slunk upon a cushion, with the look of a man who would wish to pass unnoticed. . . . A bowl of dried buffalo flesh was at last placed before us; the viands being rather tough, drew forth some remark from our host, half facetious, half apologetic. By accident it reached the hearing of the squaw, who thought that it was intended as a reflection upon her. In an instant she was in a blaze, and opened her batteries upon the chief, pouring out one continuous torrent of invective."

A hundred other subjects attract Irving and interest us. An old harridan, "with the flavour of bitterness about her tongue," at the distribution of presents clamors and shrieks and pulls and begs; finally given a piece of red ribbon, she rejects it with violent and bitter scorn and is quieted at last with a large tin kettle, which she carries off to the village. Young men paint themselves fastidiously and lounge about the village looking at the young squaws and "occasionally condescending to speak to some dirty-looking brother, with that patronising air, which, in all countries, a well-dressed person is apt to assume in conversing with a ragged acquaintance." An Indian girl, mourning bitterly, arouses sympathy until it is discovered that she had been heard to say to her mother earlier that "as she had nothing else to do, she believed she would go and take a *bawl*" over the grave of her brother—who had been killed five years before. The story of a Cheyenne girl sacrificed to the morning star, a "feast" on boiled pumpkin, the odd sight of a berdache, the dignity of an Indian council, the boasting of heroic deeds on grand occasions, the old warriors talking over old wars, the bitter rivalry of chiefs, the buffalo dance of the Otoes, the singing of the Pawnees around the campfire—for these and many other pictures of life among these prairie tribes let the reader turn to Irving's narrative.

I cannot better close than with the appreciative words of Washington Irving: "The Sketches here given are the result of his observations, and, to my mind, present some of the most spirited, lively and familiar views of Indian life that I have met with. They partake too of the youthfulness, and freshness of the author, and of a peculiar turn for the grotesque by which he is characterized. We have not had much as yet of the comic of Indian character; writers have all represented the Indians according to a conventional and artificial model; this unhackneyed youngster presents them as they are."[32]

[32] Irving to Aspinwall, New York, May 31, 1935.

Indian Sketches

Author's Dedication

TO

HENRY L. ELLSWORTH, ESQ.

Dear Sir:

Having accompanied you, throughout the whole of your bold and perilous expedition to the Pawnee Towns, permit me to congratulate you upon its success, and upon the benefits secured both to your own countrymen, and to the wild tribes beyond the border, by your enterprize and self-devotion.

With me it was the juvenile excursion of a minor, when every thing was fraught with novelty and pleasurable excitement; but with you it was an official undertaking, full of anxiety and forethought, and I cannot but fear that, to the cares of your office, was occasionally added solicitude for the safety of your young and heedless fellow traveller.

As it was partly at your own suggestion that the following pages were written, I beg you will accept this dedication of them, as a slight testimonial of my respect and esteem, and an acknowledgment of the kindness manifested by you throughout our wild campaign. If they present but imperfect sketches of the vivid scenes we have witnessed together, you will recollect that they are the first attempts of an inexperienced pencil.

THE AUTHOR

Author's Introduction

Introductory Account
of the object of the Expedition;
and the persons who composed it.

For several years past the government of the United States, as it is well known, has been engaged in removing the Indian tribes, resident within the States, to tracts of wild but fertile land, situated beyond the verge of white population. Some of the tribes thus removed, however, when they came to hunt over the lands assigned them, encountered fierce opposition from the aboriginal tribes of the prairies, who claimed the country as their own, and denied the right of the United States to make the transfer. The migratory tribes were thus placed in a disastrous predicament: having sold their native lands to the United States, they had no place to which they might retreat; while they could only maintain a footing in their new homes, by incessant fighting.

The government of the United States hastened to put an end to the bloody conflicts thus engendered, by purchasing the contested lands, and effecting treaties of peace, between the jarring tribes. In some instances, however, the aboriginals remained unappeased. This especially was the case, with a fierce and numerous tribe of Pawnees, inhabiting the banks of the Platte river, and who were backed in their hostilities by their allies the Otoes, who, though less numerous, were even more daring than themselves. These two tribes laid claim to all the land lying between the Platte and Kanzas rivers; a region comprising several hundred square miles [*sic!*]. It had long been their favourite hunting ground, in which it was death for a strange hunter to intrude. This forbidden tract, however, had been granted by the United States to the Delawares; and the latter had made it the scene of their hunting excursions. A bitter feud was the consequence. The tract in question became a debateable ground in which war parties were continually lurking. The Delawares had been attacked, while hunting, by the Pawnees, and many of their tribe had fallen. The Delawares, in revenge, had surprised and burnt one of the Pawnee towns, while the warriors were absent on a buffalo hunt.[1]

The hostile feelings thus awakened among the aboriginal tribes of the Prairies, had been manifested toward the white

[1] Irving is in error. The Pawnee country extended on both sides of the Platte from the Republican Fork of the Kansas to the Loup Fork of the Platte. The territory described by the author would run closer to thirty thousand square miles than "several hundred"; the lands assigned to the Delawares formed only a small portion of this vast extent (for the Delaware boundaries see n. 1, p. 19).

Difficulties between the Delawares and the Pawnees had existed since the arrival of the eastern tribe. John Dougherty pointed out to General William Clark (Fort Leavenworth, March 30, 1832) that the Delaware strip led out into hunting grounds claimed by the Pawnees as far back as white men had known this country and that to maintain peace it would be necessary to extinguish Pawnee claim to lands south of the Platte (*Sen. Doc. 512*, III, 308–309). The particular raid by the Delawares to which Irving refers has been placed by some writers in 1832—indeed, Irving's own statement may seem to say that—but the documents make certain that it took place in this very summer while the Ellsworth party was en route to or staying at St. Louis. The Pawnees, William Gordon reported to Clark (St. Louis, August 12, 1833), "committed depredations on the [Delawares], some fifteen or eighteen months ago, for which the Delawares fitted out, during my visit among them [June, 1833], a war party, for the purpose of redressing themselves. They were told to submit their grievances to the Government, and that proper redress would no doubt be afforded them. They replied that they had long ago done so, and as the Government had evinced no disposition to interfere, they felt authorized to resort to their own means. This party consisted of about twenty men, and had not returned when I left their country" (*Sen. Doc. 512*, IV, 308–309). By the time Ellsworth reached Fort Leavenworth the raid was over: "The Delawares have lately been out on a war party and burnt the houses or huts of the Pawnees," he wrote to Elbert Herring, August 4, 1833. The village was that of the Grand Pawnees; the Delaware leader, Souwahnock, makes a personal appearance in the council scene at Fort Leavenworth with which Irving closes his narrative. See also n. 1, p. 130, and n. 3, p. 242.

John Treat Irving, Jr., 1836

men. Several trappers and traders, had been massacred by the Pawnees, who looked upon them as intruders, and who were too far from the settlements; too confident of their own prowess, and too ignorant of the power of the whites, to care much either for their friendship or their enmity.

In this state of things, the commissioners appointed by government to superintend the settlement of the migratory tribes, were instructed to proceed to the region in question; purchase the contested lands of the Pawnees, and induce them to remove to the north of the river Platte, and effect a treaty of peace between them and their new neighbours.[2] For this purpose, in the summer of 1833, Mr. Ellsworth, the same commissioner who in the preceding year had explored a tract of the hunting grounds between the Arkansas and the Grand Canadian,[3] set out from Washington for Fort Leavenworth, a frontier post on the Missouri river, about forty miles beyond the boundary line of the State of Missouri, where he was to await the arrival of one of his fellow commissioners,[4] before proceeding to visit the hostile tribes. In this expedition he was accompanied by the writer of the following pages, who was glad of the opportunity to visit strange scenes and strange people, of which he had only heard wild and exaggerated rumours. There was another volunteer, a

[2] For this commission and its work, see the editor's introduction.

[3] See *Tour on the Prairies* by W. Irving.—JTI. *A Tour on the Prairies* had been published in England in March, 1835, and in America in April (Stanley I. Williams, *The Life of Washington Irving*, II, 74). For the elder Irving's firsthand impressions and for a history of that expedition, consult McDermott (ed.), *The Western Journals of Washington Irving*.

[4] Montfort Stokes. He was sick in St. Louis when Ellsworth arrived there and did not reach Fort Leavenworth until two weeks after Ellsworth had left that post for the Pawnee country (Stokes to Cass, Fort Gibson, October 27, 1833). Schermerhorn, the third commissioner, had returned home to New York State on a visit. For Stokes, consult Foreman, "The Life of Montfort Stokes in the Indian Territory," *North Carolina Historical Review*, Vol. XVI (October, 1939); and William Omer Foster, "The Career of Montfort Stokes in North Carolina," *North Carolina Historical Review*, Vol. XVI (October, 1939), and "The Career of Montfort Stokes in Oklahoma," *Chronicles of Oklahoma*, Vol. XVIII (March, 1940).

Scotch gentleman, travelling for information and amusement;[5] and a son of the commissioner, (Mr. Edward Ellsworth,) who acted as secretary to the expedition, made up our party.[6]

At St. Louis we hired two servants to accompany us throughout the expedition. One was a half breed, a cross between the Creek Indian and the negro; he was named Mordecai, and inherited the lazy propensities of both races, but entertained a high opinion of his own merits.[7] The other was a tall awkward boy, with a low forehead, and a dull sleepy countenance, nearly hidden by elf locks. His name was Joseph. He spoke a mixture of French and English, and would fain have passed for a full blooded white, but his mother was a thorough squaw, wife to a little creole Frenchman named Antoine or Tonish, who had accompanied the commissioner on the preceding year, in his expedition to the Arkansas frontier. Joseph inherited from his father a gasconading spirit, and an inveterate habit of lying. Like him, too, he was a first rate horseman, and a hard rider, who knocked up every horse entrusted to him. To add to his hereditary qualities, he inherited from his mother, an inveterate habit of stealing. Though a downright coward, he boasted much of his valour, and even told me in confidence, "that he could lick his daddy."[8] Being of an obstinate disposition, he was wisely appointed by the commissioner to drive a dearborn wagon,

5 Identified in the 1888 edition (p. 4) as "Mr. D." Reference in E. A. Ellsworth's letters and in signatures to treaties show his name to be John Dunlop.

6 See editor's introduction.

7 David Mordecai was paid $62.90 for his services to this commission from July 16 to December 12, 1833—four months and twenty-six days at $13.00 per month (*Sen. Doc. 512,* V, 296).

8 Joseph Deshetres. His name does not appear in the list of disbursements for the treaties of this expedition (*Sen. Doc. 512,* V, 294-97). He was the son of Antoine Deshetres and Camille Mercier, both of Florissant, Missouri, and both white. Edward Ellsworth, too, saw Joseph as a "character": "poor Joosey['s] catalogue of events would make a good appendix to Tonish['s] history as represented by your Uncle Washington Irving" (E. A. Ellsworth to J. T. Irving, Fayetteville, Arkansas, May 22, 1835). For Tonish, consult McDermott (ed.), *The Western Journals of Washington Irving,* 49-62.

drawn by two mules; and many a stubborn contest took place between him and his fellow brutes, in which he was sure to carry the day.

Such was our party when we left St. Louis, on our route to Fort Leavenworth.[9]

[9] They left St. Louis with two dearborns driven by Mordecai and Joe, according to the 1888 edition of the *Indian Sketches* (p. 7); the others were all on horseback.

CHAPTER I

The Indian Country

It was late upon a fine glowing afternoon in July, that we first crossed the Indian frontier[1] and issued from the forest, upon a beautiful prairie, spreading out as far as the eye could reach, an undulating carpet of green, enamelled with a thousand flowers, and lighted up by the golden rays of the setting sun. Occasionally a grouse, frightened at our approach, would bustle from among the high grass and fly whirring over the tops of the neighboring hills.

We had ridden for more than an hour over the green waste. The heat of the afternoon was yielding to the cool breezes of sunset; the sun itself, had just hid its crimson disk below the prairie hills, and the western sky was still glowing with its beams.

The deer, which during the scorching heat of mid-day, had nestled among the thick groves which dot the prairie, now began to steal from their hiding places, and were seen bounding over the green sward, or standing buried up to their heads among the tall flowers, and gazing wildly and fearfully at our party.

At a distance, too, we could perceive the gaunt form of a vagabond wolf, sneaking through the grass, and stealing snake-like upon his beautiful, though timid co-tenant of the prairie.

An exclamation from our guide attracted our attention to a solitary Indian, mounted upon a horse, and standing, statue like, upon a distant hill directly in our route.

Although we had often seen straggling Indians, in the fron-

1 Dates and distances were of little interest to Irving; it is seldom possible to pin him down and almost impossible to chart his course. On July 31, Ellsworth called on Isaac McCoy (at Westport) and returned to Independence (McCoy, Journal, August 31, 1833). Probably the party crossed the frontier the next day.

tier towns, they had in general so degraded an air as to attract by little attention. The appearance of this one, however, standing alone, on his own soil, where he was bowed by no feeling of inferiority, must, we thought, be as noble as the soil of which he was the master; and we pushed forward to gaze upon him. He remained unmoved, neither advancing a single pace to meet us, nor retiring on our approach. He proved to be a Shawnee; one of the remnant of that brave tribe, who under Tecumseh had made such a desperate attack upon the whites near the banks of the Wabash.

Some years since, they had been removed from their old hunting grounds and stationed about ten miles beyond the boundary which separates the state of Missouri from the territory bearing the same name. They had left the graves of their fathers, the home of their childhood, to seek in a strange land, that freedom which they could no longer enjoy in the homestead handed down to them by their unfettered ancestors; but not before the sapping influence of their communion with the whites had exerted its sway over them, and reduced them to that abject state which distinguishes the civilized from the savage Indian.[2]

A feeling of disappointment, mingled with sorrow, came over us as we rode up to this solitary being. At a distance our fancies had painted him possessed of all that was noble in the Indian character; but a nearer view dispelled the illusion. He could not have been older than thirty, but intemperance had left its mark upon his features. His hair was thick and matted, and hung nearly to his eyes. His legs were covered with leggings of deerskin, ornamented with a yellow binding. Over a dirty calico shirt he wore a long surtout coat, with immense brass buttons; and upon his shoulder he bore a very long and heavy rifle.

---

2 The Shawnee lands on the Kansas River had been provided for in the Treaty of 1825; they extended west from the Missouri state line, south of the Kansas River and the Kansas Indian lands, for one hundred miles, an area of about ten thousand square miles (Charles J. Kappler, *Indian Affairs, Laws and Treaties*, II, 262–64; *H. Rep. 474*, p. 120). The earliest migration to these lands had probably taken place in 1826.

He saluted us with the usual guttural salutation of "ugh!" and turning round rode slowly ahead of our party. His horse was one of those tough little Indian ponies celebrated for hard heads, hard mouths, hard constitutions, and a fund of obstinacy which it would puzzle Satan himself to overcome. He wriggled through the grass with a sidelong ricketty pace, that would have wearied any other than an Indian, and between the incessant drumming of the heels of the rider into the ribs of his steed, and the jerking, hitching pace of the animal, I could not well determine which underwent the most labour, the horse or his master.

He had not ridden in front of us long, before we saw at a distance, another of the same class galloping towards us. He came forward over the prairie at the full speed of a lean raw-boned nag; and we hoped to find in him a character which might redeem the first, but in this we were disappointed.

He was short and broad; dressed in a dirty calico shirt, and an equally dirty and ragged pair of pantaloons. On his head was cocked with a very knowing air, a something, which once might have been called a hat. On his shoulder he carried a long rifle, while he plied its wiping rod lustily upon the flanks of his horse until he reached the party.

After gazing at us with some curiosity, he rode off to our first acquaintance. A short conversation then took place, after which they thumped their heels into the ribs of their horses and scampered off over the prairie, rising at one moment over the top of some ridge, and then again disappearing in the hollow which lay beyond it, until at last we lost sight of them behind a grove which jutted out into the prairie.

So,—these are the Indians! This is a specimen of the princely race which once peopled the wilds of America, from the silent wilderness which still borders the Pacific, to the now humming shores of the Atlantic! We were disappointed and did not reflect that we were looking only upon the dregs of that people; that these were but members of those tribes who had long lived in constant intercourse with the whites, imbibing all their vices, without gaining a single redeeming virtue; and that the wild savage could no more be compared with his civilized brother, than the wild, untamed steed of his own prairie, could be brought in comparison with the drooping, broken-spirited drudge horse, who toils away a life of bondage, beneath the scourge of a master.

Upon their departure we urged our horses forward, for the creaking of the prairie insects warned us of the approach of night, and the place of our destination was yet some miles distant. A rapid and silent ride of an hour brought us to the wished for spot.

It was a single log cabin, built in the edge of the wood, and inhabited by a white man, the blacksmith appointed by the United States to take charge of, and keep in repair the arms paid as an annuity to the Shawnee tribe;[3] a measure of government highly pleasing to the Indians, who detest labour of all kinds, and would willingly travel a hundred miles to get another to perform some trivial job, which they might themselves accomplish with but a few hours labour.

The house of the blacksmith bore all the marks which characterize the backwoodsman. It consisted of two small cabins, formed of rough unbarked logs, and united to each other by a covered shed. One or two heavy vehicles were standing in front of it. At about a hundred yards distance was a large field of Indian corn. Two cows, two horses, and a cozy bevy of pigs, who were snuffing and grunting from a deep mud-hole a few yards from the house, made up the live stock of the establishment, and were all that were considered necessary for the comfort of a backwoodsman.

3 The blacksmith was L. Jones (Isaac McCoy, *The Annual Register of Indian Affairs within the Indian (or Western) Territory, No. 1*, p. 23).

[CHAPTER II]

The Rangers—Indian Habits—Crossing the Kanzas River

It was daylight on the following morning when we commenced our journey towards Cantonment Leavenworth.[1] It is situated in the Indian country, about forty miles beyond the line which separates the State from the Territory of Missouri. Our guide[2] took the lead, and struck into a narrow foot-path which led through the forest, while the rest of us followed in Indian file. There is a deep silence in a western wilderness. No sound is heard, not even the note of a bird to break the deathly stillness.

Occasionally a spectre-like raven would flit across our path, saluting us with his ill-omened croak; or poising himself upon his wings, to take a more minute survey of the strange beings who had invaded his secluded haunts.

The silence was thrilling. Our voices echoed beneath the leafy canopy with a sound that rendered them strange even to our own ears. Even the crackling of the dry twigs as they snapped beneath the hoofs of our horses, had a strange and solemn sound; but as we grew familiarized with it, this feeling wore off; nor was it long, before the jest and merry laugh went on as usual; and I imagine many a long day had passed since those aged forests had rung to such sounds of boisterous merriment as burst from the lips of the band, as we galloped towards the prairie, which lay but a few miles beyond.

In half an hour we reached it. A loud whoop from our guide announced that something more than usual had met his eye. At

1 In the 1888 edition Irving makes it clear that they stayed overnight at the Shawnee blacksmith's cabin. The verb should be *continued,* not *commenced.*

2 Lieutenant John Nicholls, Sixth Infantry, whom they had met in Independence and who was now on his way back to Fort Leavenworth. See editor's introduction, p. 23.

the same time he struck his spurs into his horse and galloped out into the open prairie.

At a short distance, a long troop of horsemen was trailing through the high grass, and preparing to enter a small thicket of timber which rose in the prairie at a short distance. They were a body of the United States Rangers, and had just returned from escorting the Santa Fe traders across a portion of the perilous route, which they are obliged to take, in carrying on their profitable, though hazardous trade with that inland mart.[3] When we met, they had been more than a month absent from the garrison, seeing none but their own party, or occasionally a straggling band of friendly Indians, carrying their whole wardrobe in the small valise attached to their saddles; dependent for subsistence on hunting alone, and continually on the look out for an enemy; an enemy that always came when least expected; tarried but to strike the blow, and retreated with equal celerity to the fastnesses of their own mountains.

[3] Fred S. Perrin ("Military Escorts on the Santa Fé Trail," *New Mexico Historical Review*, Vol. II [1927], 176–77) declared that there were no government records to show United States escort of Santa Fé traders except for 1829, 1834, and 1843; other sources, he wrote, suggested such action may have been taken in 1832 and 1839. It is very likely, however, that such escort was annually provided, as it certainly was in 1833. On April 23, the St. Louis *Missouri Republican* reported that "many of our enterprising young men have already left . . . to rendezvous at the Round Prairie near the Missouri line . . . whence they will be escorted as far as the boundary line between the U. States and New Spain, by a detachment of the U. S. Army." The party was not actually organized until June 19 at Diamond Grove, and probably set out for New Mexico a day or two later: "There were one hundred and eighty-four men belonging to the expedition; and ninety-three wagons, carriages and dearborns attached to it—sixty-three of which were loaded with goods. We understand . . . that the traders are under the escort of a company of Rangers" (*Missouri Republican*, July 12, 1833). Irving is further confirmed by his friend Edward Ellsworth, who wrote to his cousin Goodrich from Fort Leavenworth on August 8, 1833: "The Rangers who accompanied the Santa fee company out have come back." Louis Pelzer, in *Henry Dodge*, 67–79, gives a brief history of the ranger battalion; further information, especially about Captain Bean's company at Fort Gibson, can be gleaned from McDermott (ed.), *The Western Journals of Washington Irving* (consult index). The company now met with was that of Captain Duncan (Pelzer, *Henry Dodge*, 73). A muster roll for this Company F of the mounted rangers for June 30–August 31, 1833, is in the Richard Graham Papers, Missouri Historical Society; almost all members had been enlisted at Vandalia, Illinois, in November, 1832.

There is always a feeling of vagabond companionship engendered by travelling in the wilderness; and although we were not a day's ride beyond the settlements, we hailed the sight of this tatterdemalion band with as much joy as if we had been united by the links of a long and well tried friendship.

We spent half an hour with them; then spurring on, we soon reached the bank of the Kanzas river.

This is one of the largest tributaries of the Missouri; being from a quarter to two miles in width, and varying in depth from one to thirty feet.

Upon reaching its brink, we found attached to a tree, a large scow which was used as a ferry boat.[4] Its owner, a tall thin Delaware, was quietly seated in one corner, pouring out a flood of smoke from a small pipe which garnished one corner of his mouth.

There is always an air of gentlemanly laziness hanging about the Indians. They live they know not how, and they care not where. A little suffices them; if they can get it they are satisfied, if not, they are satisfied without it. They belong to a sect of philosophers ranging between the Epicureans and the Stoics. When pleasure presents its cup, they drink it to the dregs, and when the reverse is the case, they bear it without a murmur.

They have no objection to beg; or if it is equally convenient, to steal, for to tell the truth, they are much troubled with confused memories, and are terribly given to mistaking the property of other people for their own. It is a universal practice among them, and brings with it no disgrace. To all this is added a most gentlemanly abhorrence of labour of all descriptions, and a great store of patience in enduring the pinching hunger which is often the result of indolence. On a wet day you may travel for miles

4 W. D. Smith, a Presbyterian missionary, a few weeks earlier had found operating over the Kansas River about twelve miles from the Missouri and two miles from the Shawnee village, "a tolerably good ferry, at which the mail crosses once every week going and returning between the Shawanoe Agency and Cantonment Leavenworth" (Smith to E. P. Swift, Shawanoe Villages, Kansas River, July 29th 1833).

over the prairies, or through the thickets, and not a single Indian will cross your path; but let the sun again beam forth, and you will see them around in every direction, lounging in the long grass or sunning themselves upon some high prairie peak; with a most profound forgetfulness of the past, and lordly contempt for the future; for they are marvellously fond of fulfilling the general sense, though not the literal meaning of the old adage which says, "make hay while the sun shines."

Upon our hailing this Charon of the Kanzas, he quietly rose from his seat, and stepping to the shore, made signs for us to lead our horses into the scow. He remained upon the bank until they were all safely embarked. He did not offer to aid in the least, in getting them on board; nor did our guide appear to expect any assistance from him. When every thing was in readiness, he loosed the fastening, and seizing a long pole, thrust it into the sandy bottom, and whirled the ticklish vessel far out into the rushing current of the river. The water, at this spot, was not very deep; and by means of his pole, he soon ran the scow upon the sand of the opposite shore. He then secured it to a tree, and having received his pay, pocketed it, and strolled off, leaving the party to land, or stay on board, as they might think fit.

We disembarked and galloped up the bank. On the top was a large log house, inhabited by the blacksmith of the Delaware Indians,[5] and the last building we were to meet in the route to the garrison. We had scarcely reached it when the woods on the opposite bank of the river began to ring to the shouts of the Rangers; and the whole troop, as fantastically arrayed as a band of Italian banditti, slowly wound among the tall tree trunks, until they reached the bank which overhung the water.

There was a pause of some moments upon the brink; then a

[5] The roster of "United States Indian Agencies Affecting Kansas," *Kansas Historical Society Collections,* Vol. XVI (1923–25), 725, lists two blacksmiths attached to the Delaware Agency: B. Lawhead and Robert Dunlap. McCoy (*Annual Register of Indian Affairs No. 1,* p. 26) gave only Dunlap. In the disbursements for this expedition there is an item of $17.12 for "guns, corn, lodging &c." paid to Robert Dunlap (*Sen. Doc. 512,* V, 296).

heavy splash announced that the foremost had taken to the water; and in a moment after, his powerful animal was struggling against the swift current. The rest paused to watch his progress, then one after another dashed in; until the long line of snorting steeds, and their whooping riders, extended nearly across the river.

At that moment a dark thunder cloud, which had been hanging over the woods for several hours, opened its fire upon the band, thoroughly drenching all that the water had left untouched, and rendering them almost invisible by reason of the density of its shower.

The cloud hovered over for about an hour, but at last, one after another, a few rays were seen shooting out their bright lines from behind the dark curtain, and playing upon the tops of the distant trees. Finally the ragged masses rolling together slowly floated off to the eastward, until their dark forms were lost below the horizon, and the heaven was left in its sea of pure and spotless blue.

[CHAPTER III]

Shawanese and the Delawares

In an hour, we had left the house of the blacksmith, and were dashing through the moist and glistening grass of the prairie, in front of one of the villages of the Shawanese. It consisted of about a dozen houses or cabins, grouped together upon the top of a hill, and looking up a ragged little prairie. There was but little attraction in its appearance, and withal a most philosophic indifference to cleanliness or comfort.[1]

1 Irving may be correct in calling this a Shawnee village, but when they crossed the Kansas River the travelers had entered the Delaware country; at any rate, this was not the principal village of either the Shawnee or the Delaware tribe.

The treaty made in 1829 specified that "the permanent residence of the whole Delaware Nation" would be the "country in the fork of the Kansas and

Our approach was announced by about twenty half starved dogs, who set up a yell which brought to the doors every inhabitant of the place, old enough to be tormented with curiosity.

Presently two of them came forward to meet us. The first was a fat wheezing Indian of about fifty. He was dressed partly after the fashion of the whites, and partly in his own native style. He wore a broad brimmed black hat, ornamented with several bands of tin; a pair of large black rimmed spectacles; a blue calico shirt, and a pair of blue cloth pantaloons, secured close to his legs by several bands of yellow riband.

His companion, who was a little herring of a fellow, retained more of the Indian in his dress and appearance. His head was shaved, with the exception of a single lock[2] which luxuriated

---

Missouri Rivers, extending up the Kansas River, to the Kansas [Nation] Line, and up the Missouri River to Camp Leavenworth, and thence by a line drawn Westwardly, leaving a space ten miles wide, north of the Kansas boundary line, for an outlet . . ." (Kappler, *Indian Affairs, Laws and Treaties*, II, 304). These boundaries, surveyed in 1830 (Lela Barnes, "Journal of Isaac McCoy for the Exploring Expedition of 1830," *Kansas Historical Quarterly*, Vol. V [November, 1936], 351–75), provided about 3,450 square miles (*H. Rep. 474*, p. 120).

W. D. Smith, describing the Shawnee towns in a letter to E. McCurdy (Shawnee Villages, Kanzas River, June 19th 1833), reported: "They have mostly, as far as my observation has extended, cabin houses generally good, and some of them tolerably neat with a yard in front and a gate; neater and better in every respect than many of the habitations I have seen on Grove Creek and Ten-mile [in western Pennsylvania]. Attached to each cabin is a small field in many of which the corn is good; and the little farm as to its general appearance exhibiting signs of industry. Many of their habitations however are miserable hovels, exhibiting no signs of industry neatness or cleanliness, and I find if they progress in civilization there will no doubt be found among them as great an inequality in point of wealth and distinction as now is to be found among ourselves."

2 It is customary with all the Indian tribes, when shaving their heads, (as is the almost universal practice with the uncivilized tribes) to leave a single, long, thin lock of hair upon the crown, to aid their enemies in removing their scalp. From this it received the appellation of "scalp lock." It is considered a point of chivalry among them, to leave this unshorn. Great care is frequently bestowed upon it, and it is usually adorned with plumes of the eagle, the feathers of birds, or ornaments of deer's hair.—JTI. George Catlin describes such a scalp lock in a little more detail in his *North American Indians*, II, 23–24. For more about this custom and particularly its religious significance, consult Frederick Webb Hodge (ed.), *Handbook of American Indians North of Mexico* (Bureau of American Ethnology *Bulletin 30*), I, 524–26; II, 482–83.

upon the top of his crown, surrounded by a little pallisado of stiff bristles, left standing at its root, amid the general harvest. His face and head had been painted with vermilion, and at a distance bore a strong resemblance to a large red potato. A shirt of calico was the only article of civilized manufacture about him. His leggings were of deerskin, the edges of which were cut into a rough border: and his mocassins were made of the same material.[3]

Upon our approach, they came out with the intention of holding a conversation with us, but owing to an equal ignorance of the language of each other, we could obtain from them but little information. After wasting a short time in attempting to glean intelligence of our future route, we gave it up, and started forward at random. We rode up hills and down hollows; spattered through streams; galloped over patches of prairie, and through clumps of woodland, until, after riding for more than an hour, we found ourselves in the edge of a wood, and in the very heart of a town of the Delawares.[4]

A general barking of dogs, again announced us to the Indians. They flocked out to meet us. From them we learned our route, and passing through the village continued our journey towards the cantonment.

There is but little in the civilized Indian to excite interest, or to enlist the feelings; they are a race between the whites, and their own people as God made them. We have heard tales of those from whom they sprung; of their wars; of their contests

---

[3] These two Shawnees will reappear at the treaty council at Fort Leavenworth in November (Chap. LII).

[4] On July 3, 1834, Samuel Allis stopped at the house of the Methodist missionary to the Delawares, twenty-two miles from Fort Leavenworth: "The Delawares number about 1,000 souls, have also a Government teacher & blacksmith . . . they have a saw & grist mills—furnished by Government, raise some wheat, considerable corn & vegetables, there land is good, they also raise some cattle, horses, sheep,—& hogs. live on the north banks of the Konsas River, about 5 m- from its mouth, there land extends up the South side of the Mo River within 4 m. of the Garison" ("Letters Concerning the Presbyterian Mission in the Pawnee Country," *Kansas Historical Society Collections*, Vol. XIV [1915–16], 693).

for their soil; of their fierce and bloody defence of their villages, and of the graves of their ancestors. But where are they? Where are the braves of the nation? They have come within the blighting influence of the white man. They have been swept away, even as is the grass of their own prairie before the fire of the hunter. A spring may come, again to revive the drooping face of nature; but to them there is no spring, no renovation. It is probable, that ere two centuries shall elapse, there will be but a very remnant of their race; a few wretched beings, lingering about the then abodes of civilization, unheeded, unnoticed; strangers in the land of their fathers.

We paused for a short time, in the edge of the forest, to take a lingering look of the village; then turning away, we pursued our course until our horses again brought us to the prairie, upon which was imprinted the wide trail leading to Leavenworth.

[CHAPTER IV]

The Prairie—Arrival at Fort Leavenworth

The passing cloud which had swept over the prairie in the morning, had left nothing but beauty. A cool freshness exhaled from the tall grass glittering with its water beads. The rich, though parched foliage seemed to have given place to a young and luxuriant growth of the richest green. The clusters of flowers which had worn a dried and feverish look, now rose in renovated beauty, as if from their bed of sickness, and spread their perfumes through the morning air.

In the spring of the year, these prairies are covered with a profusion of pale pink flowers, rearing their delicate stalks among the rough blades of the wild grass. These were too fragile to withstand the scorching heat of summer; they had disappeared, and their stalks had also withered. Others had succeeded them. There was a gorgeous richness in the summer apparel of the

Fort Leavenworth in 1849

*"It is a rural looking spot—a speck of civilization dropped in the heart
of the wilderness. There was nothing here to tell a tale of war; and
but for the solitary sentinels upon their posts; the lounging forms of
the soldiers . . . or the occasional roll of the drum . . . we would
not have known that we were in the heart of a military station."*

prairie. Flowers of red, yellow, purple and crimson, were scattered in profusion among the grass, sometimes growing singly, and at others spreading out in beds of several acres in extent. Like many beauties in real life, they make up in the glare of their colours, what they want in delicacy; they dazzle but a distance and will not bear closer scrutiny.

There is a sensation of wild pleasure, in traversing these vast and boundless wastes. At one moment we were standing upon the crest of some wavelike hill, which commanded a wide view of the green desert before us. Here and there, were small clumps of trees, resting, like islands, upon the bosom of this sea of grass. Far off, a long waving line of timber winding like a serpent over the country, marked the course of some hidden stream. But a hundred steps of our horses carried us from the point of look-out. Passing down the sides of the hill, we splashed through the water at the bottom; tore a path through the grass, which frequently rose, in these hollows, to the height of eight or ten feet, and the next moment stood upon the crest of a hill similar to the first. This was again cut off as we descended a second time into the trough which followed the long surge-like swell of land.

Such is the prairie—hill follows hill, and hollow succeeds hollow, with the same regularity as the sweeping billows of the ocean. Occasionally a high broken bluff rears its solitary head in the midst, like some lonely sentinel overlooking the country. Upon the tops of these we frequently saw an Indian, standing in bold relief against the sky, or seated upon some pleasant spot on its summit, and basking in the sunshine, with that air of lazy enjoyment which characterizes the race.

Hour after hour passed on; the prospect was still the same. At last a loud cry from our guide announced that we had come in sight of the cantonment.

There was a snowy speck resting upon the distant green; behind it rose a forest of lofty timber which shadowed the Missouri. This was Leavenworth. But still, many miles intervened; for the prairie is like the ocean—the view is wide and boundless;

and it requires an eye trained by many months residence in these regions, to measure accurately the distance of objects.

It was mid day when we first caught sight of Leavenworth, but it was near sunset before we arrived there.[1] About a dozen white-washed cottage-looking houses, compose the barracks and the abodes of the officers. They are so arranged as to form the three sides of a hollow square; the fourth is open, and looks out into a wide but broken prairie. It is a rural looking spot—a speck of civilization dropped in the heart of a wilderness. There was nothing here to tell a tale of war; and but for the solitary sentinels upon their posts; the lounging forms of the soldiers, who were nearly worn out with their labours to *kill time;* or the occasional roll of the drum, as the signal for the performance of some military duty, we would not have known that we were in the heart of a military station.[2]

[1] They arrived at the fort, according to the commissioner, on August 3 (Ellsworth to Herring, Fort Leavenworth, August 4, 1833).

[2] In the 1888 edition (p. 25), Irving gave the strength of the garrison as one hundred and twenty men under the command of Major R[iley], plus the ranger company the travelers had met at the Kansas River. Available muster rolls (Richard Graham Papers) show that for June 30, 1833, Company A, Sixth Infantry, had a strength of four officers, five noncoms, two musicians, and twenty-five privates; Company F, Sixth Infantry, had four officers, six noncoms, two musicians, and thirty privates. Officers' pay vouchers in this same file indicate that two or three more companies of this regiment were then at the fort. Company F of the mounted rangers showed a strength of four officers, ten noncoms, two musicians, and ninety-four privates. It was, as Inspector-General George Croghan reported in 1836, a most unfortified fort: "There is about as much propriety in calling this Post Fort Leavenworth as there would be in calling an armed schooner a line of battle-ships, for it is not only not a fort but it is even devoid of the regularity of a common barrack—of defences it has none" (quoted in Edward R. DeZurko, "A Report and Remarks on Cantonment Leavenworth," *Kansas Historical Quarterly,* Vol. XV [November, 1947], 358).

Interesting contemporary descriptions can be found in Phillip St. George Cooke, *Scenes and Adventures in the Army,* 93 (1829); Catlin, *North American Indians,* II, 15–16 (1832); Maximilian, *Travels in the Interior of North America,* XXII, 253–54 (April, 1833), and XXIV, 113–15 (May, 1834); John Dunbar and Samuel Allis in "Letters Concerning the Presbyterian Mission in the Pawnee Country," *Kansas Historical Society Collections,* Vol. XIV (1915–16), 584–85, 693 (June, 1834); Charles Augustus Murray, *Travels in North America,* I, 250–58 (July, 1835). Young Ellsworth's interesting comments have been quoted in the editor's introduction. The survey of the Fort Leavenworth military reservation is reported in

[CHAPTER V]

The Sac Indian

On the following day we strolled through the forest which skirted the garrison and overhung the Missouri. At one moment our eyes would be caught by the dazzling plumage of the little parroquets,[1] as they whirled through the branches of the trees; at another we amused ourselves by listening to the shrill screams of a woodpecker, as he saluted some crony mounted on a neighbouring limb.

Our attention at other times would be attracted by the movements of some old antiquarian bird of the same species, who was busy peeping into the holes and crannies of some ruined trunk—to ascertain if possible the cause of its decay.

In another direction might be seen a solitary raven, sitting in silence upon the naked limb of some mouldering tree, and apparently brooding over the ruin that reigned around him.

As we passed an opening between the houses, which gave us a view of the green in front, we caught sight of a single Indian, standing beneath the shade of a tall oak.

Barnes, "Journal of Isaac McCoy for the Exploring Expedition of 1830," *Kansas Historical Quarterly*, Vol. V (November, 1936), 359–61. For the general history of this post, consult Elvid Hunt, *History of Fort Leavenworth, 1827–1927;* for the frontier in general at this time, consult Henry P. Beers, *The Western Military Frontier, 1815–1846.*

1 Parroquets (paroquets, parakeets) were once common along the Missouri, coming in great flocks in the fall and often staying until spring. Prince Maximilian of Wied, John James Audubon, J. K. Townsend, Prince Paul of Württemberg, William Faux, and Stephen H. Long reported seeing the colorful birds and noted their plentitude in the early half of the last century. In the eighteen fifties and sixties they were becoming increasingly rare, and had disappeared entirely soon thereafter, although individual birds were seen in Missouri in 1904 and 1905. The reason for their extinction is not definitely known, but all of the early accounts indicate that they were ruthlessly shot by hunters and settlers. (See "Missouriana," *Missouri Historical Review*, Vol. XXXI, No. 2 [January, 1937], 181–84.)

Whilst we were regarding him, a little red-nosed soldier came up. He informed us that the Indian was a Sac, one of those who had fought against the whites under Black Hawk. As he mentioned this, he took the opportunity of uncorking his indignation, and letting off the superfluous foam, in a volley of oaths and anathemas against the whole race in general, and this individual in particular. He threw out dark hints of what he had himself done in the war, and what he would now do, if the major[2] would only permit it. At the time we looked upon him with considerable awe; but we afterwards learned that there was little to be apprehended from him. He was a character notorious for boiling over in the excess of his wrath, especially in time of peace; but beyond this was distinguished for nothing, except a strong attachment to liquors of all descriptions.

We soon left him, and crossed over the green, to the spot where the Indian was standing.

I had formed but a poor opinion of the race from those whom I had already seen, but never was I more agreeably disappointed —never had I beheld such a princely fellow. He stood unmoved as we came up, viewing us with a calm, cold, but unwavering gaze. His eyelid never drooped; nor was the eye averted for an instant as it met our look. A large blanket, here and there streaked with vermilion, and ornamented with hawk bells, was so disposed around his folded arms, that it left bare his finely formed shoulder and half of his high and sinewy chest. A bright, steel headed tomahawk peeped from beneath its folds, and a quiver of arrows hung at his back. His legs were cased in leggings of dressed deer skin, with the edges cut into a rough fringe. He wore a pair of mocassins of dressed buffalo hide. The top of his head was closely shaven, and covered with vermilion; but his face was free from any colouring whatever, with the excep-

2 Bennet Riley, brevetted major August 6, 1829, for ten years service in grade, was commander of Company A, Sixth Infantry, and commandant of the post, according to the muster roll of April 30–June 30, 1833 (Richard Graham Papers). For him, consult Carolyn Foreman, "General Bennet Riley," *Chronicles of Oklahoma*, Vol. XIX (September, 1941).

tion of a ring of black paint, which was carefully drawn around each eye.

As we approached he drew himself up, and threw his head slightly backward with an air of haughtiness which well became his high stern features. He seemed to feel like a proud but desolate being. Upon his head was bound an eagle's plume, but it was crushed and broken. Could it be emblematic of the broken spirit of his own tribe? Their power was gone; their strength was withered; they were scattered to the four winds of heaven; the bones of their bravest warriors were whitening the prairies, and their chief was in bondage in an unknown land.[3]

And this savage—he seemed to feel that he was alone; but his stern features told that he asked no pity, and would brook no insult.

For some time he stood in front of us returning gaze for gaze, and for a moment a smile played over his features; then drawing up his tinkling blanket, he wrapped it closely around him, and walked off. We lost sight of him behind one of the buildings, as he directed his course towards the forest.

We turned away towards our quarters, but the roll of the dinner drum sounded across the green, and changing our course we obeyed its summons.

---

[3] At this time, Black Hawk was in the Eastern States.—JTI. No doubt young Irving's sympathy for Black Hawk had been aroused by his uncle, for Washington Irving had seen that chief in St. Louis eleven months earlier (McDermott [ed.], *Western Journals of Washington Irving*, 83–84). Black Hawk was still a prisoner at Jefferson Barracks when Maximilian came to St. Louis in March, 1833 (*Travels in the Interior of North America*, XXII, 228–30). In April he was taken to Fortress Monroe and held as a prisoner of war there until June 4; he then went on an extended tour of the eastern cities. By the time Irving had reached Fort Leavenworth, Black Hawk was home among the Sacs (Reuben Gold Thwaites, "The Black Hawk War," in *How George Rogers Clark Won the Northwest and Other Essays in Western History*, 194–95).

[CHAPTER VI]

The Konzas

We had been two days in the garrison. A loud shrill cry arose in the air as we were in the desolate chamber which we called "our quarters."[1] Before we had time to pass a remark as to its cause, it came again, echoing through the building, and causing the forest to ring to its sound. We knew that it proceeded from Indians, and immediately left the quarters to see them. They were at a little distance from the fence surrounding the garrison, grouped together under a large oak tree, which grew alone, upon a small level plot of ground directly in front of the quarters. They were wanderers from the Konza village, which is situated upon the Konza river, about a hundred miles beyond the line of the Indian boundary.[2]

[1] Why desolate? In the 1888 edition he stated (p. 25): "We were quartered in the same building with the family of the officer who led the band which we passed at the Kansas River, and we afterwards found him to be a genial, frank-hearted soldier, full of anecdotes of his adventures in Indian warfare and in the hunt." Edward Ellsworth told his cousin Goodrich: "We have as fine and I hesitate not to say finer provisions of all sorts & lodging than we have had at any hotel on our road" (Fort Leavenworth, August 8, 1833). The ranger officers were Captain Matthew Duncan (see n. 3, p. 16), who would soon command Company C of the First Dragoons (at this time being activated), First Lieutenant Benjamin D. Moore, Second Lieutenant William Bradford, and Third Lieutenant Henry B. Roberts. Duncan had entered the service as captain of rangers, October 4, 1832, and resigned January 15, 1837 (Francis B. Heitman, *Historical Register and Dictionary of the United States Army,* I, 388).

[2] "I mentioned in Henry's letter that the Kansas Indians were here   They have now left" (Edward Ellsworth to Chauncey Goodrich, Jr., Fort Leavenworth, August 8, 1833). The Kansas reservation began sixty miles west of Missouri, lying mostly on the north bank of the Kansas River (Kappler, *Indian Affairs, Laws and Treaties,* II, 222). The principal village was on the Soldier River near the eastern limit of the reservation. For this tribe, consult George P. Morehouse, "History of the Kansa or Kaw Indians," *Kansas Historical Society Collections,* Vol. X (1907–1908); and Waldo R. Wedel, "The Kansa Indians," *Kansas Academy of Science Transactions,* Vol. XLIX (June, 1946). For Thomas Say's near-contemporary impressions of the Kansas, see Edwin James, *Account of the Expedition . . . under Long,* in Reuben Gold Thwaites (ed.), *Early Western Travels,* XIV, 183–210.

There were about forty of them, crowded together around a small fire, which they had kindled under the shade of the tree.

Give an Indian a fire, and you give him a home. Be there one, or a hundred, a few sticks thrown together and kindled into a flame, will be the gathering place of all. It is the same in the prairies, and in the settlements; in warm weather, and in cold. When they stop from a journey or a hunt, they kindle a fire and nestle around it. From that moment they feel an ideal property in the spot upon which they have thus intimated their intention to linger.

The band before us were all finely formed men; for with the exception of the Osage Indians of the Arkansaw, they are considered the most noble of the tribes which yet roam within the neighbourhood of the settlements. As yet from their communion with the whites they have derived benefit alone. Too far from them to imbibe their vices, they have yet been able to hold sufficient intercourse to promote their own interest. They have thrown aside their buffalo skin robes, and adopted the blanket. They have become skilful in the use of the rifle, and except in hunting the buffalo, make no use of bows and arrows.

When we came up, two or three were engaged in collecting fuel to sustain the fire; the rest were lounging around, luxuriating in the most perfect laziness. Several were leaning listlessly upon their hunting spears, too indolent to bear even their own weight. Some were resting against the tree; and a band of five or six were lying upon their backs, with their feet to the fire, drumming with their fists upon their breasts, and chanting out a sleepy ditty, the chorus of which was filled up by a loud yell from every throat in the band.

They were all athletic and finely formed. Their heads were shaven with the exception of the scalp lock, which hung down between their shoulders; and their breasts were left exposed by their blankets.

There was a little squaw in company with them, a notable character, and if I might judge from the foolish look of several, and the loud laugh of the rest, gifted with a most peppery tongue. We had heard of Indian beauties, but she was not one of them, for she engrossed in her own person a concentration of ugliness, which would have more than satisfied a dozen ordinary females. There was an acidity in her black glittering eye which gave a zest to her remarks, causing them to be highly relished by the lounging crew, but rendering them unpalatable to the unfortunate scape goat at whose expense they were uttered.

We had not stood there long, before we came in for our share of her blessings. Of their nature, however, we remained in a happy ignorance. They were received with loud bursts of merriment from the graceless troop around her, with the exception of one or two of the oldest Indians. The grave faces, and wrinkled brows of these, wore a discouraging sternness. It was in vain that the little woman exhausted her wit, for the purpose of enticing a smile upon their features; their lips were as rigid as ever, nor did the relaxation of a single muscle of their swarthy faces denote that they participated in the general amusement. In spite of this, however, she appeared loath to relinquish her sport. While this had been going on, an old Indian was sitting close to the fire, with one elbow resting upon his knee, and his hand supporting his chin. His hair was white, and rested in flaky locks upon his shoulders. His eyes were fixed intently upon the blaze, and he was apparently buried in deep thought.

He had continued in this posture for some time; but at last a loud burst of laughter, which followed some remark of the squaw, seemed to call him to himself. He looked around for a moment, with a bewildered air; then starting to his feet, strode over to the oratrix, and hissed a few low, but stern words, in her ear. Her face lengthened, and her mouth closed. The rest instantly followed her example, and the faces of the whole gang were converted to a look of the most penitential gravity. What the charm was, that acted so potently in hushing the clamour of the virago I never knew, or I should have imparted it for the benefit of the civilized world.

The old man then stepped from the centre of the crowd and extended his hand to each of us. After a cordial shaking he pressed his own against his bosom, and withdrew to his former seat at the fire. From that moment the noise and jeering were hushed. The old lady turned her attention to a number of potatoes which were roasting in the fire. Parties of five or six, wrapping their blankets closely around them, sauntered off towards the quarters of the officers. Others strolled off to the banks of the Missouri; and five or six who appeared too idle even to do that, laid themselves at full length upon the grass, and joined in the drum and chorus of those who were already engaged in chanting. A few of the oldest warriors then drew together in a knot, and commenced an earnest debate, in which they were afterwards joined by the old Indian who had interfered at first in our behalf. They spoke earnestly; the matter appeared to be one of moment, and each in turn gave his opinion. There was a warmth and an energy in their tones and gesticulation as they spoke, and an earnestness in their usually calm and dispassionate features, which strongly excited our curiosity.

The little woman, too, seemed totally engrossed with the interest of the subject. She suffered a large potato to roast to coal without noticing it. She sat with her eyes intently fixed upon the varying countenances of the speakers; turning from one to the other, as each in turn delivered his opinion. Her air was not that of mere curiosity, there was a strong mixture of anxiety blended with it. She looked as if she were deeply interested in the result.

The debate continued for some time; but at length they separated, and apparently without coming to any conclusion, strolled off towards the quarters without heeding the squaw, leaving her seated alone, at the fire.

We afterwards learned, that this party of Indians had been for two days without provisions, and that they were consulting about the selection of a committee from their band, who should commence begging for a supply among the soldiers of the garrison. We forgave the little squaw, in consideration of the penance and fasting which she had already undergone.

This band hung round the garrison for several days. The imposing appearance which they bear at first sight, wears off as you become familiarized with them. The high, haughty carriage which they wear towards strangers, gradually relaxes as they become acquainted. They were constantly lounging round the quarters of the soldiers, or strolling in little parties of five or six, through the woods. Here and there, some curious fellows might be seen, peering into the windows of the dwelling houses, or stealing through some open door into the interior. Their step is so hushed and noiseless, that there is nothing to warn you of their approach. I have frequently been surprised, upon looking round in my chamber, to find a dozen of these fellows quietly seated around me, some upon chairs, others upon the floor, and all apparently as much at their ease as if they had made it their resting place for the last century. They seemed neither to care whether you welcomed them or not; they had made up their minds to visit you, and visit they would. With all this, there was an unobtrusiveness in their manners, which soon reconciled us to their presence. They would sit for hours, in the same attitude, making no remarks, holding no conversation, and were it not for their glistening, snaky eyes, which were ever fastened on your face, creating a feeling of restless uneasiness, there was little else in their company to annoy you.

It was near the close of a warm afternoon, that I had thrown myself upon a bearskin on the floor, with that feeling of listless languor which is apt to pervade a stranger, when visiting the western country for the first time. The drum was pouring out a dull melancholy roll, at the far end of the green, occasionally enlivened by the shrill tones of a fierce little fife. Under the window, a lounging soldier, half asleep, was drawling out a tedious ditty, with a strong nasal accompaniment which did not add much to the vivacity of the tune. Even the sun himself had been wrought up into a fever. With a face as red as that of a fat butcher, he crawled through the sky, as if he longed for the time when he might take his twelve hours nap in the cool bed of the ocean. The trees nodded over the bank of the Missouri with a heavy, sleepy look. The river itself scampered along its channel, as if anxious to escape from the sultry heat which filled the atmosphere.

I had lain nearly an hour upon my shaggy couch. My eyes were yielding to slumber; present things were fast vanishing, or only appeared blended with the fitful forms of a drowsy imagination.

"Ho! Ho! Ho!" shouted a dozen voices at my side. I started up—a group of Konzas were seated in a ring, around my bearskin. For a moment I was bewildered—but they soon convinced me of the reality of my situation, and of the difference between their visitations, and those of fancy.

They were a detachment who had been sent out to forage in the larders of the garrison. Although their language was unknown to me, their object was perfectly intelligible. They signified their wants with a clearness of gesticulation which could not be misunderstood, and the earnestness of which was, no doubt, enhanced by a keen appetite.

Seeing that there was no alternative, I called to our half-breed boy:

"Joseph!"

"Vat you vant?" sounded a voice from the dark cavern below, which was dignified with the name of a kitchen.

"Have you any meat or bread, for these Indians?"

"Sacre diable!" answered he. "Vare de devil I to git meat for dem? I h'aint eat none my own sef, for tree day, or Mordecai neder."

This was not altogether true, but it was conclusive, so I returned to my dusky friends with the heavy intelligence.

There are two characters in this world, whom it is impossible to convince of the truth of anything which jars with their own opinions or interests; the first is a politician, the second is a hungry Indian. I soon found it out—my red visitors were im-moveable—they were deaf both to arguments and to statements of facts. They heard me—they understood me—but they were not a whit nearer to conviction, and they made no motion to depart. There was no resource left, so I determined to abdicate in their favour, and taking up my hat I left the house, and strolled off into the woods.

It was near sun set when I returned to my quarters. I opened the door of the chamber and looked in.

"Ho! Ho! Ho!" sounded a dozen guttural voices from within. My red friends were there still, waiting for my coming. I closed the door instantly, and walked off with a hasty step to the quarters of one of the officers, nor did I return until late at night, when I found that they had disappeared.

I afterwards learned that they had been supplied with pro-visions, on the morning previous, and that they were now carry-ing on the business of begging, for mere amusement.[3]

When the night grew dark, there was a bright fire gleaming under the old oak tree where they had taken their station, and the whole group were huddled together around it. From the piazza in front of our quarters we could see their forms flitting round the blaze, and could hear their song as it rose up in the damp air, with a wildness not unmixed with melody. The day was past, and they were now enjoying the present moment with their usual happy forgetfulness of toil. In the morning we again visited the spot which they had selected for their camp; but it was deserted. The embers had fallen to ashes—the fire was ex-tinguished—and the whole wild troop had again set out upon its wanderings.[4]

[3] At this point Irving introduced in the 1888 edition (pp. 37–40) the anecdote, which has already been presented in the editor's introduction, about "Preparation No. 3," for cholera and the Kansa Indian's stealing drinks.

[4] Between the departure of the Kansa Indians and the arrival of White Plume reported in the next chapter, there was, according to Edward Ellsworth, a visit by a group of Sacs (Ellsworth to Goodrich, Fort Leavenworth, August 8, 1833). For Ellsworth's description of their painting and dancing, see editor's introduction.

CHAPTER VII

The Konza Chief

Two days after the departure of the Konza band we were seated in our chamber, when a heavy muffled tread jarred upon the piazza in front of us. A large Indian passed the window, and a moment after he entered the room.

He was tall and muscular, though his form through neglect of exercise, was fast verging towards corpulency. He wore a hat after the fashion of the whites, a calico hunting shirt and rough leggings. Over the whole was wrapped a heavy blanket. His face was unpainted, and although his age was nearly seventy his hair was raven black, and his eye as keen as a hawk's. He was the White Plume, chief of the Konza nation.[1] He had spent much time among the whites, and had gradually become familiarized with their manners. Upon entering the room he lifted his hat from his head and placed it upon the table; then advancing towards the Indian commissioner, who was seated near the door,

1 On August 8, Edward Ellsworth wrote from Fort Leavenworth to his cousin: "The Kansas Indians . . . have now left but their head chief has just arrived   he is a very clever old man   he is accompanied by his squaw & his son." Fourteen years earlier, members of Long's expedition had found "Wom-pa-wa-ra, *He who scares all men,* more commonly known to the whites as Plume Blanche or White Plume, a man rising rapidly in importance, and apparently destined to become the leader of the nation" (James, *Account of the Expedition under Long,* XIV, 177). "Nom-pa-wa-rah, or the White Plume" was the first of the Kansas chiefs to sign the treaty of June 3, 1825 (Kappler, *Indian Affairs, Laws and Treaties,* II, 225). Catlin (ca. 1832) described him as "a very urbane and hospitable man, of good portly size, speaking some English, and making himself good company for all white persons who travel through his country and have the good luck to shake his liberal and hospitable hand" (*North American Indians,* II, 23). Victor Tixier reported meeting White Plume in 1840; the chief then had two wives, though the one Tixier sketched was probably not the one Irving saw. The Frenchman's description does not tally with Catlin's: ". . . a short, wiry man with an aquiline nose and piercing eyes. . . . He had two wives, one of whom had an air very seldom found among the Kanza women. I obtained permission to draw a portrait of her. . . . I learned [later] that the young woman died shortly after her return to the village" (McDermott [ed.], *Tixier's Travels on the Osage Prairies,* 201).

he offered his hand to him; after which he shook hands in turn with the rest. Having done this, he stepped into the centre of the room, and wrapping his blanket closely around his body beneath his arms, commenced an address—not that he had any thing in particular to say, for he had come to the garrison by accident; but he was one of those windy characters, who take great delight in listening to their own speeches, and who, unfortunately for the ears of many a civilized man, are not confined to savages alone. By his side stood his interpreter, a white man, who had spent many years among the tribe, and who translated the sentences, as the chief paused for that purpose.[2]

The address lasted for about ten minutes, by which time he was completely out of breath, and seated himself from mere exhaustion. The most of it was dull and a mere repetition of the same ideas; but once in speaking of the loss of his children, who had died of the cholera during the fall previous, his language was even poetical.

"My children," said he, "have gone from me. The Great Spirit has called them. They have disappeared like the snow that melteth on the prairie. I was lonely; I returned to my lodge, but it was desolate, for they were not there."

When he had rested himself for a few moments, he rose up; and after throwing out several hints of so broad a character that they smacked strongly of beggary, he received several presents and left the building, winding his way over the prairie, along the narrow trail which led to his village.

[CHAPTER VIII]

The Forest—The Kickapoos

Day after day waned by, still we lingered in the white-washed cottages of Leavenworth. Urgent preparations were making for

2 Clement Lessert.

our departure to the western wilds, but as yet they were un-finished. To the commissioner who had charge of the expedition, every moment was fraught with interest and anxiety, but to several of us who had accompanied him from curiosity alone, there was but little occupation. Still, there was a feeling of dreamy pleasure in wandering through the tall moss-grown groves which surrounded the garrison. There was a calm quiet pervading them, which stole soothingly over the mind, drawing it away from dwelling upon things present, and wrapping it up in its own wild musings. The thick arches of overhanging trees, threw a dark and night-like shade over the ground. Here and there a solitary ray of sunshine, like a pilgrim in a strange land, strayed through some crevice in the thick foliage, playing in a bright hazy streak through the gloom, and casting a golden spot upon the dark creeping plants beneath. There was a vastness in the size of the mighty trunks, that seized forcibly upon the imagination. What was America when those veteran trees were but saplings? Who were her children? Where are they? The tale is a sad one, and fraught with little that reflects credit upon the white man.

The forest is full of ruins. It gives many a touching memento of the work of time. Hundreds of gigantic trees which have weathered the storms of ages, and for centuries have kept their silent watch, have yielded to its power; have been hurled from their stands, and their lumbering wrecks are decaying upon the ground—the green moss is their covering, the wild ivy their shroud. Thousands of dead trees are still standing, shooting up their tall gray forms, stripped of bark, of foliage, and of branches; still, they cling with a lingering tenacity to their old abiding places, as if loath to resign themselves to the ruin which is every where reigning around them, and although despoiled of foliage, as if they still loved to linger on the spot which once bore witness to their magnificence.

Occasionally in our rambles we would fall upon a solitary Indian, roaming through the woods, or seated in deep meditation upon the wreck of some prostrate tree. It was the place for him. Let him look upon the forests and read his own fate; they are united—their destinies are the same; alike they have lived and flourished in the wilderness of nature, and alike they are disappearing before the approach of civilization. Let the Indian grieve at the sound of the woodman's axe, for at the fall of every tree, the hour of his own ruin draws nearer.

From the time of our arrival at the garrison, small parties of Indians had been constantly coming and going. They belonged to the Kickapoo tribe, another band of emigrants from the states.[1] There were many manly forms among them, and some of their females were even beautiful. Scarce a day elapsed that we did not catch a glimpse of the gaudily dressed figures of some band, their tin trinkets glistening in the sunbeams, and their bright garments fluttering in the wind, as they galloped over the prairie towards the garrison. They carry on a species of traffic with the sutler at the post;[2] exchanging furs and skins for ribands, and such other showy articles as are likely to catch the eye of a savage. This tribe, from long intercourse with the inhabitants of the settlements, have become accustomed to driving bargains, and are looked upon by the generality of traders as pretty hard customers; yet even from them, the profits derived by the whites are great.

From seeing these different bands constantly coming and going, to and from their village, we conceived a desire to visit them; and accordingly, upon a fine clear morning we started.[3]

[1] The Kickapoo reservation lay adjoining that of the Delawares and immediately to the west and north of the military reservation, according to the provisions of the Castor Hill Treaty of October 4, 1832 (Kappler, *Indian Affairs, Laws and Treaties*, II, 365–67). James Kennerly, in June, 1833, brought out a band of 375 Kickapoos and 119 Potawatomi and settled them on their lands six miles above Fort Leavenworth (*Sen. Doc. 512*, I, 644).

[2] Alexander G. Morgan.

[3] This was a pleasure excursion by the young men. Irving does not comment on an official visit made to the Kickapoos, though he no doubt attended. "Our course will probably be to go to the Kickapoo Indians first   they are about 5 miles off & we shall have 'talk' with them here   then we prepare for our Pawnee expedition" (Edward A. Ellsworth to Chauncey Goodrich, Jr., Fort Leavenworth, Au-

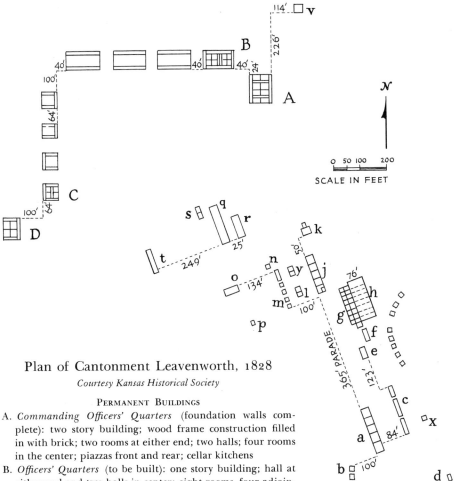

Plan of Cantonment Leavenworth, 1828

Courtesy Kansas Historical Society

PERMANENT BUILDINGS

A. *Commanding Officers' Quarters* (foundation walls complete): two story building; wood frame construction filled in with brick; two rooms at either end; two halls; four rooms in the center; piazzas front and rear; cellar kitchens

B. *Officers' Quarters* (to be built): one story building; hall at either end and two halls in center; eight rooms, four adjoining; piazzas front and rear; cellar kitchens

C. *Soldiers' Quarters* (completed): one story building; center hall, two rooms on either side; piazzas front and rear; cellar kitchens

D. *Hospital* (completed): two story building; hall at either end; four rooms; piazza in front; cellar kitchens

TEMPORARY QUARTERS

a. *Soldiers' Quarters Left Wing:* tent, four company rooms, one for guard

b. and c. *Huts for Laundresses*

d. *Sink for Left Wing*

e. and f. *Sutler's Store Houses*

g. *Officers' Quarters:* one story building, built of logs

h. *Officers' Yards and Kitchens*

j. *Soldiers' Quarters Right Wing:* hut, four rooms for the companies; one room for the guard, prisonary, and staff guard

k. *Smith's Shop*

l. *Kitchens for the Four Companies of the Right Wing*

m. *Huts for Laundresses of the Right Wing*

n. *Board Kiln*

o. *Bake House*

p. *Sink for the Right Wing*

q. and r. *Commissary Store Houses*

s. *Hut for the Commissary Sergeant and Sergeant Major*

t. *Sand Pit*   v. *Ice House*

NOTE: The Commanding Officers' quarters are 300 yards from the river and about 200 feet above low water mark.

The path was for the most part through the woods. We rode about an hour, crossed several brooks, traversed several small patches of prairie, and at last found ourselves upon the summit of a high bluff which overlooked the little Indian town, and commanded a fine view of the whole neighbouring country. At our feet lay a small green prairie, dotted with clusters of wild flowers. Three of its sides were enclosed by a ridge of hills, at the foot of which meandered a clear, sparkling brook, brawling in low murmurs over its rocky bottom.[4] A long range of trees stood upon its borders, leaning over the stream, and shading its waters from the noontide sun. The fourth side of the green was hemmed in by a dark thick forest, which extended back to the banks of the Missouri.

In the edge of this stood the village of the Kickapoos.[5] It fronted upon the variegated green. It was a retired, rural spot,

gust 8, 1833). Because a band of Kickapoos led by Kishko had objected to the reservation selected for this tribe, the western commissioners had been instructed by Elbert Herring, commissioner for Indian affairs, on June 1, 1833, "to visit those lands, and make such alterations as they may find just" (*Sen. Doc. 512*, III, 706–707). A talk with the Kickapoos was held at their village on September 2; this was the commissioner's second official visit to that town (*ibid.*, IV, 640).

4 Salt Creek in Leavenworth County.

5 The Reverend W. D. Smith, exploring for the Presbyterian Mission Society, visited the Kickapoos a few weeks before our travelers saw them: "I should perhaps say something of the Kickapoos. . . . They are not yet settled and it is uncertain to what part of their lands they will go. They live at present in the only unhealthy place I have seen in the country. Their village is situated on the northern edge of a low wet Prairie which runs up along a creek from the low bottoms of the Missouri. Their huts are built so closely as to prevent a free circulation of air, and to accelerate the accumulations of filth" (Smith to E. P. Swift, Shawanoe Villages, Kanzas River, July 29th 1833). Dunbar reported on June 27, 1834, that the Kickapoos then had two villages about a mile apart, "one . . . is inhabited by the prophet's band, which consists of those who have embraced the prophet's religion, or are friendly to it. The other . . . [is] occupied by a band of irreligious Indians" ("Letters Concerning the Presbyterian Mission in the Pawnee Country," *Kansas Historical Society Collections*, Vol. XIV [1915–16], 585–86). Like young Ellsworth (n. 3 *supra*), John Dunbar placed the principal village five miles from the cantonment. Samuel Allis ("Letters Concerning the Presbyterian Mission," 693) placed the two villages a mile apart and four miles from the fort; at that time (1834) he estimated them as having about four hundred people each.

shut out from the world, and looked as if it might have been free from its cares also.

As we stood upon the bluff, a small party of inhabitants from the village moved towards a tree growing alone in the prairie, about a quarter of a mile from the town, and collected together beneath its shade. Presently, two young Indians made their appearance, mounted on horseback. Suspecting that there was to be a race of some description, we left the bluff, dashed through the brook at the bottom of the hill, and in a few moments were under the tree where the group had assembled. They received us in their usual calm manner, and we were satisfied; for the welcome of an Indian is shown more by actions than words. There is no superfluous expression of feelings which he never had—he never makes use of hypocrisy—he receives you with a good will, or not at all.

By the time we reached the spot, the preparations were finished. A little, hard headed, old Indian was appointed umpire, and the two riders were at their posts. They were both young men, dressed in hunting shirts and cloth leggings. Their horses were not of the class, that might strictly be denominated racers. One was black, the other cream colored. The black one had fierce little eyes glittering like fire, beneath a long shaggy forelock, which reached nearly to his nose. The eyes of the other were water coloured, and had a sneaking slyness about them— an air which seemed to insinuate that their owner "knew a thing or two." Both horses were round bodied, bull necked, and the thick legs of both were garnished with fetlocks of matted hair, extending from the knee joint down to the hoof, and trailing on the ground as they walked. There was not much show of spirit about them. They appeared but little ambitious of distinguishing themselves in the coming contest, and if their own inclinations had been consulted, it is probable would have declined it altogether. Not so their riders; they sat as eager as grey hounds in the leash. Their eyes were intently fixed upon the umpire, who seemed to take the matter with wonderful coolness. At last he gave the signal—there was a hard, quick thumping of heels, against the ribs of the horses—the next moment they had vanished from their posts. There was a great clattering over the hard course—their bounds were short but rapid. At last the legs grew invisible, and the bodies looked like two balls, moving through the air. The riders whooped and screamed, and the band of lookers-on shouted as loud as either.

The little cream coloured pony was working wonderfully hard, but the black was gaining ground. There was a tree at some distance, which they were to pass round, and return to the starting place. They reached it—the black taking the lead by a length—his legs were invisible as he turned, but the cream coloured pony pushed him hard. They now approached the goal.

"Two to one on the black!" shouted one of the whites.

"Lay it on, old boy, or you're beaten!" halloed another.

Both riders exerted themselves to the utmost. They flew over the ground like lightning. The black still kept the lead, but both horses seemed to be eaten up with fury, at being driven at such a rate. They rushed snorting in—the crowd shouted, and opened a passage for them—they dashed through, running nearly a hundred yards beyond the mark, before they could check their speed. The black pony had won, but he appeared too angry to enjoy his victory. I looked at the other. *There* he stood—*there* was that self-satisfied, water coloured eye, which said, "I may have been beaten, but still I know a thing or two."

When the race was finished, we rode on and entered the town. About thirty huts constructed of bark, compose the village. It is impossible to describe their architecture, for no two were built alike, and as far as I was able to judge, they had no particular shape. A strong gale of wind would have prostrated even the best of them, had it not been for the shelter of the forest in which they were built.

As we rode along, the troops of naked children who followed at our heels, convinced us, that among the sundry and manifold cares of the world, this tribe had not forgotten to perpetuate their race, and notwithstanding their laziness, had contrived to start a fresh growth of papooses, that constituted the "rising generation," and were then undergoing the education, usual to the Indian child. From what we saw, there is little doubt, that when the present race shall pass away, the rising tribe will be fully qualified to inherit in a creditable manner, the laziness of their forefathers.

Here and there, winding through the woods, or strolling over the prairie, might be seen a couple of cooing, greasy lovers; full of affection and slovenliness; unwashed, but devoted. What a fund of affection there must have been to have overlooked such a world of defects. A loud cry broke out in one of the hovels, and a couple rushed out. The first was a fat blowzy squaw. After her followed a diminutive, spider-legged Indian, who looked as if he had withered away under the gall of his own disposition. He was the lord and master of the lady. In his hand he flourished a stick, with which he had been maintaining that discipline, by some deemed proper in a family, and which he now seemed inclined to continue. The woman, however, escaped, and made for the woods. The bystanders paused for a moment to look on, for there was an agreeable excitement about this, which did not occur every day, and which therefore was not to be lost. Upon the escape of his wife, the little man looked around, as if he longed for some other object, upon which to vent the remainder of his wrath; but finding none, he disconsolately entered his dwelling.

In the centre of the town is a small log house, the residence of the agent, appointed by the United States to reside with the tribe, and attend to the payment of the annuities forwarded by the government to this nation.[6] We were cordially welcomed by him. We found the chief and prophet of the tribe with him. The former was a corpulent man, and in his youth must have

6 Richard W. Cummins was agent for the Kickapoos as well as the Shawnee and Delaware Indians; ordinarily he lived at the Shawnee Agency, which must have been the first stop of the travelers after crossing the frontier. The man met at the Kickapoo village may have been F. W. Miller, subagent to Cummins.

been peculiarly handsome.[7] The prophet [Kanakuk] was a tall bony Indian, with a keen black eye, and a face beaming with intelligence. He was leaning upon the muzzle of a long rifle when we entered. This he laid aside, and with the assistance of an interpreter,[8] commenced a conversation with us. It was something unusual for him, as he generally kept aloof from intercourse with the whites. He had been converted to Christianity, and on Sundays delivered addresses upon this subject, to the tribe.

There is an energy of character about him, which gives much weight to his words, and has created for him an influence greater than that of any Indian in the town. From the little we saw it was evident that the chief yielded to him, and listened to his remarks with the deference of one who acknowledged his superiority. There was however no appearance of jealousy or heart burning between them.[9]

[7] Presumably Pat-sa-che-haw, since he was the only Kickapoo other than Kanakuk, the Kickapoo prophet, to sign the treaty at Fort Leavenworth on November 12 (*Sen. Doc. 512*, IV, 728).

[8] Lawrence Pinsonneau (Gilbert J. Garraghan, *Catholic Beginnings in Kansas City, Missouri*, 53–54).

[9] The most detailed account of Kanakuk (Kanacuk, Kan-ne-kuh-kah, Kee-an-ne-kuk, Kenekuk, Kennekuk) is that of James Mooney in *The Ghost-Dance Religion* (Bureau of American Ethnology *14th Annual Report* [1892–93]), 694–700. Mooney characterized him as "the direct spiritual successor of Tenskwatawa and the Delaware prophet," noted that he had risen to strong power in the tribe by 1827, and reported that he died of smallpox in Kansas in 1852. Catlin painted his portrait in 1831 before his removal from Illinois (*North American Indians*, II, 98–99). One of the first to describe the prophet and his religion on the new lands was W. D. Smith: "They are it is true partly religious but wholly Heathen. They have their peculiar forms of worship to which they have become attached and which it would be impossible to break down. Their religion and worship in all their parts seem to bear a striking resemblance to that of the Roman Catholics, and whatever notions of Christianity they may have they are as far as I could discover decidedly of that character. Their leader, or Prophet, is a man of a strong mind, and considerable eloquence, and rules his people in a manner which would reflect honour on an enlightened statesman. They are moral in their deportment, and seem very sincere in their religion. I endeavored to acquire a knowledge of the meaning attached to each of their ceremonies, and hyerogliphic characters used in prayer like the Roman beads, but owing to the inefficiency of the interpreter, what I acquired was far from satisfactory" (Smith to E. P. Swift, Shawanoe Villages, Kanzas River, July 29th, 1833). Other contemporary accounts will be

It was late in the afternoon before we left. The sun was fast sinking in the west, and his last beams were resting on the tree tops, as we rode out of the woods. One hour's ride, brought us again to our quarters at the cantonment.

CHAPTER IX

Departure for the Pawnees—Prairie Life

Several weeks had elapsed, since our arrival at the garrison; yet the other commissioner had not made his appearance. Mr. Ellsworth determined therefore, to set out without him, for the Pawnee villages.[1] The state of the garrison, enfeebled by sickness, did not allow of a sufficient escort to overawe the savages. He therefore took the bold alternative of throwing himself among them, in a manner unarmed, piquing their honour and hospitality by this mark of confidence.[2]

Seven soldiers constituted the whole of the military escort: merely sufficient to protect us from any petty, prowling band. The two servants, Mordecai and Joseph, who had hitherto accompanied us, were to have charge of the two light wagons—in

---

found in Garraghan, *Catholic Beginnings in Kansas City, Missouri*, 49–50, 53–54 (Father Lutz, 1833); Jerome C. Berryman, "A Circuit Rider's Frontier Experiences," *Kansas Historical Society Collections*, Vol. XVI (1923–25), 215–17 (first Methodist missionary among the Kickapoos, 1833–34); "Letters Concerning the Presbyterian Mission in the Pawnee Country," 586–87, 693, 695 (Dunbar and Allis on the prophet and his religious ceremonies, June and July, 1834); Isaac McCoy, *History of Baptist Missions*, 456–58; Murray, *Travels in North America*, II, 77–80 (September, 1835).

1 On August 28, 1833, Edward Ellsworth wrote to his uncle, Chauncey Goodrich, that "Gov. Stokes remains sick at St. Louis   He will not go with us of course to the Pawnees as we go in a few days." It was not merely the nonarrival of Stokes that held up the expedition: young Ellsworth had had cholera and was at this date of writing still so weak that he could "walk only 80 or 90 feet from the house." For more detail, see editor's introduction.

2 "25 rangers were detailed, and ready to start with me. . . . The rangers were suddenly ordered to Jefferson Barracks—I took, therefore, a few soldiers only . . ." (Ellsworth to Cass, Fort Leavenworth, November 4, 1833).

which were packed our bedding, baggage and camp furniture. We had also engaged the service of a negro as cook.[3]

Our own mess was increased by the addition of Major Dougherty[4] from St. Louis, the agent for the Pawnee Indians, and Dr. May, a surgeon resident in Missouri.[5]

On the morning previous to the day of departure, the soldiers commenced loading two heavy ox wagons, with kegs of gunpowder; barrels of flour; sacks of bacon; tents and cooking utensils, besides boxes and bales, containing presents for the Indians.[6] Towards evening, a cessation of swearing in the neighbourhood of the store-house, gave token that the task was accomplished. In the course of an hour, half a dozen oxen were yoked before each wagon, and conducted by two wild teamsters. They departed under escort of the seven soldiers. The whole were to encamp on a small stream a few miles distant, and await our

3 In the 1888 edition his name was given as Jones (p. 49). Later in the narrative he is renamed Little Black Bear by the Indians.

4 Major John Dougherty (1791–1856), Pawnee-Oto-Omaha agent since 1827, was a St. Louisan, but he had now come down from his agency at Belle Vue. "The cholera confined him a considerable time in the early part of the fall," Ellsworth wrote on December 3, "and he entered into my service as soon as he was able to ride" (*Sen. Doc. 512*, IV, 744). He probably arrived at the fort only in time to start out on the expedition, for Joshua Pilcher, in charge of the American Fur Company post among the Omahas, wrote to Pierre Chouteau, Jr., on August 21, 1833: "The cholera was very fatal at *Belle Vue*: the Sub Agent [John Beauchamp], both Blacksmiths, Mrs. Cossner [?], the Interpreter & wife all went off in a few hours, and Major Daugherty escaped narrowly and is still in verry bad health—he is & has been here for some days *by my invitation*" (Chouteau-Maffitt Collection, Missouri Historical Society). For Dougherty, consult Margaret Stauf, "John Dougherty, Indian Agent," *Mid-America*, Vol. XVI (January, 1934), 135–46.

5 Dr. William S. May was paid $100 a month and allowed $7 for medicines from September 1 to November 4, 1833. "He was much needed, for all were sick more or less during the tour" (*Sen. Doc. 512*, IV, 647; V, 295). "The Doctor was clad in a buck-skin coat, with high boots, and a soft, broad-brimmed hat, which turned up all around, and assumed any shape which the owner might wish. He rode a small mule named Kitty Keero, upon whom he lavished various terms of endearment. As he was a pretty lusty fellow, it is probable that Kitty would have preferred a rider who was more crusty and less heavy" (*Indian Sketches*, 1888, p. 58).

6 "The Commissioner, with prudent care for our creature comforts, had added a cow, remarking that coffee was always improved by the addition of milk, a remark in which we all concurred" (*Indian Sketches*, 1888, p. 50). In all probability the cow was intended for a present to the Indians.

[45]

coming. Our party, six in number, were to follow their trail, on horse back on the succeeding morning.[7]

The sun rose cheerily over the tops of the trees, on the day following, and we prepared to leave. There was quite an excitement in the garrison. Kind wishes and farewells were exchanged. Many who had been anxious to join the troop, in their journey through this unknown land, now hung round with longing eyes. There was a mystery and shadowy danger, which threw a high excitement around the whole expedition. Nothing was positive about the wild tribes we were to visit. It was known, that their numbers were large; it was reported, that they were cruel and unsparing in their nature; that they looked upon the whites as their bitterest enemies, and carried on a war of extermination against the whole race. By way of adding to the agreeable excitement, two or three, had collected all the tales of murder and bloodshed, committed by the Indians since the discovery of America, and poured them into our ears, with a most edifying accompaniment of long faces and evil prophecies. They foretold that we would never again be seen at Leavenworth, or at all events, that if we did, it would be stripped of our scalps. They thought, as these were the most desirable trophies, perhaps the Indians would have the generosity to permit our return, provided we left them behind. These, and many other predictions of an equally comforting nature, were conveyed to us, by a number who buzzed around as we were getting ready. They, however, at last took their leave, not forgetting to give us the rather unnecessary caution, to "take care and not get killed."

It was near mid-day when we set out. Our little cavalcade clattered over the hard walks until we reached the road. Galloping over the prairie, we at length came upon the broad trail left by the heavy baggage wagons, as they had passed through the high grass.

[7] The two dearborns with the three servants apparently had gone with the heavy wagons. The latter carried, among other things, $1,655.29 worth of "blankets, cloths, beads, paints, kettles &c" as presents for the Otoes and Pawnees (*Sen. Doc. 512*, V. 296).

A number of the officers accompanied us several miles, but at length they took their leave, and left us to journey onward in our pilgrimage. As long as we were in the garrison, where the busy face of man was seen, where active forms were moving around us, and the every day concerns of life were going forward, we felt that though distant from home, we were still connected with society; but when we had started on our journey, and bade farewell to those who had accompanied us; as we watched their forms until they were hid by the distant hills, we felt that the last link was broken, which had hitherto united us to the world and its occupations.

It was intended, first to strike up in a northerly direction, until we reached the village of the Otoe and Missouria Indians,[8] situated upon the Platte river, about twenty miles north-west of its junction with the Missouri. Thence the Platte was to be our guide, until we came upon the Pawnee towns. They are seated on its banks, some five or six days' journey further to the westward.

During our stay at the garrison a change had come over the face of nature. The bright and luxurious summer flowers had disappeared, a growth of yellow and blue, the harbingers of the departing year, supplied their places. Here and there might be seen a single red flower, the survivor of those which had flourished in the summer, shooting up its head amid clusters of golden hued blossoms, still lingering, though a stranger among them. The deep richness of foliage, which graced the trees, had departed, and the brown tinge of autumn was creeping among the leaves. The bright soft green was disappearing from the prairie grass, giving place to a colour of greenish brown. The geese and pelicans had left their lives of solitude, and forming themselves into large flocks, were winging their way to the north;

8 The remnants of the Missouri tribe had settled with the Otoes by 1829; at that time they numbered eighty souls (Hodge [ed.], *Handbook of American Indians*, I, 911). The village was nearer forty than twenty miles above the Missouri.

the wind swept over the rustling grass with a moaning sound that spoke strongly of the approach of winter.

At this season we commenced our travel.[9] It was late in the afternoon when we reached the spot where the soldiers had encamped. It was on the side of a small prairie hill. Within a few yards of their tents, a scanty run of water stole through the grass, and at the distance of about a hundred yards stood a grove of timber, which supplied the fuel necessary for their night fires.

There is but little variety on the prairie. The life of one day is the life of a month; yet there is an excitement about it. The killing of a deer is an era in the day. The appearance of a hunter upon a distant hill, would give birth to a thousand speculations, as to his success in the chase. The sight of a deer standing upon an eminence, or reclining in some hollow, was a signal for bustle. There was an intense interest excited, in watching the movements of the hunters, as they stole down upon him; as they drew near every eye was fixed, even the breath was restrained: the animal scents them in the tainted air; the hunters crouch in the tall grass and creep onward—the deer rises to his feet; his nose is raised high in the air; he begins to walk off. Now is the time! Crack!—sounds the rifle. In five minutes he is far beyond sight, or two hunters are staggering beneath his weight, as they bring him to the camp.

The sight of foot prints in the grass, would be the foundation of a hundred wild fancies. By whom were they made? by members of what tribe? were they friends or foes? where were they going? was it a war party or a hunting party? These and a hundred other conjectures would be offered, by a knot collected around the suspicious mark, denoting that others besides ourselves had passed in that direction, and that we were not the only beings wandering upon that waste.

9 They did not start until after September 2 at the earliest, for on that day Ellsworth had a talk with the Kickapoos at their village; Edward Ellsworth, as secretary pro tem of the commission, kept the record (*Sen. Doc. 512*, IV, 640–43).

CHAPTER X

The Party of Sac Indians

We had been absent about a week, from the garrison, and had traversed nearly a hundred miles of prairie and woodland.[1] Our encampment during the night previous, had been upon the borders of a small prairie rivulet, which meandered through the country, overhung by a fringe of bushes and trees. Several times during the day previous, foot prints had been observed in the grass; and the whole party were on the look out for Indians. At night, lest the horses should stray from the camp, and be driven off by lurking marauders, they had been secured by long ropes to stakes. The night, however passed without disturbance; and in the morning the tents were struck, and the party resumed its journey.

As the movements of the wagons were necessarily tardy, four of us strolled forward on foot. We were several miles in advance of the party. We travelled slowly that they might overtake us, amusing ourselves by discharging our rifles at the ravens or vultures which soared over our heads. Sometimes we diverged a little from our path, to get a shot at the deer, which we now and then, saw standing at a little distance, gazing with surprise at our appearance.

We were out of sight of the wagons. In front of us, at the distance of a quarter of a mile, rose a swelling, cone-like hill. From each side of it extended a long ridge, effectually shutting out the view beyond. Presently a black object rose over its top. Gradually it grew larger and larger, until the tall, stately form of an Indian appeared, and stood watching our movements. A moment after, another joined him; he was followed by a third,

1 They must have been somewhere between the Big and Little Nemaha at this time. Philip St. George Cooke, two years earlier, had traveled over this route and described it in much greater detail than does Irving (*Scenes and Adventures in the Army*, 95–104).

who took his stand by the side of his comrades. For some moments there appeared to be a consultation among them, then seating themselves they waited for us to come up. The position which they had taken was directly upon the narrow trail we were following, so that whether friends or foes, there was no possibility of avoiding them. But as there were only three, there was little to be apprehended. Before advancing, however, the soldiers took the precaution to hammer their flints, and renew the priming of their guns. While thus engaged, one of them named Wolf,[2] a tall, gigantic fellow, with a neck like a bull's, who had fought against Black Hawk, took the opportunity to bestow a little of his advice and opinion upon the others, and turning round he commenced:

"You see them ar Ingens; well, them is Sacs and Foxes. I know 'em, for I *fit* agin 'em when Black Hawk led 'em on. And now I think on't: it's dreadful aggravating to see how the folks at the east'ard are honouring that ar rascal for killing and murdering the whites, while we who *fit* agin him to prevent it, a'int taken no notice on; its monstrous aggravating. But that a'int nothing to the *pint*. You see them ar Ingens on that ar hill. Now you think there's only three on 'em. There you think a lie—bekase there's more behind 'em;—for if there wa'rnt they would come on to meet us, and would'nt be squatting like so many woodchucks in the *parara*. They'm waiting for the rest to come up, to see whether they think it best to rob us or not. That's my opinion, and I know something of Ingen natur, for I *fit* agin 'em. Now I know one what they wont rob, and that's me; first, bekase I ai'nt got nothing to lose; and second, bekase I intend to make my yager[3] speak to the first red skin what tries to take it. And

---

[2] Probably Elijah Wolf, Company F, Sixth Infantry. He had enlisted at Nashville, Tennessee, November 8, 1828; the company muster rolls for February 28–June 30, 1833, show him in confinement (for desertion?) under a general court-martial order (Richard Graham Papers).

[3] This is a short rifle, and carries a very large ball. They are used by the U. S. dragoons, on account of the convenience of their length.—JTI. The First Regiment of Dragoons was created by an act of March 2, 1833; between May and September of that year ten companies reported to Colonel Dodge at Jefferson

now my boys, move ahead—keep a stiff upper lip, and don't be in a hurry to use your *wepons*. If the worst comes to the worst, we can keep 'em off until the wagons come up, and then we'll lick 'em."

After finishing his address, he shouldered his yager and strode on, followed by the rest of us. Notwithstanding his knowledge of "Ingen natur," we did not place as much confidence in his experience as he might have supposed; nor did we expect to push matters to the extremity, which he seemed to take for granted, would be the result of our meeting. In five minutes we were at the bottom of the hill. The savages maintained their sitting posture on the summit, nor did they rise until we came within about ten yards of them. Upon reaching them we found that the soldier had been correct in one of his conjectures; for at the distance of little less than a quarter of a mile, were about seventy more of the same band, driving in front of them a large drove of horses. They were all wild, uncouth looking fellows. Some few were dressed in blankets, but the most of them in robes of buffalo skin. At the sight of us they raised a loud yell, and leaving their horses to the charge of one or two squaws, scampered over the prairie to meet us.

"I told you so," said Wolf. "Look to your guns, and when they crowds around, keep a tight grip on the *wepons,* but don't fire till it comes to the pinch."

The crowd poured on towards us, each endeavoring to out-run his neighbour. Many threw from them the robes which impeded their motions, and several pulling them from their shoulders, packed them under their arms. Yet they appeared to be actuated by curiosity alone. But one of them had a gun; the rest were armed with bows and tomahawks. Upon reaching us, they pressed round, fingering our different articles of dress with much curiosity, though without any appearance of hostility towards the owners. At length they drew round in a closer

Barracks. Irving may have seen some of these in July, but there were none on duty at Fort Leavenworth during his stay in the Indian country.

crowd, and began to hustle us. Suddenly a tall, thin fellow grasped hold of Wolf's yager.

"No you don't *stranger!*" shouted Wolf, jerking the gun from his grasp, with the look of a nettled bull. At the same time he whirled the Indian off, with a violence that fairly made him spin, and nearly prostrated two others, whom he encountered in his involuntary movement. "Keep off, you red devils," said he, stepping back, "I wants none of your *neighbourship*." Seizing his gun by the muzzle, he whirled the breech around with a violence which caused the Indians to draw back, and cleared a small circle around him.

At this moment the chief, or person who seemed to have charge of the party, made his appearance. He spoke a few words to the band, which caused them to draw off; then walking his horse up to us, he cordially shook hands with all. He was an old man, dressed in Indian style, with the exception of a plaid handkerchief, tied round his head. Upon the top of this was mounted a broad brimmed black hat, shadowing a little, dried up, French-looking physiognomy. Agreeable as his presence was at that moment, there was but little about him, to justify the high idea we had formed, of the leader of a wild band of savages; and there were many nobler men in his troop. As they stood in a large circle around us, I think I never beheld such a number of proud spirits, as were there. It seemed strange that they should all be at the command of such a miserable looking little leader.

While we were standing thus, a loud whoop from one, attracted the attention of the whole band. The next moment the unwieldy wagons came toiling along a ridge at a distance, followed by the light dearborns, and a train of four soldiers.

At this discovery the Indians broke away, scampered towards them, and in a short time were all clustering round the vehicles. They remained there about half an hour, and then resumed their journey along the prairie.

[CHAPTER XI]

The Journey—Saline River

Another week had elapsed, but still we were on our journey.[1] With the exception of the band of Sac and Fox Indians, we had met with no other savages. We were the only human beings, who lived and moved upon the wide waste. Nothing else was visible—not a deer, not a tree—all was prairie—a wide unbroken sea of green—where hollow succeeded hollow, and the long grass waved on the hills, with a heavy surge-like motion, until at last it was blended with the hazy atmosphere, which met the horizon. The power of sight was shut out by nothing; it had its full scope, and we gazed around until our eyes ached with the very vastness of the view that lay before them. There was a degree of pain, of loneliness, in the scene. A tree would have been a companion, a friend. It would have taken away the very desolation which hung round us, and would have thrown an air of sociability, over the face of nature; but there were none. The annual fires which sweep over the whole face of the country, during the autumn of every year, effectually destroy any thing of the kind. There will be no forest, as long as the Indians possess these regions; for every year, when the season of hunting arrives, they set fire to the long dry grass. Once fairly on its errand, the destructive messenger speeds onward, licking up every blade and every bush; until some strip of timber, whose tall trees protect the shrubbery, by the dampness which they diffuse beneath; or some stream, stops it in its desolating path. The object of burning the grass is to drive the deer and elk, that are roving over

---

[1] Dodge took thirteen days to cover 172 miles between Fort Leavenworth and the Otoe village in 1835 (G. P. Kingsbury, "Journal of the March of a Detachment of Dragoons, under the Command of Colonel Dodge," *American State Papers, Military Affairs,* Vol. VI, 130–31).

the broad extent of prairie, into the small groves of timber scattered over the surface. Once enclosed within these thickets, they fall an easy prey to the hunters.

We at last reached the Platte[2] river, about forty miles distant from the Otoe village; then striking off to the west, we followed the course of this powerful tributary of the Missouri.

On the first night, our little camp was placed upon a high bank of the Saline river, which flows through the prairie until it empties into the Platte.[3] During the spring of every year moisture exudes from the soil near its source, covering the prairie for the distance of many miles. This is dried up by the heat of summer, and leaves in its place a thick incrustration of salt. This is in turn dissolved by every successive rain, and carried off into the Saline river, giving to its water the brackish taste, from which it has derived its name. There is a barrenness around the stream, contrasting strongly with the other rivers that grace the prairie. Around *them* is always a rich forest of the deepest, rankest green. Every thing marks the luxuriance of

---

2 The Indian name for La Platte is *Nie-borah-ka,* signifying the shallow river; as also the word *Nieagaruh* signifies the broken river. This last word might lead one to a pretty correct conclusion as to the meaning of the name Niagara, given to the celebrated river and falls connecting Lake Erie with Ontario; for the word is the same among several of the different tribes, who, though they now dwell in the "far west," may nevertheless have once roamed in the neighbourhood of our eastern waters.—JTI. Irving's etymology is no better than a guess: according to Hodge [ed.], *Handbook of American Indians* (II, 68), the word "Niagara" is derived from a phrase signifying "bisected bottom-land." The Platte was very commonly called the Nebraska in that day, and sometimes the Flatwater.

3 Irving's mileage cannot be correct since the Saline or Salt enters the Platte less than forty miles above the Missouri; had they reached the Platte forty miles from the Otoe village they would have been very close to the Missouri. It is more likely that they struck the Platte a little below the Saline. Kingsbury ("Journal of the March of a Detachment of Dragoons, under the Command of Col. Dodge," *American State Papers, Military Affairs,* Vol. VI, 131) described it as "a small shallow stream of about one hundred and fifty yards wide, the water of which has a saline taste." Lemuel Ford, on the same expedition, reported it "thirty or forty yds wide two or three feet deep" ("Journal," *Mississippi Valley Historical Review,* Vol. XII [1925–26], 554). In "A Summer on the Prairie," *Army and Navy Chronicle,* Vol. II (May and June, 1836), 278, the latter writer gave its width as twenty to thirty yards!

GEORGE CATLIN   *Courtesy the Smithsonian Institution*

Kanakuk, the Kickapoo Prophet, 1831

"The prophet was a tall bony Indian, with a keen black eye, and a face beaming with intelligence. . . . There is an energy of character about him, which gives much weight to his words, and has created for him an influence greater than that of any Indian in the town. From the little we saw it was evident that the chief yielded to him, and listened to his remarks with the deference of one who acknowledged his superiority."

the soil, and the nourishment yielded by the streams, to the lofty trees, which hang like guardians over their waters.

But the Saline is far different. There are no groves to fringe its banks. Here and there, the huge, grey forms of a few dead trees, may be seen leaning with a melancholy grandeur over its surface, or lying prostrate in the river, while its waters gurgle with a mournful sound, around the branches of these fallen giants. There is a cheerless look about it. It winds its way through the prairie with a withering influence, blighting every green shrub; and seems to bear an ill will to all the bright beauties of creation.

I strayed some distance down the stream, pattering my rifle bullets on the water, to the great annoyance of several ducks who were quietly dozing upon its surface, and some sprawling old terrapins who were floating down the stream, enjoying an evening sail.

A loud hail from the camp, and the voice of Mordecai announcing that supper was ready, recalled me to the spot. The roasted shoulder and ribs of a large buck were impaled upon a stake of dog-wood, planted in the ground in front of the mess. They had already commenced their meal, with knives of all sizes and descriptions, and the mass of meat disappeared like magic, before their reiterated attacks. Though at all times very well qualified to act a conspicuous part, in a warfare of that description, they were now more than usually fitted for the task, owing to their eating only two meals a day—one at sunrise and one at sunset—the rest of the time being occupied in journeying over the prairie. By the time that we finished, the sun had sunk in the west, and the stars were glimmering in the sky. Our party collected round the large fire of blazing logs, and our guide [Dougherty] having lighted his Indian pipe, related to us an Indian tale, of which the following is the purport.

"About forty miles above the spot where we are now encamped, lie the great salt plains, which cause the brackish taste of the Saline river. In one part of these plains, is a large rock of pure salt of dazzling whiteness,[4] which is highly prized by the Indians, and to which is attached the following story."

CHAPTER XII

The Legend of the Saline River

Many years since, long before the whites had extended their march beyond the banks of the Mississippi river, a tribe of Indians resided upon the Platte, near its junction with the Saline. Among these was one, the chief warrior of the nation, celebrated throughout all the neighbouring country, for his fierce and unsparing disposition. Not a hostile village within several hundred miles, but wailed for those who had fallen beneath his arm; not a brook, but had run red with the blood of his victims. He was forever engaged in plotting destruction to his enemies. He led his warriors from one village to another, carrying death to the inhabitants, and desolation to their homes. He was a terror to old and young.

Often, alone and unattended, would he steal off, to bathe his hands in blood, and add new victims to the countless number of those whom he had already slain. But fearful as he was to the

4 According to Alice C. Fletcher and Francis La Flesche (*The Omaha Tribe,* Bureau of American Ethnology, *27th Annual Report* [1905–1906], 342), this must have been near present-day Lincoln on upper Salt Creek, "the waters of which left on the grassy banks a white saline deposit. This fine salt the women brushed into piles by means of feathers and afterwards it was deposited in bladder bags for future use." The "large rock of pure salt" was a standard part of Plains legend, but there were extensive salt deposits in Oklahoma, Kansas, and Nebraska. McCoy (*History of Baptist Missions,* 411) described a salt spring on the Solomon River. Ford ("A Summer on the Prairie," *Army and Navy Chronicle,* Vol. II [May and June, 1836], 321) was interested to observe "in passing over the immense plain, bordering on the Platte . . . that the ground in many places, appeared to be covered with a white crust, and in some spots which bore the appearance, it seemed to be elevated some inches above the surrounding level. Curiosity led me to examine some of these spots, and to my astonishment I found them to be formed almost entirely of pure salt. We passed over hundreds and hundreds of acres where these formations of salt were within a few feet of one another."

hostile tribes, he was equally dreaded by his own people. They gloried in him as their leader, but shrank from all fellowship with him. His lodge was deserted, and even in the midst of his own nation he was alone. Yet there was one being that clung to him, and loved him, in defiance of the sternness of his rugged nature. It was the daughter of the chief of the village; a beautiful girl, and graceful as one of the fawns of her own prairie.

Though she had many admirers, yet when the warrior declared his intention of asking her of her father, none dared come in competition with so formidable a rival. She became his wife, and he loved her with all the fierce energy of his nature. It was a new feeling to him. It stole like a sunbeam, over the dark passions of his heart. His feelings gushed forth, to meet the warm affection of the only being that had ever loved him. Her sway over him was unbounded. He was as a tiger tamed. But this did not last long. She died; he buried her; he uttered no wail, he shed no tear. He returned to his lonely lodge, and forbade all entrance. No sound of grief was heard from it—all was silent as the tomb. The morning came, and with its earliest dawn he left the lodge. His body was covered with war paint, and he was fully armed as if for some expedition. His eye was the same, there was the same sullen fire that had ever shot from its deep sunk socket. There was no wavering of a single feature; there was not the shrinking of a single muscle. He took no notice of those around him; but walked gloomily to the spot where his wife was buried. He paused for a moment over the grave— plucked a wild flower from among the grass, and cast it upon the upturned sod. Then turning on his heel, strode across the prairie.

After the lapse of a month he returned to the village, laden with the scalps of men, women, and children, which he hung in the smoke of his lodge. He tarried but a day among the tribe, and again set off, lonely as ever. A week elapsed, and he returned, bringing with him a large lump of white salt. In a few words he told his tale. He had travelled many miles over the prairie. The sun had set in the west, and the moon was just rising above the verge of the horizon. The Indian was weary, and threw himself on the grass. He had not slept long, when he was awakened by the low wailing of a female. He started up, and at a little distance, by the light of the moon, beheld an old, decrepit hag, brandishing a tomahawk over the head of a young female, who was kneeling, imploring mercy.

The warrior wondered how two females could be at this spot, alone, and at that hour of the night; for there was no village within forty miles of the place. There could be no hunting party near, or he would have discovered it. He approached them; but they seemed unconscious of his presence. The young female finding her prayers unheeded, sprang up, and made a desperate attempt to get possession of the tomahawk. A furious struggle ensued, but the old woman was victorious. Twisting one hand in the long black hair of her victim, she raised the weapon in her other, and prepared to strike. The face of the young female was turned to the light, and the warrior beheld with horror, the features of his deceased wife. In an instant he sprang forward, and his tomahawk was buried in the skull of the old squaw. But ere he had time to clasp the form of his wife, the ground opened, both sank from his sight, and on the spot appeared a rock of white salt. He had broken a piece from it, and brought it to his tribe.

This tradition is still current, among the different tribes of Indians frequenting that portion of the country. They also imagine, that the rock is still under custody of the old squaw, and that the only way to obtain a portion of it, is to attack her. For this reason, before attempting to collect salt, they beat the ground with clubs and tomahawks, and each blow, is considered as inflicted upon the person of the hag. The ceremony is continued, until they imagine she has been sufficiently belaboured, to resign her treasure without opposition. This superstition, though privately ridiculed by the chiefs of the different tribes, is still practised by them, and most devoutly credited by the rabble.

CHAPTER XIII

The Otoe Messengers

On the afternoon following, a little before sunset, we encamped within ten miles of the Otoe village. Several times during the day, we had observed the heads of Indians, peering over the hills, but they had instantly disappeared upon being remarked, nor had an Indian ventured to approach. Our place of encampment was on a small knoll. At its foot, a meagre run of impure water was struggling through the grass, while a long line of tall, rank weeds marked its course, as it wound a passage along the different hollows. A solitary tree grew over a small puddle, which had formed in the prairie; and a cluster of wild plum trees were knotted together around its trunk. With these exceptions, there was not a tree or a bush in sight.

At a little distance from us was the site of a deserted Indian village.[1] It had been uninhabited for many years, and the stations where the lodges once stood, were overgrown with weeds and creeping vines. A short distance off, was the burial ground of the place, which evidently, had not been visited for many a year. The tall grass waved upon the large mounds, and the frightened prairie hen started up from the resting places of the dead.

We had scarcely encamped, and fixed up the largest tent, when the loud cry, "Indian ahead!" was bellowed out, by the stentorian lungs of one of the soldiers.

The savage was on a hill, about five hundred yards distant. He was mounted upon a small black horse; clothed in a scarlet blanket, and in his hand held a long spear. He sat for some moments watching our movements; then thumping his heels into the sides of his horse, he dashed across a hollow that inter-

---

1 Possibly one of the deserted Otoe villages described by Prince Paul of Württemberg in 1823 (*First Journey to North America in the Years 1822 to 1834*, 419–25, 426–28).

vened, and galloped to the door of the tent. He sprang from the animal, and turning him loose, walked up to the guide. They were well acquainted; but his salutation was calm and cold; a slight smile played over his face, for a moment, as he recognised him, then all was quiet. His features were like stone; and whatever passions may have lurked within his bosom, his countenance was not the mirror that reflected them. He was attired in the wild garb of those Indians, who as yet have had but little intercourse with the whites. A pair of rough leggings were drawn over his legs, and a piece of blue cloth was secured around his hips. The rest of his body was unclothed, unless the red blanket, which most of the time, lay on the ground at his feet, might have been considered part of his apparel.

The chief of the Otoe village had been apprised of our approach, and had sent this warrior to watch, lest we should come upon the town before it was prepared for our reception. He hung around the tent for some time, saying little; but we could see, that while his face was apparently turned towards the ground, his dark eyes were moving with restless activity in every direction, scanning every action of the party. He remained with us a short time; then having received a few presents for the chief, and one or two for himself, he caught the end of the buffalo tug, which though secured to the neck of his horse, was long enough to trail twenty feet after him in the grass—and with a sudden jerk brought the animal to him, and sprang upon his back.

He had scarcely mounted, before another Indian appeared on an opposite hill, and galloped towards us. He exchanged a slight salutation with the first comer, and passing him, shook hands with the guide. There was more cordiality about him, than we had observed in the other, and his face wanted the cold reserve, which marked that of the first. Upon reaching the tent, he immediately signified his intention to remain during the night, and accordingly turned loose, the small white horse upon which he rode. Then lighting his pipe, he wrapped his blanket round him, and quietly seated himself near the fire—watching the cook, who was busily engaged in preparing supper.

The other, finding what was his intention, started off towards the village, and in a few moments was out of sight.

CHAPTER XIV

An Otoe Warrior—The Iotan Chief

The whole prairie was glowing with the rays of the morning sun, when we started for the Otoe village. Our journey lay for the whole distance, along the borders of the Platte. It was a soft golden morning, and the water danced with a very air of happiness, sparkling and bubbling in silver and rainbow brightness, as it scudded along its broad channel. Its surface was studded with islands teeming with verdure, and tinted with all the various hues of autumn. The birds were piping out their matin hymns, and the fish were splashing sportively beneath their watery covering, sending a thousand silver circlets eddying onward to the shore. The prairie grass was bending beneath the dew drops, which hung like strings of crystal upon their withering blades.

The heavy wagons were now kept closely together. The whole party, which during the first part of the journey had straggled widely apart, were collected. Our Otoe friend rode in front, accompanied by Major D[ougherty], the Indian agent. We had travelled for several miles, when we observed a single Indian galloping towards us on a large spotted horse. In a few moments he came up. He was one of the principal braves of the Otoe nation. He was completely naked with the exception of a small piece of cloth secured around his hips. His head was shaven, and to the scalp-lock was attached an ornament of deer's hair, resembling the crest of an ancient helmet. His whole person, head, face, and body, had been covered with vermilion, until it was the colour of blood, and at a few yards distance, he looked as if he had been skinned alive. But notwithstanding his bloody appearance, his countenance, though calm and grave, had a mild expression not usually met with among the Indians. His whole demeanour was prepossessing, and when he spoke, his voice was like soft music. He was a favourite with most of the wild traders in that part of the country, on account of his generous character. If a stranger entered the village, he was the first to welcome him to his lodge, and to protect him from the insults of the meaner spirits of his nation. Yet even with this chivalrous nature, he was an Indian warrior, and an Indian warrior is little better than a murderer. He had counted as many scalps, as any of his nation; but those of hoary age, of the woman, and the child, were hanging in the smoke of his lodge, in companionship with those of the war worn warrior.

In an hour's time we arrived within a short distance of the village, though as yet it was hidden from our sight by a high bluff. Suddenly, a horseman dashed from behind it, and came towards us, plying his lash and urging his horse forward at a mad speed. The cry of "The Iotan!" burst from several who had before seen him; and in a few moments this redoubtable chief was by our side.[1] He had evidently brought into service, the whole of

[1] This noted warrior was most commonly known as Ietan (L'Ietan, Iatan, Iotan, Jutan); his other name was Shaumonekusse (Chonmonicase), the Prairie Wolf. In James, *Account of the Expedition under Long* (XIV, 235), he was referred to as a "youthful leader." Prince Paul of Würtemberg in 1823 identified him as second chief of the Otoes: "Schock-mo-no-koch-fi, a fine-looking, tall man. He wore only a waistcloth which was most becoming to his dark skin" (*First Journey to North America*, 427). Cooke (ca. 1831–32) though him "a fine distinguished man, of great prowess, and profound judgment, or craft; perhaps his most remarkable quality was, a close observation and penetration of character and motives. . . . But deep beneath the calm exterior of his character burned a lava of impetuous passions which, when strongly moved, burst forth with a fierce and blind violence" (*Scenes and Adventures in the Army*, 111). W. D. Smith met him at Fort Leavenworth in July, 1833: "Shaw-mun-e-cusse, or as he is more generally called, *Iatan* which name he has acquired from his successful wars against the Iatan tribe, exhibits a great deal of the true Indian character. His frame is large and muscular yet stately and well proportioned. His dark keen eye whilst

his wardrobe, much of which he had received from the whites. His hair was long, and round it was bound a large piece of skin from the head of the grisly bear. Round his neck, hung a necklace of the claws of the same animal; and what was of more importance in his estimation, he was clothed in a long surtout coat, of blue cloth, adorned with red facings, and enormously large brass buttons, and garnished upon each shoulder, with a pair of tarnished, sickly-looking silver epaulettes. From beneath the skirts of the coat, appeared two bare legs; and he wore a pair of coarse mocassins of buffalo hide.

There was a look of comic slyness, lurking around the eyes of this chief, united with an irascible twinkle, which bespoke a character habitually good natured, but prone to occasional gusts of passion. The most prominent feature of his face, however, had suffered mutilation. The end of his nose was wanting.[2] I was curious to learn, whether this singular wound had been received

it indicated depth of observation and keen discernment lurked beneath a heavy brow, with an expression of deep cunning and intrigue, and looked as if it might be easily made to assume the very savage scowl. Sometimes it was permitted to wear a playful expression, which with a peculiar motion of the lips seemed to manifest a propensity to wit. His figure brought forcibly to my mind the description of the Knight. 'His square turned points and strength of limb / Showed him no carpet Knight so trim / But in close fight a champion grim, / In camps a leader sage' [Marmion]. He is said to rule his people with absolute authority" (W. D. Smith to E. P. Swift, Shawanoe Villages, Kanzas River, July 29th 1833). Kingsbury in 1835 reported "Jutan . . . a bold and successful warrior, and is considered one of the most intelligent Indians on the frontier . . . tall, well made, with a fine and intelligent cast of features" ("Journal of the March of Dragoons under Dodge," American State Papers, Military Affairs, Vol. VI, 131). Captain Lemuel Ford on the same occasion ("A Summer on the Prairie," Army and Navy Chronicle, Vol. II [May and June, 1836], 292) thought him "probably, at this time the most noted and popular Indian belonging to any tribe under the protection of our government. His stature is somewhat above the ordinary size and well proportioned. His countenance indicates much good humor. . . ." Thomas L. McKenney and James Hall, Indian Tribes of North America, I, 156–64, give an account of Ietan.

2 "Old Ietan with his nose off. Don't forget that story & the cause of this catastrophe," Edward Ellsworth urged his friend Irving in a letter from Fayetteville, Arkansas, May 22, 1835. The portrait painted in 1821 shows a complete nose either because the artist wished to please his subject or because the incident occurred after this date.

in battle or private brawl—and my inquiries, made me acquainted with a curious tale of Indian revenge. There are a dozen different versions of the story, in circulation among the traders and trappers, but as far as I could ascertain, the following is the most correct.

CHAPTER XV

The Iotan and His Brother—or Indian Revenge

It was some years before the Iotan had reached the rank of a chief, that he was despoiled of his nose in the following manner:

Several Otoe Indians, by dint of paying fifty times their value, had become possessed of a number of kegs of whiskey. As this was rather a rarity, a council was called, and a general carousal of the male portion of the village resolved upon. The females were excluded: it being deemed necessary that they should remain sober, to exercise a conjugal care over their husbands, when so inebriated as to be unable to take care of themselves. In the meantime a person was appointed as guard, whose business it was, to keep watch over the liquor, and drive off all interlopers, who might be inclined to test its quality, before the time appointed. After three long, and to them lingering days, the time came round; and at the appointed hour not a soul was behindhand.

The signal was given; and the revel commenced. As the liquor began to work upon the passions of the revellers, they grew furious. They howled, yelled, and fought. The females fled from the building. All weapons had been removed beforehand; for they knew their own ungovernable nature, when under the influence of liquor, and therefore, had taken precautions, to prevent the occurrence of mischief.

But when the whiskey commenced its work; the savage was changed to a demon, and the lodge resounded with their screams and howling; there was a hell within its bosom.

[6 4]

The giant warrior fixed his gripe upon the trembling frame of the aged; brother smote brother; friends fought with bitter fury, and the weak and decrepit were trampled under foot.

It was in this stage of the riot, that the Iotan and his brother had a furious scuffle. They grappled and rolled upon the ground. In the frenzy of strife and intoxication, his brother bit off the end of his nose, and instantly extricating himself, rushed out of the lodge.

The Iotan was perfectly sobered; he paused for a moment, looking intently in the fire, without uttering a word; then drawing his blanket over his head, walked out of the building and hid himself in his own lodge. On the following morning he sought his brother, and told him that he had disfigured him for life; "to-night," said he, "I will go to my lodge and sleep; if I can forgive you when the sun rises, you are safe; if not, you die." He kept his word; he slept upon his purpose; but sleep brought not mercy. He sent word to his brother that he had resolved upon his death, and that there was no further hope for him; at the same time he besought him to make no resistance, but to meet his fate as a warrior should.

His brother received the message and fled from the village. An Indian is untiring in his pursuit of revenge, and though years may elapse, yet he will obtain it in the end. From the time that it became the fixed purpose of the Iotan to slay his brother, his assiduity never slept; he hunted him for months. He pursued his trail over the prairies; he followed his track from one thicket to another; he traced him through friendly villages; but without success; for although he was untiring, his brother was watchful, and kept out of his way. The old warrior then changed his plan of action. He laid in wait for him in the forest, crouching like a tiger, in the paths which he thought he might frequent in hunting, but he was for a long time unsuccessful. At length, one day, while seated on a dead tree, he heard the crackling noise of a twig breaking beneath a cautious footstep. He instantly crouched behind the log and watched the opposite thicket. Presently an Indian emerged from it, and gazed cautiously around. The Iotan recognized his brother instantly. His care-worn face and emaciated form, evinced the anxiety and privations that he had suffered. But this was nothing to the Iotan; as yet his revenge was unsated, and the miserable appearance of his brother touched no chord of his heart. He waited until he was within a few feet of him; then sprang from his lurking place and met him face to face. His brother was unarmed; but met his fiery look with calmness and without flinching.

"Ha! Ha! brother;" cried the Iotan, cocking his rifle, "I have followed you long, in vain,—now I have you—you must die."

The other made no reply; but throwing off his blanket, stepped before him, and presented his breast. The Iotan raised his rifle and shot him through the heart.

His revenge was gratified; but from that hour a change came over him. He became gloomy and morose; shunned the society of his fellow men, and roamed the woods, where he was nearly driven to suicide by the workings of his feelings, and the phantasies of his brain. It was not until many years had elapsed, that he recovered from the deep anguish, caused by this unnatural act of vengeance.[1]

[1] Irving dressed up this story of revenge more than did his contemporaries. Cooke declared that this episode in Ietan's life had been "so perverted by an Indian story-monger [Irving?]" that he could not refrain from giving it "rightly." In a drunken carouse in 1822, the brother, Blue Eyes, "had the misfortune to bite off a small piece of I-e-tan's nose." The victim told his brother he would kill him, went after his rifle, returned to find Blue Eyes waiting his fate stoically, and shot him through the heart. Ietan was then seized with remorse: "He retired from all intercourse with his race, abstaining wholly from drink, for which he had a propensity; as if under a vow he went naked for near two years; he meditated suicide, and was probably only prevented from committing it by the influence of a white friend; but he sought honorable death in desperate encounters with all enemies he could find, and in this period acquired his name or title from a very destructive attack he made on a party of the I-e-tan tribe. He lived a year or two with the Pawnees, acquired perfectly their difficult language, and attained great influence over them, which he never lost. After several years of such penance I-e-tan returned to the villages of his nation . . ." (*Scenes and Adventures in the Army*, 111–12). Captain Ford, who met Ietan in 1835 and published his "A Summer on the Prairie" the following year, disagreed with our author: "Since the above was written," he declared in a footnote, "I have read a work by John T. Irving, Jr.,

[CHAPTER XVI]

The Reception—The Town

It was many years after this savage deed that the Iotan was appointed chief of the Otoe tribe, and his after conduct fully justified the choice of the nation.[1] To an ingenious skill in devising and planning war parties, he added a desperate daring in carrying them into effect. And though now well stricken in

entitled 'Irving's Indian Sketches.' His version of the affair differs in some respects from the one here given. Believing, however, that this account will be found strictly true, I have not thought proper to make any alterations." Ford asserted that "the detached part of the nose found its way into the kettle of whiskey. Here it was discovered at the end of the debauch, in a fine state of preservation." The next morning, taking his rifle, Ietan went to his brother's lodge and wakened him to say that he was going to kill him. Blue Eyes asked that Ietan should sleep one night and then "if no change was wrought upon his mind, he would submit to his fate." Ietan refused and shot him dead. This act of revenge made him "extremely odious to his tribe . . . it became necessary . . . that he should seek protection from a neighbouring tribe." He then so managed to stir up trouble for the Otoes that they recalled him to become their chief ("A Summer on the Prairie," *Army and Navy Chronicle*, Vol. II [May and June, 1836], 292–93). Charles Augustus Murray, who hunted with Ietan in 1835, said he heard the story often, and once from an eyewitness. He gave it briefly, declaring that Ietan shot his brother, did not fly, but "awaited the sentence of the council of the Braves, which terminated in his being elected chief in his brother's place" (*Travels in North America*, I, 340–41). The usual difficulties at reaching a common truth are illustrated here. The portrait of 1821 shows a complete nose. Cooke placed the incident in 1822 and declares he won the name of Ietan *after* this time. But Edwin James used the name in September, 1819. It is interesting to note in James the report of a similar incident in which (previous to 1819) "Ha-she-a, called Cut Nose . . . [had] lost the tip of his nose in a quarrel with Ietan" (*Account of the Expedition under Long*, XIV, 235).

[1] Charles Augustus Murray declared Ietan became chief immediately after killing his brother, Blue Eyes (*Travels in North America*, I, 341). According to Cooke, he was elevated to the headship in 1830 on the death of his elder brother, La Crinière (*Scenes and Adventures in the Army*, 112). His signature first appears on an Otoe treaty in 1825 (Kappler, *Indian Affairs, Laws and Treaties*, II, 257). Some of his early exploits are mentioned in James, *Account of the Expedition under Long*, XIV, 232. Ford devoted a paragraph to his political and military skills ("A Summer on the Prairie," *Army and Navy Chronicle*, Vol. II [May and June, 1836], 292–93).

[6 7]

years,[2] there is no warrior more constantly lurking in the path of the enemy, and when it comes to the deadly struggle, no voice is raised in a louder war whoop, and no arm falls heavier upon their foes, than that of the Iotan chief.

The old warrior welcomed us cordially, then turning round he rode with us in the direction of his village. While he was speaking with the commissioner, several dusky forms clambered the high bluff before us, and stood upon its dizzy verge, watching our movements. Suddenly the Iotan galloped a few yards in front, and waved his arm, uttering a long, shrill yell. It was answered by a loud whoop from those on the hill; who instantly commenced whirling their blankets around their heads. Then all was silent.

For a few moments we were in doubt as to the meaning of the manoeuvre; but suddenly a loud roar rose from behind the bluff, and a dark troop of wild horsemen burst round its base, and came pouring down upon us. There must have been several hundred of them. Every man was naked, but glaring with paint. They flooded onward, pealing out scream upon scream, brandishing their spears, and whirling their tomahawks around their heads. It seemed as if old Pluto had given a holiday, and that his crew were revelling upon the earth, under the forms of these snorting steeds and their wilder masters. Still they came on, and the din increased. The old chief was unmoved and sat like a statue upon his horse. I looked around upon our little band, there were several lowering brows and tightly compressed lips, and the fingers of two or three were on their gun triggers. They were not accustomed to the Indian welcome; and to them, all this long parade of yelling warriors wore a menacing appearance. The band had now approached within a hundred yards. We could perceive the flashing eyes of the straining horses, the bare teeth, scowling brows and starting muscles of the riders. Bow

[2] Murray in 1835 guessed his age as fifty-five or sixty (*Travels in North America*, I, 341); Kingsbury (also 1835) thought him about fifty years old ("Journal of the March of a Detachment of Dragoons under Dodge," *American State Papers, Military Affairs*, Vol. VI, 131). After all, Irving was not yet twenty-one!

clattered against bow; tomahawk clashed against tomahawk, and voice was blended with voice, until the whole din rose in the air, like the wild tumultuous roar of a raging sea. They were close upon us;—another moment—and we were lost. The eyes of the soldiers began to flash fire, their teeth were clenched, and there was an expression about their faces, which told, that in spite of numbers, their resistance would be bloody. At that moment, at a signal of the Iotan, the wild horde separated, and whirled around, enveloped in a cloud of dust.[3]

The old chief smiled with an air of grim satisfaction, as he observed the effect produced upon us by his warriors; then raising his voice, he joined in the wild melée around us. Horse dashed against horse, as the band swept onward in a large circle. Some were hurled from their seats; others clung to the manes of the maddened horses. The strong poured down upon the weak and brushed them from their paths. Ever and anon, some little pepper-spirited horse, vexed with the hustling, would pause to discharge his heels into the ribs of his next neighbour; but before it could be done, the crowd would press upon him, and again he would be borne onward, in the rushing course of the living whirlpool. No one regarded his neighbour; each was under the influence of a mad excitement. A giant Indian was dashing round, upon a horse as powerful as himself, at the inner verge of the ring. In front of him was another, on a little nag, who kept near the border for safety. Suddenly they came in contact. The powerful steed swept onward as if he had met with no obstacle. The little horse spun out of his path, and his rider

[3] This alarming show was a customary form of greeting by the Plains Indians. The Dodge party, within a few miles of the Otoe village, found itself "literally surrounded by Indians; some were dressed from head to foot in all the gaudy colors of the rainbow; while others could boast of nothing but a small piece of cloth or strouding about the loins. The deficiency of clothing, however, was generally made up in red paint, with which they were completely covered, giving them much the appearance of men destitute of their skins. Many of their horses had evidently been decorated for the occasion, some with eagles' feathers tied to their tails, foretop and mane, with a scalp hanging from the bits of the bridle, and their bodies fantastically painted with various kinds of paint" (Ford, "A Summer on the Prairie," *Army and Navy Chronicle,* Vol. II [May and June, 1836], 292).

threw a somerset in the air, landing in the very midst of the throng. Fifty hoofs clattered over his head; but he scrambled out, caught his horse, bounded on his back with a loud whoop, and flourish of his tomahawk, and pursued his course as if nothing had happened.

After this scene of hubbub and confusion had continued for about fifteen minutes, the crowd gradually ceased its clamor, and formed in a large circle round us, with their horses' heads towards the party. Presently the ring broke and was extended in two lines, through which a band of about thirty warriors slowly advanced, to a long solemn chant, sung by the whole troop, and accompanied by a kind of drum. This band was formed of the flower of the Indian village. None were admitted except those who could boast of having taken a certain number of scalps, or of having performed an equally honourable service, in stealing a large number of horses. These warriors were highly ornamented; paint of every hue was laid upon their bodies. Their heads were decorated with feathers and the variegated plumage of the gaudy birds of the Platte islands. Long strings of wampum hung from their necks and ears. Each bore a calumet adorned with feathers and tinkling bells. Some wore glittering armlets and collars of tin. Their heads were shaven, and covered with vermilion, and from the top of each hung the chivalrous scalp lock, generally adorned with an eagle's plume. As much care had been bestowed upon the horses as upon their riders, and they had been selected from the whole village. They now moved forward with proud step, as if conscious of the haughty character of those who guided them; but this was as much owing to the horsemanship of the riders, as to the spirit of the animals themselves; for there is no class of people better able to show off the points of a horse than the Indians, for they almost live in their saddle from childhood.

The band moved slowly forward, and then commenced walking their horses round, abreast, in the space between the multitude and our party; still keeping up their loud and not inhar-

Courtesy M. Knoedler and Company

Ietan (Chon-mon-i-case or L'Ietan), an Otoe Chief, 1821

"His hair was long, and round it was bound a large piece of skin from the head of the grisly bear. Round his neck, hung a necklace of the claws of the same animal. . . . There was a look of comic slyness, lurking around the eyes of this chief, united with an irascible twinkle, which bespoke a character habitually good natured, but prone to occasional gusts of passion."

monious song, which we afterwards learned, was in praise of the whites—that is, of their liberality.

At length the chief gave a signal, and this troop fell back into the general crowd. Several horses were then presented to the party by the braves and distinguished warriors.[4]

While this was going on, one old warrior, who was notorious for being the greatest thief, and for having killed more men than any other in the village, rose up to boast of what he had done in his younger days; and to let us know that he was not a man to be overlooked—a thing which seemed very likely to happen in the bustle which prevailed. He was lean and shrivelled, but his strength must have been prodigious in his prime, for every muscle rose like a rope, upon his withered frame. He spoke for about fifteen minutes, and then drew back. When he had concluded, another old man rose up, and in like manner vaunted his former exploits, many of which savoured strongly of the marvellous. These speeches were translated with great gravity by the interpreter, who, to confirm our wavering belief, took an opportunity of whispering into our ears, that, "in boasting of his exploits an Indian was always scrupulous in adhering to the truth." This was perfectly convincing; and while he travelled

4 In the 1888 edition Irving expanded this little paragraph describing the custom of "smoking horses": Ietan and several other chiefs sat down on the grass and produced their pipes. "Presently the Iotan advanced to the Commissioner and Major Dougherty, and drawing a few whiffs from his pipe, presented it to them in turn. Each drew a few whiffs and handed it back to him. The Iotan then made a brief address, and returned to his seat. Major Dougherty informed us that by this 'smoke and speech' he and the Commissioner had each been presented with a horse. Several other chiefs and braves followed the example of the Iotan, and by the time they had got through these smoking performances, the Commissioner and Major Dougherty were each the prospective owner of five or six horses. I may add here, that when the fulfilment of these promises was carried out several days afterwards, on the part of some of the minor braves, a great deal of the enthusiasm which led to the gifts had evaporated, and the old, the halt, and the blind were among the horses which found their way to our tents as presents to the Commissioner and Indian Agent. On a future occasion of a similar kind, at another tribe, an enthusiastic brave who had promised beyond his means, seized the occasion to visit a friend who lived in a village about thirty miles off, taking his horse with him. We never heard of him or his present afterwards" (pp. 89–90).

[71]

along within the verge of possibility, we were resolved to give credence to all that he uttered.[5]

After listening to a few more of these worthies, and smoking a few pipes of kin-ne-ka-neek, with the different chiefs, Iotan rose up, and the party prepared to move onward towards the town.

In crossing the prairie, which separated us from the village, our course was stopped by a deep gully, which about a dozen squaws were engaged in filling with bushes and weeds, to render it passable for the heavy wagons. While this was going on, the old Indian who had first delivered his address, came sweeping up at a full gallop. He did not pause at the hollow; but probably for the purpose of showing off his horsemanship, dashed down into it. His horse made a vigorous spring up the opposite bank, but lost his footing on its slippery verge, and after a desperate scrambling, rolled with his rider floundering in the mud at the bottom. There was a loud shout of laughter at his expense. For a moment he stood glaring about him like an angry tiger; then raising his withered arm, he shook it at the crowd. "Laugh on! laugh on!" exclaimed he, "I am old and feeble now; but there was a time when you would not have dared to have done this." Having given vent to his impotent rage, he sprang upon his

[5] An amusing instance of this was reported in James, *Account of the Expedition under Long*, XIV, 232–33: "After several rounds of dancing, and of striking at the post by the warriors, Mi-a-ke-ta, or the Little Soldier, a war-worn veteran, took his turn to strike the post. He leaped actively about, and strained his voice to its utmost pitch whilst he portrayed some of the scenes of blood in which he had acted. He had struck dead bodies of individuals of all the red nations around, Osages, Konzas, Pawnee Loups, Pawnee Republicans, Grand Pawnees, Puncas, Omawhaws, and Sioux, Padoucas, La Plais or Bald Heads, Ietans, Sauks, Foxes, and Ioways; he had struck eight of one nation, seven of another, &c. He was proceeding with his account when Ietan ran up to him, put his hand upon his mouth, and respectfully led him to his seat. This act was no trifling compliment paid to the well-known brave. It indicated that he had still so many glorious acts to speak of, that he would occupy so much time as to prevent others from speaking, and put to shame the other warriors by the contrast of his actions with theirs." For other references to this custom, consult John Francis McDermott, *Glossary of Mississippi Valley French*, 78 (*frapper au poteau*).

[7 2]

horse, scrambled up the bank, and galloped forward to the village.

In the course of an hour we reached the town.[6] A large concourse of women and children followed at the heels of the party, and clustered like bees around the heavy wagons as they toiled along.[7] We passed through the town, and fixed upon a small hill at about five hundred yards distance, as our camping ground. Accordingly the heavy wagons were drawn up; the tents were pitched around them, and the horses and oxen, being released from their labours, were sent off to a thick bottom of timber at a short distance, where the wild pea vines were matting together in the greatest luxuriance.

The village of the Otoe Indians is situated upon a ridge of swelling hills overlooking the darkly wooded banks of the Platte river, about a quarter of a mile distant.[8] There is but little beauty

6 They arrived on September 17, Ellsworth reported to Herring from the Otoe village, September 18, 1833.

7 Ford stated that when the Dodge expedition passed through the town "the tops of their dirt houses were literally covered with women and children, while a thousand meagre, half starved dogs kept up an incessant yell below" ("A Summer on the Prairie," *Army and Navy Chronicle*, Vol. II [May and June, 1836], 292).

8 You may take your choice without paying any money: how close was the Otoe village to the Platte? Kingsbury wrote: "The Otto village is situated on a high prairie ridge, about two miles from the river, and overlooks the surrounding country for many miles. In front lay the green valley of the Platte. The broad river running through the middle, and the valley terminated on the opposite side by hills covered with groves of timber. In rear nothing could be seen but an extension of the vast prairie until its smooth, undulating surface became almost blended with the distant horizon. To the right and left the river could be seen for many miles wending its course along through the valley, its broad shining surface here and there darkened by island groves of timber, the whole element combined forming the most beautiful landscape I had ever seen" ("Journal of the March of a Detachment of Dragoons under Dodge," *American State Papers, Military Affairs*, Vol. VI, 131). Ford, perhaps standing beside Kingsbury, reported that "the Ottoe village is situated about one mile from the right bank of the Platte, upon a beautiful bluff, or second bank. It commands a full view of the surrounding country and the river with its hundreds of islands, covered with cotton wood and willow. The Elk-Horn, a large stream falling into the Platte near its junction with the Missouri, can also be seen stretching off to the North West . . ." ("A Summer on the Prairie," *Army and Navy Chronicle*, Vol. II, [May and June, 1836], 292).

or neatness about an Indian town. The lodges are built in the shape of a half egg. They frequently are twenty feet in height, and sometimes sixty in diameter. The roofs are formed of long poles, which diverge like the radii of a circle, from one common centre. The ring of the circle is formed of upright posts, driven closely together in the ground, and projecting upward about five feet. These are interwoven with brushwood and the smaller branches of trees, and form the support of the outer end of the poles composing the roof, the interstices of which are also interwoven with twigs and brushwood. The whole is then covered with earth, and when finished resembles a large hillock. The town contained about seventy of these lodges, standing singly or in groups, without any attention to order or regularity. Within, they are capacious, but dark, being lighted, merely by a small aperture at the top, which serves both as window and chimney. The fire is built in a cavity in the centre, directly under the hole in the roof, by which the smoke escapes after floating in easy wreaths about the interior.[9]

As the lodges are very spacious, a little back from the fire there is a circular range of tree trunks standing like columns, and connected by timber laid in their forks, forming a support for the roof, which otherwise, from the great length of the poles that form it, and the heavy mass of superincumbent earth, might

[9] Compare Kingsbury: "The village was very neat in its appearance. The lodges were built of wood, thatched with prairie grass, and covered with dirt. They were of a circular form, with a pointed roof about ten or twelve feet high to the break of the roof, and about fifteen or twenty feet high in the centre" ("Journal of the March of a Detachment of Dragoons under Dodge," *American State Papers, Military Affairs*, Vol. VI, 131). Ford said the ground was first excavated to a depth of two to three feet, that the upright timbers were ten to fifteen feet long, and that upon the frame for the roof "a netting of willows, bound together by strips of bark, is placed. Over the whole dry grass is thrown, to prevent the dirt from falling through. The roof is then covered with dirt to the thickness of from two to three feet. These lodges are from fifty to seventy-five feet in diameter" ("A Summer on the Prairie," *Army and Navy Chronicle,* Vol. II [May and June, 1836], 292). Cooke thought the village (1831) contained about fifty lodges; he too mentioned the excavation for the lodges (*Scenes and Adventures in the Army*, 104). Paul of Württemberg in 1823 also described typical Otoe lodges (*First Journey to North America*, 421–22).

fall in, and bury the inhabitants. Around the wall of the building, are ranged cribs or berths for sleeping, screened from view by heavy mats of grass and rushes. Over the fire is inclined a forked stake, in the hook of which hangs a large kettle, generally filled with buffalo flesh and corn. This, to judge from its looks, is never removed from the fire, even for the purpose of cleaning it.

[CHAPTER XVII]

Indian Habits—The Escape

We had been a week in the village, and had become familiar with all the antiquated gossips of the place. The old warriors would stop us as we lounged around, to listen to some sly joke, which as in duty bound, we relished most highly; though the wit of it was for the most part beyond our fathom, as it lay hid in the arcana of their language. The old squaws would hold us by the button, and whine into our ears some lugubrious tale of misery, equally unintelligible. The children soon lost the shyness, which had at first marked their conduct; they were continually hanging around the tents, teasing the black cook, or frightening the oxen. When not thus engaged, they were scampering like deer across the prairie, in the enjoyment of their wild games. Here and there, too, a knot were busily engaged in gambling away arrows, which they had received from their parents; discussing with the most earnest eagerness, the fairness and unfairness of each toss of their competitor.

Our tents became the gathering place of the whole tribe, where they assembled to discuss the news of the day. Here they would light their pipes, and talk over the deeds of former times; of scalps taken—of horses stolen—of buffalo hunts, and of hair breadth escapes from the Sioux and Osage Indians. All the incidents which tend to variegate the desultory life of a savage, were here brought into review by the gossiping group; receiving their

[75]

meed of praise or censure, as they deserved it. Among the rest they spoke high in praise of a young Indian, who stood at a little distance. He was leaning against a wheel of one of the wagons, gazing, though with an evident air of abstraction, upon the group collected round the fire. He was scarcely twenty; yet he was already a brave, and stood high among the older warriors. A long feather hung from his scalp-lock, and was his only ornament. A blanket was thrown loosely over the lower part of his body, and was his only covering. Among various things related of him, was the following.

A few weeks before our arrival at the village, he was returning one afternoon, from an unsuccessful hunting excursion, which had taken him to a great distance from his home. The crimson disk of the sun was scarcely visible above the tops of the prairie hills. The burning heat of a hot summer's day was mellowing down into the mildness of a July evening, and one by one, the ravens and vultures were winging a steady course towards their roosts in the thick forest skirting the Missouri.

The Otoe had yet twenty miles to travel, and it would be night-fall before he could reach his village; but he would not push his generous steed, which was already much fatigued. He therefore, rode slowly across the prairie, occasionally chirruping to the horse, or humming some Indian song.

Suddenly his quick eye was caught by the appearance of a black speck, which rose over the edge of a distant hill, between himself and the setting sun. In a moment after, the whole figure of a mounted Indian emerged to view, followed by four others, also mounted. They did not observe the Otoe, but continued riding along the top of the ridge, in the same direction with himself. Supposing them to be some of his own tribe, he checked his horse, and raised a loud whoop to attract their notice.

At first they did not hear him; but a second shout raised at the full pitch of his lungs, brought them to a halt. A short consultation seemed to take place; after which they rode slowly, and carelessly towards him, as if they by no means intended to hurry themselves in obeying his call. As they were some distance off, he dismounted from his horse, laid his rifle in the grass in front of him, and lighting his pipe, prepared to smoke until they should reach him. He lay intently watching them, as they drew nearer. He however, soon discovered from some peculiarity in their dress, that they were not Otoes, but as he supposed Konzas, who were then at peace with his tribe.

Fearing nothing, therefore, he continued lolling on the grass, and smoking. As they approached still nearer, their cautious movements awakened suspicion, and he began to doubt their being Konzas. Raising himself, he sat earnestly watching them with every sense on the alert, though he continued to smoke his pipe with apparent tranquillity.

He now observed that they gradually separated, as if their object was to surround him as he sat. Another glance, showed that they were Osages, the deadly foes of his tribe. Dashing his pipe to the ground, he bent hastily forward to seize his rifle. It was fortunate for him that he did so; for at the instant, a bullet aimed at his heart whizzed past him, cutting a deep gash in his shoulder. In an instant he sprang upon his horse. The Osage war whoop rang in his ear; but with that daring that never forsakes an Indian, he brandished his rifle in the air, and raising his own answering war cry, dashed off like the wind. He had the start by only a hundred yards. Everything depended upon the speed and bottom of his horse; but he was a tried one, and nobly did his duty. Hill and dale disappeared behind him. Scarcely had he vanished from the top of one ridge, ere his hoofs clattered over the top of the next. But his enemies pressed on at the same mad rate. The clang[1] of their horses' hoofs rang in the ear of the Otoe with a fearful clearness. Luckily they could not pause to take aim with their rifles. At two miles' distance was a skirt of forest; it was growing dark, and could he but reach this, he would be safe. His horse, however, was nearly broken down; he panted, and staggered. The rider plied the lash

1 *Clang* seems a doubtful word for unshod horses.

[77]

with phrenzied fierceness; the generous animal taxed his strength to the uttermost; but nature was exhausted. Within a quarter mile of the timber, he began to fail, when his rider sprang from his back and bounded forward on foot. A loud cry burst from his pursuers, as they saw him abandon his horse; but there was little cause for the shout; for his speed nearly equalled that of their jaded steeds. He was within about a hundred yards of the thicket, when finding that they could not overtake him, the Osages drew up and discharged their pieces. The bullets pattered among the leaves of the grove, but missed their mark. The Otoe turned half round, when on the border of the bushes, shook his rifle in the air, and raising a yell of triumph, plunged into the thicket.

The advantage was now on his side, for the Osages dared not approach, lest he should fire upon them from his covert. They rode up and down for a time, at a distance, vainly endeavouring to catch a glimpse of his figure; then returned across the prairie, contenting themselves with carrying off the deserted horse.[2]

[CHAPTER XVIII]

The Rival Chiefs—Indian Feasts

Besides the Iotan, there are two other chiefs, inferior in rank, and far less popular. It was amusing to see how jealous a watchfulness each held over the actions of the other—each afraid to take a single step in the transaction of any business whatever, lest it should give some advantage to his rival. They reminded me strongly of two belligerent cats, mounted on the top of some gutter, glaring in each other's eyes, and growling deep muttered

[2] Could this be part of the Osage raiding party mentioned in the report of the Commissioners West, Fort Gibson, February 10, 1834: "The Osages . . . had just been [1833] at the Ottoe village with one hundred warriors to destroy the town; and this village only escaped by the timely arrival of an express from Fort Leavenworth, announcing their danger" (*H. Rep. 474*, p. 80).

sounds of wrath; but neither venturing to attack or retreat, lest by some unguarded movement, he should expose some unprotected part to the fangs of his adversary. The Indian names of these two worthies I have forgotten; but they are known to the trappers by those of the Big Kaw[1] (or Kanzas) and the Thief.[2]

This last honourable badge of distinction, was bestowed upon the father of the present possessor; but in process of time, the old Thief was gathered to his fathers, and the young Thief reigned in his stead. He inherited his name, his worn out blankets, and so large a number of grudges and private quarrels, that, in acting as executor and revenging his father's injuries, years had elapsed before he could fairly say that the debts of the deceased were paid off.

The young Thief had, however, now become the old Thief. His hair was silvered by age; and he had arrived at that period of life which old folks are apt to call "the years of discretion." That is, he had passed the prime of his usefulness, and had reached that age, when strong attachments are usually formed to easy comforts and chimney corners.

The Big Kaw is a short thick Indian, rather good natured, but gifted with a large supply of mulish obstinacy, and a temper like gunpowder. Oppose him—flash!—he is in a blaze; the children scamper; the squaws scatter; the rabble vanish. None stay to listen to the outpourings of his wrath, unless it may be one or two old fellows, who are too decrepit to get out of his way,

1 Choncape (Shunk-co-pee, Schon-ka-pe, Tschon-co-pee), or Big Kansas. Paul of Württemberg in 1823 mentioned him as one of the foremost chiefs of the Otoes, whereas he named Schoch-mo-no-koch-fi (Ietan) "the second chief" (*First Journey to North America*, 427 ff.). In 1821 Choncape visited Washington and had his portrait painted by Charles Bird King. His signature first appears on the treaty of 1825 (Kappler, *Indian Affairs, Laws and Treaties*, II, 257). McKenney and Hall have a very brief account of him, and the bulk of Frederick Webb Hodge's notes to it are from Irving (*Indian Tribes of North America*, I, 218–22). He was still a chief of importance in 1844 (Clifton Wharton, "Journal of the Expedition of Major Clifton Wharton in 1844," *Kansas Historical Society Collections*, Vol. XVI [1923–25], 292).

2 The Thief was third signer on the Otoe treaty of September 21, 1833 (Kappler, *Indian Affairs, Laws and Treaties*, II, 401).

or are blessed with so happy a sadness of hearing, as to render it agreeable to them to be conversed with, even though by a man in a passion.

The family of this chief consists of several wives, and a son, who, is one of the most intelligent young men in the village. He, however, is the very counterpart of the old man in disposition; and when the two get fairly excited, the village is in an uproar. If the quarrel is commenced in a lodge, the building is instantly vacated by the rest of its occupants, until the silence which reigns within, gives notice that the storm has blown over. Upon these occasions, it is said that those who return, generally find the old man looking very foolish, and the son very angry. From this it is suspected that the former is held in subjection by his graceless offspring. Be that as it may, the young warrior still retains a strong affection for his fond old father. Although in his anger, he sometimes oversteps the bounds of propriety, and conducts himself in an indecorous manner towards him, yet upon the whole he is looked upon as a pattern of filial piety—particularly, as he permits nobody to bully his father, but himself. The Thief was in every respect the reverse of his rival. He was tall and wiry—of that construction which denotes extreme hardiness of constitution, united with a great lack of superfluous flesh. He was calm and quiet in all his movements, and would sit for hours in the same posture, his eyes alone keeping watch. He slid in and out of our tent, with a noiseless step, which frequently caused us to be unaware either of his presence or his absence. We were often startled, when least expecting it, by hearing his deep sonorous tones at our elbows.

The Iotan chief is the lord paramount of the village. With that cunning policy for which he is noted, he contrives, by balancing the interest of the two inferior chiefs, to keep them so constantly engaged in watching each other, that they have no time to turn their attention to himself.

On the first day of our arrival, we were invited to feast with about half the village. The first lodge which we entered was that of the Iotan. We found him sitting cross-legged upon some cushions, to receive us. Upon our coming up to him, he presented the commissioner with a seat next himself. Then turning to his wife, he called for the feast, which consisted of dried buffalo flesh, boiled with a large quantity of hard corn.[3] The interior of his abode wore but a dull, dingy look. The rafters were almost invisible for the eddying clouds of smoke, lazily seeking the hole in the roof, which served for the chimney. This old chief had divided his affections among five wives. They were seated in different parts of the lodge engaged in pounding corn, or chattering over the news of the day. They were evidently under but little subjection. While we were eating with him, the old man took the opportunity to disburthen his heart. He let us into a knowledge of the miseries to which he was subjected from their caprices; and the difficulties which he found in maintaining a proper discipline where there were so many mistresses and but one master.[4]

[3] Prince Paul of Württemberg had had a less happy time "feasting" with the Otoes. "We had to accompany the first chief into his hut, where the ceremonies prescribed by the Indian code of civility took place. This hut was also clean, and in this regard differed from the rest. I could not stay in it long, however, because the smoke of the fire in the hut was driven back into it by the strong wind. To this inconvenience was added the preparation of a most repulsive meal, which was being prepared in my honor. It consisted of dog meat and jerked, dried buffalo meat. This tempting meal was boiled with corn. The kettle in which the ingredients were contained was badly in need of scouring. The scum was being skimmed off with a most unappetizing horn spoon. . . . I left the hut for a few minutes. Mr. Riley [Captain Bennet Riley], however, called me back and said that the Indians would be very much offended if I should disdain their meal. He said I should control myself, and at least pretend to partake of it. I therefore returned, but was again seized with revulsion when an old dirty woman picked up the meat out of the kettle with her dirty hands, and greedily sipped the meat broth out of her hollowed hands. I exerted all my will-power to suppress the terrible repugnance I felt, but could not force myself to swallow an entire spoonful of the food which Schon-kape handed me. When I sipped of it the Indians were content . . ." (*First Journey to North America*, 427–28).

[4] Moses Merrill (1834) noted that Ietan had "five wives; two only live in his own lodge; the others have lodges of their own, to which they often invite the chief to eat with them. . . . At evening was invited out to eat with another of Itan's wives, in company with himself. She is not more than twenty-five years of age, while he is more than fifty" ("Diary of Moses Merrill," *Nebraska Historical*

Upon leaving the lodge, we next visited that of the Big Kaw. He guided us himself through the intricacies of the town, until we reached the building and entered through its low funnel-mouthed door. We had scarcely seated ourselves, before we found that we had got into warm quarters. The lady of the house had not expected company, and was unprepared for visitors. There was evidently a storm gathering. I read it in her lowering eyes, and in the uneasy, stealthy look of the Indian. He made no parade, but glided across the building, and motioned us to a seat, with a guilty air; then slunk upon a cushion, with the look of a man who would wish to pass unnoticed. Occasionally he cast towards his helpmate a deprecating glance, like that of a whipped dog—his eye seemed to say, "I know I was wrong in bringing them; but I beseech you to keep quiet now, and you may scold as much as you please when the visiters have gone."

A bowl of dried buffalo flesh was at last placed before us; the viands being rather tough, drew forth some remark from our host, half facetious, half apologetic. By accident it reached the hearing of the squaw, who thought that it was intended as a reflection upon her. In an instant she was in a blaze, and opened her batteries upon the chief, pouring out one continuous torrent of invective. Hot headed and irascible as he naturally was, nevertheless for a moment he shrank under it; and if it could have been done with credit to himself, probably would have

---

Society Transactions, Vol. IV [1892], 164). According to Ford, he had once had six wives; in 1822 his favorite wife, who had accompanied him to Washington the year before, died, and he was so grief-stricken that he had three of his best horses killed to carry her and her goods to the land of the departed ("A Summer on the Prairie," *Army and Navy Chronicle,* Vol. II [May and June, 1836], 293). McKenney and Hall (*Indian Tribes of North America,* I, 165–67) give a brief account of this woman and include her portrait. In April, 1837, Cooke informs us, Ietan took two of his youngest wives with him to a trading house near the mouth of the Platte, got drunk, and drove them out of doors in the night. Two men of his tribe, one of whom he had formerly stabbed, seduced them. Eventually the men brought the women back to the village, and in the resulting fight Ietan, as well as a number of others, was killed (*Scenes and Adventures in the Army,* 113–15).

evacuated the field; but in the present case that was impossible; and to be thus lorded over by his wife, and before strangers was intolerable. Though for a moment overawed by the attack, his touch-paper temper began to take fire. At first it only evinced itself by a few sulky shakes of the head; but at last it burst through all restraint, and sent back a fire as hot as was given. The war was furious for some moments, and apparently carried on with equal vigour on both sides; but at length the bursts from the chief grew fewer and fewer: he was evidently getting worsted; his lips grew closer—more resolved, and his look began to wander round the dwelling, until at last it rested upon a large stick which lay on the floor at a little distance. A glance of his eye called the attention of his wife in that direction. It is probable that she understood its meaning, for after a few sulky looks, and a few sullen mutterings, her words grew more and more rare, and at last ceased altogether.

We remained but a short time longer, and after visiting the lodges of several others, returned to our tents.

[CHAPTER XIX]

Domestic Grievances

Among the number of our daily visiters, were three old squaws, hideously ugly, and filthy in the extreme. Wrinkle upon wrinkle, covered their faces, and layer upon layer of dirt, covered the wrinkles. Their long, gray, uncombed hair, hung in thick, matted locks, reaching nearly to their waists; and each of their long skinny arms, with which they coaxingly patted us, resembled in appearance and delicacy, the trunk of a grape vine. These old harridans, were perfect nuisances. They were constantly lingering about the door of the tent, on the look-out for plunder. They seemed to possess the power of ubiquity; it would have puzzled Argus to keep track of their movements. They were shuffling around all day long, peeping into every hole and cranny. One of them even stole meat from the frying pan, while the black cook had turned his head to drive off the other.

Come upon them when we would, they were always sure to greet us with a half-smirking, half-piteous look; but the moment we turned away, they were at their old occupations. They were so constantly at work, that there was some talk of appointing a person, whose sole employment should be, to keep an eye to their movements. They lived at our tent doors, and for aught we knew to the contrary, might sleep there too; for we left them there in the evenings, and we found them at their posts before sunrise. Indeed so constant was their presence, that the sight of one of them moving off towards the town, was the signal for a general search, as they seldom made their disappearance, without taking with them some article which did not belong to them.

They had taken a particular fancy to Jones, the black cook. This unlucky wight was yet young in years, and inexperienced in the ways of the world. He had a fond and foolish heart, and acknowledged that he always felt a sort of sneaking kindness for the other sex. When dwelling upon the subject, he used to open his eyes, until the small speck of a pupil, was almost lost in the immense field of white, and exclaim, "I ai'nt afeared of no man; but I can't stand the wimmen."

To the young urchins, who intruded into his domains, he was not so indulgent, but kept a keen eye and a long stick for their especial benefit. This, however, only subjected him to ten times more annoyance. They would pull him by the coat tail, or jerk his ragged pantaloons, until they worked him up into a passion. Then their greatest delight, was to be hunted over the green by the Black Bear, (the name which he had received among them.)[1] He might as well have followed a cloud. They sprang like fawns over the prairie, scarcely appearing to rustle the grass

[1] Compare James, *Account of the Expedition under Long*, XIV, 287: "A negro belonging to the Fur Company coming in on an errand, they [the Omahas] spoke of him as the *black white man*, and one of them jokingly said, he was a Wasabajinga, or little black bear."

in their flight. They played around him like swallows, until completely exhausted by his own lumbering movements, he was fain to give out, and return unavenged to his occupations. Wo to the unlucky urchin, however, who, having once been guilty, should venture at any subsequent time within his reach. A hearty cuffing would convince him, that the memory of the Black Bear was more tenacious than his own, and would warn him in future to keep clear of so dangerous a neighbourhood.

During the whole of our journey from fort Leavenworth to the Otoe town, Mordecai, the driver of one of the dearborns, had kept his fellow servants in a state of constant tribulation. He gave such bloody accounts of Indians, and Indian murders, that they regarded death as almost inevitable; and I suspect would have deserted at the first opportunity, had there not been more danger in leaving than in remaining with the party. When, however, we had been received by the Otoes, and the danger was past, Mordecai forgot his tales of terror. He pretended a kind of fellow-feeling for the Otoes. He talked Creek to the old women, who were willing to understand any language, so they might but remain sufficiently near the tents, to get an opportunity of stealing. He regarded the children that hung round, with a kind of parental affection, and thoroughly discountenanced the thwackings which Jones so liberally bestowed upon them.

When we were perfectly settled in our camp, the horses which he had driven, were turned adrift with the rest. He then took upon himself the duties of cook, devolving upon Jones the less honourable employment of cutting wood for fuel. He would stand by the hour, with a red flannel night-cap stuck upon the side of his head; his butcher-knife in one hand, and his arm akimbo, descanting upon the arduousness of the office.

He had a high opinion of his own importance, and made no hesitation in saying, that he ranked next to the Commissioner, in the estimation of the Indians; that Mr. Ellsworth was respected by the chiefs on account of his having charge of the presents. As for himself, that he was popular among the vagabonds of the village; for they had no hope of presents, and therefore, were delighted to come in for a share of the tit-bits and choice morsels which it was in his power to distribute, while cooking.

Notwithstanding the altered tone of Mordecai, and the cordiality of our reception, there was one individual who remained inveterate in his prejudices against them. This was the French boy, Joe. He never spoke of the Indians without some qualifying expression of ill will. Whenever any thing was stolen, he at once attributed it to them. Frequently, however, his loud vociferation on these occasions, caused us strongly to suspect that he was the delinquent, and that this clamour of indignation was raised, that he might escape unsuspected.

His sole occupation was, to spread the bearskins at night, and remove them in the morning. During the rest of the day, he strolled about abusing the Indians, cracking his whip, or halooing at the stray curs who were skulking around.

"Mordecai," said he one day, to that worthy, who was standing in the midst of a group of Indians, in his usual stately attitude, with one hand tucked in his side, while the other held a frying pan, "Mordecai, dere is no good in having dese Ingens around you; dey'm all d——d rascals any how."

Mordecai gave a self-satisfied smirk, threw a compassionate glance at Joe, then extending his arm with an impressive air, "Joe," said he, "don't abuse the Indians, it hurts my feelings— I'm an Indian myself."

"Yes, a nigger von," replied Joe, turning upon his heel.

It seems too, that the Iotan was of the same opinion; for whenever Mordecai spoke of his Indian descent, the old warrior quietly shook his head, remarking "that he had never seen an Indian with wooly hair."

It was evident, however, that his contempt was engendered by seeing him perform menial offices; for like all Indians, he had a great distaste for labour, and respected those only, who, like himself, did nothing.

[86]

From an engraving after Seth Eastman, in Henry R. Schoolcraft,
The Indian Tribes of North America, III, *Plate* 6.

Striking the Post

To gratify the Indian desire to publicize his deeds of valor in war, a post was erected where the entire tribe could witness the ceremonies of "striking the post." His military ardor excited by singing and dancing, the warrior stepped forward and struck the painted post with his club or lance. The recital of his exploits was detailed and dramatic, accompanied with gestures appropriate to the narration, and when he finished the whole assembly of warriors united in yells of victory and defiance.

[CHAPTER XX]

A Man of the World

A number of idlers usually assembled in front of our tents, during the fine, sunshiny afternoons, to sing their songs, smoke their pipes, and regale themselves by listening to the adventures of their neighbours, which they had heard recounted a hundred times before. Among them was a tall, thin Indian, with a wrinkled, hard-looking face, and a head covered with a profusion of long, knotty hair, which he occasionally combed, by raking it with his fingers. He seemed as if he had been smoke-dried for a century, until his flesh had hardened into gristle; and looked as if further shrivelling was an impossibility. He had a very small, busy eye, which twinkled with an incessant play of humour. It overcame even the grave disposition of the oldest warriors, and surprised them into as broad a laugh, as was ever known to proceed from the mouth, of the most scape-gallows Indian of the tribe, or even from the broader mouth of that vociferous character, the Black Bear.

He usually made his appearance at the door of the tent, a little after sunrise, and continued in its neighbourhood, during the whole day. Though he shifted from the fire to the tent door, as the process of cooking, and carrying the meals within, went forward.

His usual dress was an old buffalo robe, worn almost bare of hair, and in his hand he carried a long handled pipe, as antiquated as himself. He was one of those poor, but merry dogs, who are found in all countries—taking the world as it goes, laughing at care, and free from all of those disturbances which fret their fellow men. He had never held any property of his own, he had never burthened himself with a wife, he had never built a lodge to shelter him. He was a perfect man of the world, and supported himself by visiting his neighbours. The lodges of the whole tribe he looked upon as his own property; the children of the whole nation, were equally under his charge. His bed was his time worn buffalo robe; and the abode in which night surprised him, was his usual resting place, until the next morning sun awakened him. He was a welcome visiter at the stately dwelling of the chief, and in the less noble, though to him equally prized wigwam, of one of the lowest of the town; for in wealth, they were all superior to him, and he thought that a poor devil like himself, with scarce a tatter to his back, had no right to sneer at the good will of any individual, who, however needy, was better off than himself. Notwithstanding the apparent easiness with which he slid through the world, his life had not been without its spice of adventure. Nor had the lapse of fifty years flown over his head, without bringing in its train, a host of those mishaps both by "flood and field," with which the history of a savage, is ever teeming. These he was accustomed to relate in the different lodges, to the assembled group of old and young, with a degree of humour which completely enraptured the women, and rendered him a welcome guest in every dwelling in the town.

He was sitting as usual, one fine afternoon, at the door of the tent. After finishing his pipe, he related an account, of his having been chased by a party of Sioux Indians, across the prairie which lay between the Elk Horn river and the Missouri, on his way to the Otoe Agency. After laughing heartily, the interpreter[1] translated it for the benefit of the rest.

[1] A man named Oloe signed as interpreter at the Otoe Treaty of September 21 (Kappler, *Indian Affairs, Laws and Treaties*, II, 401), but it is far more likely that Irving meant Dougherty in this instance.

[CHAPTER XXI]

The Chase

The Otoe Agency is situated upon the banks of the Missouri river, at thirty-five miles distance from the Otoe village. It consists of half a dozen rough buildings, tenanted by as rough inhabitants. The most of these are half breed Indians, with full blooded squaws for wives, and an immense number of mongrel children. The latter may be seen from morning till night, lying on the ground in front of the agent's dwelling; and basking in the sunshine, with that listless enjoyment which they inherit with their Indian blood.[1]

Early one clear morning, the Indian mentioned in the last chapter, left the Otoe village on a visit to the agency. After swimming the Platte, and fording the pure still waters of the Elk Horn, he strapped his time worn buffalo robe tightly round his body and proceeded onward.

As he was on a friendly visit, to gossip with his old cronies at the agency, he had no weapon, but carried under his arm his inseparable companion, his pipe. As this pipe is destined to bear a conspicuous part in the adventure which is to follow, it would perhaps be worth while to describe it. The stem was of ash, about four feet in length, half an inch in diameter, and charred in the fire, until it had acquired a dirty brown colour. The bowl was

[1] Earlier this year (May 3) Prince Max, traveling up the Missouri in the *Yellowstone*, noted: "Belle Vue, Mr. Dougherty's post, is agreeably situated. The direction of the river is north-west. Below, on the bank, there are some huts, and on the top the buildings of the agents, where a sub-agent, Major Beauchamp, a blacksmith, and some servants of the company, all lived with their families, who attend to the plantations of the company. These men are mostly married to women of the tribes of the Otos and Omahas; all, on our landing, immediately came on board. Their dress was of red or blue cloth, with a white border, and cut in the Indian fashion. Their faces were broad and coarse, their heads large and round, their breasts pendent, their teeth beautiful and white, their hands and feet small and delicate. Their children had dark brown hair, and agreeable features" (*Travels in the Interior of North America,* XXII, 266).

of stone, to contain the kinne-ka-neek,[2] which an Indian uses as a substitute for tobacco. He usually carries it about him in a small pouch, formed of the entire skin of a young otter, muskrat, or fox squirrel.

The route to the Otoe Agency, lay across a range of steep, ragged ridges. The Indian sauntered slowly along. He had a whole summer's day before him, and was never in a hurry in his movements. Arrived at the summit of a hill which commanded a wide prospect, he paused to cast a wary look around him. The country lay spread out at his feet. Here and there it was broken by small patches of timber and brushwood, which served to give relief to the otherwise barren appearance of the prairie. There was nothing to be seen wearing a hostile garb— not even a wolf. Notwithstanding this apparent security, his watchfulness never slumbered. He had been too often hunted and harassed by foes, to relax for an instant that vigilance, which from necessity, becomes a constant habit with an Indian.

He travelled for several hours, and his journey was nearly at its end. The tall, thick timber, which darkened the bank of the Missouri, was now seen raising its dusky outline above the summits of the distant ridges. The groves, and tangled thickets, were becoming more and more frequent, and every thing bespoke a near approach to that king of rivers, the mighty Missouri.

A smooth prairie about two miles in width, alone separated the Indian from the groves in which the agency was nestled. A few yards in front of him, was a low hillock, between two thick clusters of bushes. He sauntered to the top and looked around.

2 *Kinne-ka-neek* is a substance used by the Indians as a substitute for tobacco. It is made by crushing to fineness the dried leaves or bark of the wild sumach. This is then mixed with plug tobacco, cut fine, and is smoked by them. The proportion of tobacco to sumach is about one fourth. The tobacco pouch of the Indians, is always formed of the skin of one of the animals above mentioned. The head is left appended to it, and the bones, intestines, and fleshy substance are removed from the body through a small hole cut in the throat, which afterwards serves as the mouth of the pouch. These pouches are often highly ornamented, with stained porcupine quills, beads, and if their owners can obtain them, hawk's bells.—JTI.

To the left was a small clump of bushes fringing the bottom of the hill; but beyond, in that direction, there was no object to break the spotless green of the prairie. It stretched far off to the northward, until its distant verge was mingled with the haze of the sky. To his right, was another clump of thicket, which clustered at the base of the hill, and swept off to a distant ravine. At a short distance beyond this, a long line of lofty timber, rising above a crowded underbrush, stretched off through the prairie, until it joined the forest of the Missouri. All appeared clear of enemies. So, wrapping his robe still closer around him, the Indian was preparing to quit his stand, when his quick eye was caught by the quivering motion of a bush, in the thicket at the bottom of the hill, on his left. In an instant every sense was on the alert; —it might be a deer, or it might be a lurking foe. He paused, and watched in breathless silence. The bush was again agitated, the painted head of an Indian emerged from among the leaves, and the form of another was dimly seen crouching in the bushes.

The Otoe at once recognized them for Sioux, the bitterest and most powerful foes of his tribe. His loud taunting laugh, accompanied by the Otoe war cry, announced to the lurking savages that they were discovered. In an instant they sprang forth and raised the well known war cry of their tribe.

The Otoe fled down the opposite side of the hill, making for a thicket of bushes and vines at its foot. As he ran he grasped the stem of his pipe in one hand, and the stone bowl in the other. He protruded the end beyond his side, in such a manner as to lead his enemies to suppose that he was armed with a rifle, and carrying it at full cock, ready to be discharged.

His pursuers, to the number of four, followed at his heels, like a pack of hounds in full cry. They gained upon him, for age had stiffened his joints; but by dint of hard straining he gained the covert of brushwood, leaving them full two hundred yards behind. A shout betrayed their disappointment. The wary old savage now threaded his way, swiftly, but with great caution through the thick maze of bushes. He scarcely bended a twig or rustled a leaf, lest it should catch the observant eyes or quick ears of the Sioux, whom he could perceive lurking round, though keeping out of rifle shot distance.

At last the motion of a large bush, through which he was endeavouring to force a passage, revealed his position. In an instant each Indian fitted an arrow to his bow, and stood ready to let fly his shaft the moment he could get sight of the game; but they were still careful to keep beyond the reach of the supposed rifle. At length they drew nearer, and stood upon the edge of a ridge, not more than a hundred yards off. An arrow could not be sent with certainty at that distance; but a bullet could. The Otoe suddenly raised his wild looking head above the bushes and levelled his pipe. A loud yell burst from the Sioux, and they darted below the ridge of the hill, beyond his sight, to escape the dreaded shot. The moment that they disappeared, the Otoe sprang forward and ran. He had succeeded in gaining several hundred yards through the underwood, when his route was again detected. He again raised his head above the bushes; his pipe was again to his shoulder, and pointed in the direction of the hostile group. Once more they disappeared beneath the ridge, and he pushed forward in his course. This manoeuvre was repeated several times, till the Otoe came to where the thicket terminated, and was only separated by about three hundred yards of open prairie, from the wooded bottom of the Missouri.

Seizing the moment of another dispersion of his foes, he burst from the bushes and fled for the timber. He had nearly reached it, when a loud whoop announced that his flight was discovered. His pursuers were obliged to force a path through an intervening skirt of brushwood. This gave him some advantage, and he gained the timber just as they were emerging from the thicket which he had deserted. After rushing rapidly through the underwood, for a long distance, and after several turnings and doublings, he gradually lost all sounds of pursuit, and reached the Agency in safety, all glorious at having beaten off a war party by means of a pipe.

[CHAPTER XXII]

The Metamorphosis

We had been attending a feast, given at the lodge of the Iotan chief; and were returning through the town, towards the little eminence, on which the white canvas of our tents was fluttering in the wind. As we passed one of the lodges, we observed a group of females in front of it, busily engaged in exposing to the heat of the sun, a large quantity of shelled corn. This was done by scattering it upon a buffalo-skin tent, spread upon the ground for the purpose. One squaw attracted our attention, from her gigantic height; most of the Indian females being under, rather than above the middle size. As we approached her, there was a masculine coarseness in the features of her face, which rendered her hideously ugly, and formed a contrast, highly in favour of the group around her. We afterwards learned that this strange being, though now clad in the garb of a female, and performing the most menial of their offices, was in reality a man, and had once ranked among the proudest and highest braves of the Otoe nation. His name had once stood foremost in war, and in council. He had led on many an expedition against their noble, but bitter foes, the Osages. In the midst of his bright career he stopped short; a change came over him; and he commenced his present life of degradation and drudgery.[1]

1 "Among some of the uncultivated tribes to the north, there are instances, though rare, of men assuming the office of women. They put on women's apparel, and mingle with them, and affect the manner and appearance of females as much as possible and continue this folly during life" (McCoy, *History of Baptist Missions*, 360–61). Victor Tixier reported a similar instance among the Osage in 1840: "In the Head Chief's lodge lived a warrior named *la Bredache*. This man, who a few years before was considered one of the most distinguished braves, suddenly gave up fighting and never left Majakita, except when the latter went to war" (John Francis McDermott [ed.], *Tixier's Travels on the Osage Prairies*, 234). For other references, see McDermott, *Glossary of Mississippi Valley French*, 22–23 (*berdache*).

The cause of the change was this. He had been for several weeks absent upon a war expedition, against his usual enemies, the Osages. At a little before sunset, on a fine afternoon, a band of Indians were seen coming over the hills, towards the Otoe village. It was a troop of way-worn warriors. They counted less than when they started; but their tale of scalps, and their fierce brows when they spoke of the death of their comrades, told that those comrades had not been unavenged. In front of them strode the stately form of the brave. He was wearied with fatigue and fasting; and without staying to receive the greetings of his fellow-townsmen, he hastened to his lodge, and threw himself upon one of the bearskins which form an Indian bed; and there he remained for the night. In the morning he arose from his couch; but he was an altered man. A change, fearful and thrilling, had come over him. His eye was quenched; his proud step wavered; and his haughty frame seemed almost sinking, beneath the pressure of some heavy calamity.

He collected his family around him. He told them that the Great Spirit had visited him in a dream, and had told him that he had now reached the zenith of his reputation; that no voice had more weight at the council fire; that no arm was heavier in battle. The divine visitant concluded by commanding that he should thenceforth relinquish all claim to the rank of a warrior, and assume the dress and avocations of a female. The group around him heard him in sorrow; for they prided themselves upon his high and warlike name; and looked up to him as the defender of their hearths. But none attempted to dissuade him from his determination; for they listened to the communications of the deity, with a veneration equal to his own.

After speaking with his own family, he made known his intention to the nation. They heard him gravely, and sadly, but they too, assented to the correctness of his resolution. He then returned to his lodge, and took down his bow, from the place which it had occupied, and snapping it in two, threw the fragments into the fire; and buried the tomahawk and rifle, which had often served him in battle. Having finished this, he washed the war paint from his face, and drew the proud eagle's plume from the scalp-lock. From that hour he ceased to be numbered among the warriors of the nation. He spoke not of battle; he took no part in the councils of the tribe; and no longer raised his voice in the wild war-whoop. He had relinquished everything which he had formerly gloried in, for the lowly and servile duties of a female. He knew that his allotted course was marked out for him; that his future life was destined to be one of toil and degradation; but he had fixed his resolution and he pursued his course with unwavering firmness. Years had elapsed since he first commenced this life of penance. His face was seamed with wrinkles; his frame was yielding to decrepitude; and his ever scowling eye, now plainly showed that the finer feelings of his nature, had been choked by the bitter passions of his heart. His name was scarcely mentioned; and the remembrance of his chivalrous character, was a dream in the minds of his fellows. He was neglected and scorned, by those who had once looked up to him, with love and veneration. He had the misery of seeing others fill the places, which he once filled; and of knowing, that however exalted he once might have been, and however they might have respected his motives, that he was now looked upon as one of the lowest of the nation.

[CHAPTER XXIII]

Indian Dogs

There are no greater thieves in existence than the Indian dogs; not even excepting the old squaws, who have made it their amusement for half a century. With the last, it is a matter of habit, and practice; but with the former it is instinct. It is also necessary for their existence, that they should be at the same time accomplished thieves, and practised hypocrites. They are never fed by their masters, who are always particularly careful to keep every eatable from their reach, their own appetites being generally sufficient to dispose of every thing of that nature. As far as I was able to judge, the only act of pastoral kindness which they ever exerted over their canine flock, consisted in flogging them, whenever a chance offered itself.

There is scarcely a lodge which does not patronise at least a dozen of these hangers on, who, with all their thievishness, are the most pious-looking dogs in existence.[1] Frequently, have I observed some gaunt, greedy fellow, who looked as if he had been dieted for a fortnight, steal with a meditative air into the building, as if he had strolled in without observing what he was about, so much were his thoughts occupied with more weighty matters. But notwithstanding his absence of mind, the moment his look fastened upon any article of food, a change came over him. The air of abstraction passed away; every latent faculty was called into play; and his eye fairly blazed with a concentration of thievish longing. Then, with a fixed gaze, but with an indifferent, lounging step, he would sidle towards the object of his wishes, waiting only for a favourable opportunity to seize his prize, trusting to fortune to make good his retreat. But should he at that moment catch your eye, his flashing, eager look, instantly disappeared, and was succeeded by a meek, deprecating, and unpretending slouch, which seemed to beg that you would not place any improper obstruction upon his actions.

It was not long before it became known to these gentry that a band of strangers had arrived among them, who were as yet unacquainted with their evil practices. Accordingly they deserted the town, to linger around our tents. The first day was

---

[1] Murray, who traveled with the Pawnees on their summer hunt, estimated that in the village "there were more than six hundred tents, and that each tent owned, upon an average, seven dogs, so that there were upwards of four thousand dogs in the encampment, all of them mongrels and curs, very slightly differing from the wolf in appearance, and scarcely at all in voice" (*Travels in North America,* I, 288). Tixier, too, wrote feelingly on the subject of Indian dogs (McDermott [ed.], *Tixier's Travels on the Osage Prairies,* 163–64).

one of jubilee to them, and truly exemplified in us the scriptural saying of "certain men fell among thieves." But we soon became initiated into their customs; and removed from their reach, every thing which we apprehended might be in the slightest degree palatable, or even digestible.

There appeared to be a most cordial hatred existing between them and the old squaws; who above all things detested opposition in their line of business, and were unwilling that any interlopers should come in to assist in carrying off a share of those spoils which they considered their own peculiar property.

Among the number of our canine visiters were two who seemed to carry on a co-partnership. The one was a little rakish-looking dog, of a dirty white colour, with pinkish-green eyes, who had quite a buckish way of carrying his tail. He was a mighty pragmatical, self-important little body, and was apparently endeavouring to pass himself off for more than he really was. He ranged between the gentlemen dogs and the rabble dogs of the village. There was a swaggering, self-important air about him, which reminded me strongly of those individuals of the human kind, who are generally to be found in all places, attempting to hide their own natural vulgarity under a great show of daredevil, rakish gentility. The boon companion of this dog was his reverse in every respect. He was a lean, shaggy fellow, with a drooping slouch to his tail, and quiet, pensive expression of countenance. No one would have suspected him of being the greatest thief in the village; yet such he was; and as such his approaches were most thoroughly discountenanced by all the old squaws, who looked upon him as a most formidable rival. He never attempted to resist their attacks, but fled howling away at the slightest appearance of danger; though half an hour would not elapse before he was as busy as ever. We found that in stealing he far excelled his companion; who made ten times as much bustle in carrying off ten times as little; and who was frequently left to receive the share of punishment due to both.

They continued together for several days. But at length the

partnership dissolved, and each went on to steal for his own private benefit. Many were the sly bits which disappeared, and great was the caution used by the occupants of the tents to keep out of their reach every article which they thought would be acceptable. They continued their visits for several days after their real character had been discovered. But having been detected in the act of dragging off a large bag, which contained some twenty pounds of bacon; and having been several times flogged for their evil practices; and finding that the party had now grown quite cautious of their provisions; they deserted us altogether—betaking themselves to the town, and leaving their places to be filled by other dogs, equally ravenous, but less experienced in this art of gaining a livelihood.

[CHAPTER XXIV]

Indian Life

To dress and ornament himself with trinkets and gewgaws, is the delight of a savage. The glittering presents of the whites, bear as strong an attraction to the warrior as to the female or the child, though his disciplined habits prevent those loud bursts of pleasure which escape unrestrained from them. Scarcely a day elapsed but a little group would collect before our tents for the purpose of ornamenting themselves. They were apparently very fastidious in their taste; for when hours had been spent by an Indian beau in laying on one streak of paint after another, and in ogling himself by piecemeal in a small scrap of looking glass, some defect would appear, and with an exclamation of dissatisfaction the whole would be rubbed off. The work would then be recommenced with unabated perseverance until he succeeded in daubing and ornamenting himself to his entire satisfaction.[1]

[1] "I have seen some dandies in my life—English, Scotch, French, German, ay

When the toilette was completed, a surprising change came over the young warriors. They would fling their blankets ostentatiously around them, and with a lordly air lounge through the town; looking first at one of the young squaws, then at another; and occasionally condescending to speak to some dirty-looking brother, with that patronising air which, in all countries, a well-dressed person is apt to assume in conversing with a ragged ac-

and American dandies too; but none of them can compare with the vanity or coxcombry of the Pawnee dandy. Lest any of the gentry claiming this distinction . . . doubt or feel aggrieved at this assertion I will faithfully narrate what passed constantly before my eyes in our own tent; namely, the manner in which Sâ-ní-tsa-rish's son passed the days on which there was no buffalo hunt. He began his toilet, about eight in the morning, by greasing and smoothing his whole person with fat, which he rubbed afterwards perfectly dry, only leaving the skin sleek and glossy; he then painted his face vermilion, with a stripe of red also along the center of the crown of the head; he then proceeded to his 'coiffure,' which received great attention, although the quantum of hair demanding such care was limited, inasmuch as his head was shaved close, except one tuft at the top, from which hung two plaited 'tresses' . . . He then filled his ears, which were bored in two or three places, with rings and wampum, and hung several strings of beads round his neck; then, sometimes painting stripes of vermilion and yellow upon his breast and shoulders, and placing armlets above his elbows and rings upon his fingers, he proceeded to adorn the nether man with a pair of mocassins, some scarlet cloth leggins fastened to his waist-belt, and bound round below the knee with garters of beads four inches broad. Being so far prepared, he drew out his mirror, fitted into a small wooden frame, (which he always, whether hunting or at home, carried about his person,) and commenced a course of self-examination. . . . I have repeatedly seen him sit, for above an hour at a time, examining his face in every possible position and expression; now frowning like Homer's Jove before a thunder-storm, now like the same god, described by Milton, 'smiling with superior love;' now slightly varying the streaks of paint upon his cheeks and forehead, and then pushing or pulling 'each particular hair' of his eyebrows into its most becoming place.' . . . His toilet thus arranged to his satisfaction, one of the women or children led his buffalo-horse before his tent; and he proceeded to deck his steed, by painting his forehead, neck, and shoulders with stripes of vermilion, and sometimes twisted a few feathers into his tail. He then put into his mouth an old-fashioned bridle . . . from the bit of which hung six or eight steel chains, about nine inches long; [with] some small bells, attached to the reins. . . . All things being now ready for the promenade, he threw a scarlet mantle over his shoulders; thrust his mirror in below his belt; took in one hand a large fan, of wild-goose or turkey feathers, to shield his fair and delicate complexion from the sun; while a whip hung from his wrist, having the handle studded with brass nails. Thus accoutred, he mounted his jingling palfrey, and ambled through the encampment . . ." (Murray, *Travels in North America*, I, 317–21).

quaintance. When they had finished their perambulations, they would mount upon the top of one of the highest lodges, and stand for hours to be gazed at by the different idlers; a term which, in truth, might be applied to the whole of the male portion of the town.

In war and in hunting there is no being more untiring than the Indian. He will spend days, and weeks, in search of an enemy. If in the course of his travel he meets with a strange track crossing his path, his journey is at an end, until he has satisfied himself whether it is that of a friend or a foe. If it is ascertained to be that of an enemy; and if there is any prospect of gaining a scalp; the main pursuit gives place to this. He follows upon the trail, rapidly and surely, and nothing is left undone to in-sure the successful accomplishment of his purpose. He endures fatigues of all kinds; fasting and peril are unheeded by him; he has but one aim: it is murder. There is but little chivalry in the Indian warfare. The pursuer steals like a snake upon his foe. He gives him no warning—no opportunity to resist his fate. Often the death-scream of the victim is simultaneous with the crack of the rifle, that gives him the first notice of a foe.

In peace, and in his own village, the Indian is a different being. He lounges about listlessly; he will sit for hours watching the children at their games; or will stop at the different lodges to hear the floating rumours of the town. Sometimes a knot of five or six will gather together, for the sake of talking over their own domestic grievances, and abusing their wives behind their backs; or they will assemble in the prairie, and relate to the young men their exploits in battle; their success in hunting; the deeds of the different noted men of the village; always wind-ing up with the injunction of, "Go thou and do likewise." At a little distance from these, a single warrior may be seen lolling in the grass; warming himself in the sunshine; and drawling out a dull, sleepy song, with an air of the most perfect indiffer-ence to all things, past, present, and to come. Further on, two or three may be observed strolling along the summits of the different prairie hills, and apparently keeping watch over the neighbouring country.

In war an Indian is all activity—the creature of excitement; but there is not a more listless being in existence, when this grand object does not call into play the latent energies of his nature.

[CHAPTER XXV]

The Indian Guard

During our stay at the village, the crowd of visiters and pilferers, increased from day to day. The chief, therefore, stationed one of the warriors at the encampment, to keep off the idlers and intruders of all descriptions, and above all to have a keen eye to the movements of the dogs and old women. At the same time he took occasion to let us know, that though the warrior had been selected by himself, his pay would be expected to come from the hands of the Commissioner. On the following morning the guard made his appearance, and prepared to enter upon his office.[1] He was tall and thin, with a shaved head, and a body highly painted with vermilion. He wore, or rather carried with him, a dirty blanket; which, with a small piece of blue cloth, around his hips, and a ragged pair of mocassins, completed his dress, and the whole of his worldly possessions. Like most men in office, he began to hold his head higher than the rest of the world; and to look with a patronising air upon his former cronies. He forthwith commenced the discharge of his duties, with that assiduity which fully verified the trite, but true proverb, "a new broom sweeps clean." He routed the droves of vagabond children. He hunted the old squaws over the prairie, till nothing in the shape of a petticoat, dared venture in the neigh-

[1] Such a guard was commonly called a "soldier" (McDermott, *Glossary of Mississippi Valley French,* 138 [*soldat*]. In James, *Account of the Expedition under Long,* I, 235, will be found a much more formal picture of a "soldier." Murray described their duties in the buffalo hunt (*Travels in North America,* I, 336).

bourhood. A perpetual whining and howling of curs, accompanied by the hearty thwacks of a cudgel, informed us that this portion of our visiters, had also been treated with all the respect due to so numerous and busy a community.

This lasted for a day; after which, a perfect calm reigned throughout the camp. There was no excitement; for the guard had monopolized it. There was no squabbling, or howling; for the women were driven off, and the dogs knew better than to venture a second time, within the reach of a cudgel, whose favours were bestowed with such an unsparing liberality.

The office now became a sinecure. The guard sat for hours, upon the head of an empty pork barrel, drumming his heels against its sides, and trolling out some Indian ditty; or occasionally bellowing out a threat, at some urchin, who ventured to steal a distant look at the forbidden premises. When this became tedious, he stretched himself at full length, on the grass, and resumed his old occupation of singing. An hour spent at this, exhausted his patience. He then rose up, threw his blanket across his shoulders, and swaggered off to the village to hear the news, and to take a chat with the old folks, who treated him with the greatest deference, now that he was in office. After paying one of these visits, he always returned to his post, and regaled us, as well as he was able, with the news of the day. By degrees, his jurisdiction seemed to increase, until at last from the charge of our goods and chattels, it reached to the charge of ourselves; and none of the party could leave the tent, without receiving a very inquiring look, as to what might be the nature of the business which called him forth. All these things tended vastly to raise him in the estimation of the village; though I verily believe, that at the bottom, he was one of the most arrant vagabonds breathing; and that the chief, acting upon the principle usually followed by politicians of the present day, had promoted him to office, because it was necessary that something should be done for him, and because there was no other way of doing it.

From a lithograph after Charles Bird King, in Thomas L. McKenney
and James Hall, The Indian Tribes of North America, I, 218.

Choncape, or Big Kansas, 1821

*"The Big Kaw is a short thick Indian, rather good natured, but
gifted with a large supply of mulish obstinacy, and a temper like
gunpowder. Oppose him—flash!—he is in a blaze; the children scamper; the rabble vanish. None stay to listen to the outpourings of his
wrath, unless it may be one or two old fellows, who are too decrepit
to get out of his way, or are blessed with so happy a hardness of hearing, as to render it agreeable to them to be conversed with, even
though by a man in a passion."*

Great as had been his display of diligence for the first day, it soon disappeared; and at the end of three days, there was little difference in the appearance of the camp, from that which it wore previous to his appointment. According to his notions, he had performed all that was necessary to entitle him to his pay, and any further labour, he considered as altogether super-fluous. Before a week had elapsed, he was nearly as great an annoyance as any of the idlers, whom it was his business to remove.

[CHAPTER XXVI]

The Otoe Council

A day had been appointed for holding a council with the nation, for the purpose of forming a treaty, with respect to the lands lying in the neighbourhood of the Nemahaw river.[1] The hour determined upon, was three o'clock; and at that time, we pro-ceeded from the tent to the town, with a string of children at our heels.

We found nearly the whole tribe assembled, and seated in circles, in the large lodge of the Iotan chief. At the far end of the building, was the Iotan; and by his side, were stationed those two worthies, the Big Kaw, and the Thief. Next them, were the stern forms of the older warriors and braves. There was something solemn in the unyielding features of these war-worn veterans. They sat, as motionless as stone—moving not a single muscle of their dusky countenances. They had thrown aside

1 Ellsworth had arrived on September 17 and had expected to hold the treaty council the next day. However, it was not until September 21 that the commis-sioner and the Otoes met in formal session. The Otoes (and the Missouries living with them) were to cede all lands below the Little Nemaha and to live thereafter between that stream and the Platte (Kappler, *Indian Affairs, Laws and Treaties*, II, 400–401). Merrill entered in his diary that the treaty was made on the afternoon of September 20 and signed on September 21 (p. 160).

their usual careless deportment, and all were prepared to listen, with intense interest, to the terms of the treaty. This was observable, not only in the principal braves, but throughout the whole assembly. Even the veriest scapegrace assumed an air of dignity, befitting the occasion.

The lodge was excessively crowded. One ring was formed beyond another; one dark head rose behind another; until the dim, dusk outlines of the more distant were lost in shadow, and their glistening eyes alone could be seen. The passage which led to the air was completely crowded with women and children; and half a dozen curious faces were peering down through the round hole in the roof.

The most of them had adorned themselves for the occasion. Plumes were floating from their scalp-locks; their heads and breasts were painted with vermilion, and long strings of wampum hung from their necks and mutilated ears. But at the present moment there appeared to be no thought of their appearance. Every sense was wrapped up in an intense interest in the approaching council; every breath was held; and every eye fixed with eagerness upon the face of the Commissioner, as he arose to address the meeting.

He stated simply and clearly the terms of the treaty.[2] There was not a sound to interrupt his voice—not a limb stirred—not a muscle. Their chests seemed scarcely to move, so suppressed was their breathing; they were like statues; and their steady stare into the face of the speaker; and the eagerness with which every eye turned to the interpreter, as he translated each sentence; showed their deep interest in the scene. At length the speaker concluded, and a loud groan, or grunt of approbation, followed from the throats of the whole meeting.

2 The principal terms of the treaty guaranteed that previously established annuities of $3,000 would be continued to 1850, that $500 a year would be paid for education, that a horse-mill would be built, that two farmers would be sent to live among them for five years, and that $1,000 in stock would be left for them in care of the agent or the farmers (Kappler, *Indian Affairs, Laws and Treaties,* II, 401).

The old chief remained in grave deliberation for a few moments; then lighting his pipe, he drew a few puffs, and passed it to his neighbour, until it had completed the round of the whole assembly. He then rose and addressed the council. He spoke but a short time. The speech was intended as an answer to that of the commissioner, though it was addressed principally to his warriors. He spoke warmly of the liberality of the whites. He threw out hints as to the contents of the heavy wagons which they had brought with them; and that the less difficulty they made in agreeing to the terms of the treaty, the greater would be their share of the presents. He then dilated upon the advantage to be derived from a friendly intercourse with the whites; and wound up his whole address, with a most pathetic lamentation about the distance between their village and the buffalo hunting grounds. What this last portion of his speech had to do with the rest of the address, I could not well make out; but it appeared to be received with keen satisfaction by his audience; and when he resumed his seat he was greeted with a grunt of applause, which would have done credit to a sty of full-grown porkers.

After him, one of the warriors rose up to address the meeting. He was a lean, sinewy old man; his hair, which was unshaven, was now beginning to whiten with the frost of years, and hung in long tangled locks upon his shoulders. He rose slowly until he had attained his full height; then, gathering his robe closely round his waist, he commenced his harangue. At first he spoke in a low, tremulous tone; his gestures were feeble but impressive; but at length he grew warmed with his subject, and his voice rose from its weak tones, until it sounded through the building with a startling clearness. His withered face lighted up; and his filmy eye seemed to kindle with a new lustre, as he proceeded. The whole dusky crowd listened in silence to his words; but they did not last long. The eloquent spirit, which for a few moments illumined him, passed away. Like the last, leaping flash of a dying flame, it was transient, and expired. For a moment the old warrior seemed endeavouring to recall his train of thought, but without success. Then with a melancholy shake of the head, he drew his blanket over him, and sank into his seat.

None rose after him. The pipe was again passed round, and the terms of the treaty having been assented to, by the chiefs and principal warriors, the crowd poured from the lodge, and scattered through the town.[3]

[CHAPTER XXVII]

Distribution of Presents

On the day following the council, the packages containing the presents for the tribe, were given to the chief, who prepared to divide them among the different members of his village. A large circle, composed of every man, woman and child, had collected in the prairie. In the centre of this, sat the chiefs, and five or six of the principal warriors. The packages were opened, and they commenced separating the different parcels for the purpose of distribution.

There was a great anxiety evinced by the crowd. Every eye was strained with an expression of strong hankering towards the distributors; who quietly proceeded in the business of opening bundles of knives; boxes of kettles; tin cups; packages of beads; cloths; ribands, and other articles, without paying the slightest attention to the imploring, anxious looks of the restless bystanders. When this had been completed, the chief commenced cutting up the pieces of cloth, calico and ribands, and sending off the warriors to distribute them.

Until this moment there had been silence, but now arose

3 The treaty was signed by Jaton, Big Kaw, The Thief, and twenty-three other chiefs and warriors. Edward Ellsworth signed as secretary pro tem, and Dougherty, Dr. May, Dunlop, and Irving as witnesses. J. D. Blanchard, Charlo Mobrien, and Oloe, interpreter, were also witnesses (Kappler, *Indian Affairs, Laws and Treaties*, II, 401).

a deafening clamour. The young squaws begged, the old crones scolded, screamed, and poured out torrents of abuse. The boys whooped, and the papooses bawled. Never was there such a scene of confusion. When a warrior approached the edge of the circle, a dozen hands were reached out, to seize upon the article which he held. But those who had been appointed, had been carefully selected for their coolness. For amid all the scrambling, they maintained the most philosophic calmness, and listened to the invectives of those who were disappointed with the most composed indifference. The distribution was managed with great impartiality; though we observed that a low word or an imploring look from some of the young girls, had their weight; and more than once changed the destination of a gaudy riband, or string of richly coloured beads. A loud outcry was always raised by the neighbours, on each of these occasions; and a few hard epithets were bestowed, by the old viragos, who thought they had lost, by this change of intention.

During the distribution, our attention was attracted by the manoeuvres of one of the many antiquated squaws who crowded in the ring. She was a diminutive little being, clothed in a dirty flannel jacket, and a tattered piece of dress resembling a petticoat. As for her years, they must have been countless. There must have been a strong flavour of bitterness about her tongue; for we observed that all the warriors seemed to shrink from collision with her. Although they evidently neglected her, still their neglect was of a more deferential nature than that exhibited towards the rest; and whenever they passed her, it was with a shuffling, apologetic air. There was no more active being in the assembly. She flew round in every direction; at one moment, she was at one part of the circle, and at another moment she was in the opposite. She scolded, screamed, and begged. She writhed with an eel-like slipperiness, through the crowd. Whenever one of the distributors passed across the circle to present some peculiarly tempting article, a terrible hustling and jostling would be observed at the point to which he appeared to direct his steps, and before he could reach it, the convulsed face and straining eyes of the little squaw, would force a passage through the mass; and her shrill voice would be heard above the general clamour. She never obtained the prize, but the donor, after disappointing her, always moved off, with a hurried step; until he had placed as much space as possible between himself and her vigorous tongue. As the distribution proceeded, finding herself no better off than before it had commenced, she grew furious, and the clamour of her tongue was incessant. At last one of the distributors, an old dried up Indian, with one eye, marched up to her, and either from compassion, or for the purpose of hushing her abuse, reached out a small piece of red riband towards her. She snatched it eagerly; but after looking at it for a few seconds with an air of deep chagrin, her face began to swell like a roasting pippin; and shaking the little fragment of a riband towards him, with an air of the greatest contempt, she opened a torrent of apparently bitter invective. This raised a loud shout of laughter, at the expense of the old man. He, however, did not wait to hear it, but walked off with a cool step, until he had got beyond the reach of her fire. At length another present was given her, but without effect. Her tongue was as inveterate as ever; and to get rid of her, she was finally presented with a large tin kettle, with which she marched off to the village, to the great relief of the whole assemblage. After her departure, the business went on with a degree of good humour, which had not previously existed.

During the distribution, we observed that those of the females who were troubled with large families of children, were particularly well provided for. They were presented with those articles most suited to their domestic economy. To the young squaws, were given only trinkets and ribands, which were of small value in themselves, but possessed the strongest attractions for them. The knives and guns, were bestowed upon those of the young men who were the most distinguished. The chiefs however were particular to lay aside one or two of the best of each article for their own private use.

In turning over the piles of blankets, a few small ones had been discovered. These were given to several of the wild-looking little fellows who were peering in through the ring. For a moment they seemed to doubt the reality of the gift; they appeared bewildered; then forcing a passage through the crowd, they raised a loud whoop, and started off for the town, at full speed; occasionally looking back, as if they feared a change might have taken place in the intention of those who presented them, and that some one might be in pursuit to take away the prize.

After about an hour's chattering, laughing and scolding, the ceremony was finished, and the crowd dispersed—some with sour and sullen looks, some with an air of indifference—while the smiling, pleased countenances of others denoted they at least were fully satisfied with the portion allotted to them.

Most of the discontent was evinced by the old folks of both sexes. The men restrained themselves, and walked off with lowering brows. The women however gave full exercise to their tongues, and continued it, until the sound of their sharp, shrill voices was lost in the distance, as they travelled in Indian file towards the town. Notwithstanding the show of discontent, there were but few who had not obtained some trifle in the general distribution.

Shortly after this, we observed a troop of Indians coming up from the village. They were fantastically dressed, in buffalo skins, so as to bear a strong resemblance to that beast. They retained the head, beard, and legs of the animal entire; and were so well disguised, that several of them at a little distance, might have been mistaken for the brute itself. They had prepared themselves to give us the buffalo dance.[1] They drew up in a large circle,

---

[1] John Mix Stanley ten years later painted such a dance among the Creeks: "This dance is enacted every year during the season of their busk or green-corn dances; and the men, women, and children, all take an active part in the cere-

at a little distance from a skin tent, which had been lent to us by them, our own marquee having become much tattered in a heavy gale a few nights previous. The leader of this band was the Big Kaw, who frisked behind the grave head and beard of an enormous buffalo bull. In the centre of the circle were seated a number of buffalos, whose business it was to sing, while the rest, consisting of chiefs, squaws, and pappooses, or in other words, of bulls, cows, and calves, danced to their music. The chorus commenced with a low, mournful ditty, which set the whole herd of dancers in motion. They began moving slowly round the singers; but as the chant grew more and more animated, the vivacity of the herd increased. From a walk they quickened their pace to a trot; from a trot, it ambled off into a full gallop. Now the spirit of the beast, began to show out. The cows bellowed; the bulls frisked, roared, and fought; they kicked up; they tore up the ground, and chased each other round the circle. This lasted some time, until they grew uproarious, and the butting of horns was furious. At this sight the cows drew off; and several calves, after bursting out into a loud bawl, raised up from all fours, and mounting upon their two hind feet, started for the village—too much frightened to take any further share in the day's diversions. The dance lasted for about two hours, after which, the Big Kaw, under the form of a seven-year-old bull, came and seated himself upon a billet of wood, at our sides. He appeared perfectly satisfied with his performance, but was grievously out of wind.

After this followed several other dances of a similar character. They received their appellations from different animals; and the merit of a dance consisted, in imitating as nearly as possible, the

---

mony. They invest themselves with the scalp of the buffalo, with the horns and tail attached, and dance about in a circle, uttering sounds in imitation of the animal they represent, with their bodies in a half-bent position, supporting their weight upon their ball-sticks, which represent the forelegs of the buffalo" (*Portraits of North American Indians*, 10). James's report of this dance among the Otoes is principally a description of the costume (*Account of the Expedition under Long*, XV, 127).

actions of the beast from which it received its name.[2] They continued until late in the afternoon; when the Indians, one after
another, departed to their homes; and long before nine o'clock,
the busy hum was entirely stilled, and a deep silence hung over
our tent, and the surrounding prairie.

[CHAPTER XXVIII]

Departure of Otoes for the Hunting Grounds

Several days had elapsed, and the growing coldness of the weather, warned us that it was time for the expedition to be on its
move towards the Pawnee villages.[1]

The Otoes had consumed their supply of provisions, and
were preparing to desert their town and start for the hunting
grounds. The Iotan offered to accompany us, with about twenty
of his principal warriors, that he might exert his influence with
the Pawnees, to prevent any hostility towards us. Although chief
of a different and but a small tribe, still his influence with these
wild hordes, was equal to that of any of their own leaders.[2] His
desperate courage had rendered him popular with the chiefs,
and older warriors; and his sociable manners, though tinged
with a dash of grimness, had rendered him a favourite with the
less distinguished of the nation. In addition to this, the character

2 Allis the following year saw at Belle Vue "20 of the Otoes, with one of the
Pawnee chiefs & 2 of his sons . . . dance in the evening, what they call the beardance,
[they] prepared them a drum, & commenced singing & dancing, one of there number was dressed in the skin of a white-bear, & would keep time with the musick,
I never saw the beardance before, I was greatly annoyed by there noise until
midnite. I have sinc ben greatly annoyed by there singing. What a *blessed day*
when thes heathen shall sing the songs of Redeemin love . . ." ("Letters Concerning
the Presbyterian Mission in the Pawnee Country," *Kansas Historical Society Collections*, Vol. XIV [1915–16], 696).

1 Irving telescopes his narrative here: a party of Omahas under Big Elk came
in for a talk with the commissioner on October 3. See editor's introduction.

2 The Otoes and Missouries numbered sixteen hundred at this time; the
Pawnees eleven thousand (*H. Rep. 474*, p. 39).

of the Otoe tribe for furious courage, and pre-eminent skill with the rifle, gave great consequence to their chieftain.

It was for this reason that the proposition of the Iotan was gladly acceded to. And our preparations for departure, were forthwith commenced.

In the meantime, a change took place in the village. Every family was busily engaged in making ready for its departure, to the distant haunts of the buffalo. Large droves of horses, poured in from every direction. The town rang with noises of all descriptions. Squaws were scolding; children were squalling; pappooses, too young to shift for themselves, like so many little mummies, were suspended in baskets, round the inside of the lodges, where they would be out of harm's way, while their mothers were engaged in packing up. The dogs had probably learned from disagreeable experience, that this was one of the ill-humoured seasons of the tribe. Many of them had withdrawn to a short distance in the prairie, where they sat, demurely waiting until the bustle should be finished, and good humour restored to the town. The warriors laid aside their usual indolence, and assisted their wives in loading the horses. The only idlers in the town, were children and old men. The first stood in droves, looking on, equally aware with the dogs, of the souring effect of all this bustle, upon the tempers of the grown-up portion of the community; and equally cautious in avoiding all contact with them. The last strolled up and down; kicking every stray cur they chanced to meet, and bellowing out advice to all who chose to listen.

Here and there, a long train who had finished their labours, were slowly wending their way, over the western hills, towards the wished-for hunting grounds. A long suite of dogs, lounged after them, and disappeared with them, behind the distant ridges.

As one family after another dropped off, the town began to wear a lonely air. Wild and uncouth as were its inhabitants, we had formed a companionship with them. When, however, we entered their lodges, found the fires extinguished, the buildings stripped, and silence and solitude reigning, where we had been greeted with kind looks and smiling faces, we experienced a dreary feeling, which increased our desire to be once more on the wing towards our still distant goal.

[CHAPTER XXIX]

Departure from the Otoe Village

It was about ten o'clock, on a rich golden morning, that we started from the Otoe village.[1] The baggage wagons had left it some hours previous, and had long since passed the hills which rose behind the town. A crowd of gazers collected round us, as we saddled our horses. At length every thing was completed, and bidding farewell to the dusky group, we mounted, and galloped off in the direction taken by the wagons.

Our course lay along the [south] borders of the Platte, which soon began to lose the luxuriant verdure, that had fringed its banks in the neighbourhood of the Otoe town. Scarcely a tree or shrub grew upon its borders, or threw a shade upon the glare of its waters. It moved sullenly along, with now and then the gloating trunk of some ponderous tree, drifting towards the still more murky waters of the Missouri.[2]

1 Ellsworth wrote Herring from the "Otoe Village on the Platte" on October 4. They probably started for the Pawnee village the same day.

2 Dodge's expedition two years later must have followed much the same route. Kingsbury ("Journal of the March of a Detachment of Dragoons under Dodge," *American State Papers, Military Affairs*, Vol. VI, 132–33), wrote then: "Our course to the Pawnee village lay along the valley of the Platte, in some places approaching close to the river bank, at others keeping at a distance of half a mile or a mile. The valley is of variable width, from one mile to three or four miles wide, and terminated on both sides by a high prairie ridge. From one of the high points near the river the eye could wander over a vast extent of country, possessing almost every variety of feature. Could view the broad surface of the river, studded with islands covered with groves of timber; the green level valley, terminated by hills of every variety of shape, beyond which there was a successive range of hills, until

Our party now counted about thirty, including Indians, and although, on account of the scarcity of provisions, four of the soldiers had been sent back to the garrison, still the reinforcement of Otoes, more than compensated for their loss. They were a noble race of men, with more pride of character, than we had observed in any of the Indians we had as yet met with. They had all prepared themselves for the journey. Their blankets were thrown over their shoulders and strapped round their waists, in such a manner as to leave a short skirt, extending half-way down to the knee. Their legs were protected by coarse leggings of buffalo skin. Each man carried a short scabbard, containing a knife; and several pair of mocassins were strapped upon the back of each. They had left their rifles at the village; and a short thick bow, with a well stocked quiver of arrows, supplied their places. This was the usual equipment of an Indian warrior, when starting on a peaceful journey.

The leader of the band, was the Iotan chief. Next followed the short, thick figure of the Big Kaw, succeeded by the long form of the Thief; and after them came the inferior warriors. They moved in front of us, with limbs that seemed not to know fatigue; and although we travelled over many miles of prairie before nightfall, their pace was the same, and their step as unflagging as ever.

Take an Indian upon the prairies, and he is in his element. An air of wild freedom breathes around him. His head droops not; his eye quails not; and not a single feature yields in submission to his fellow man. He is unrestrained in body; unfettered in spirit; and as wayward as the breeze, which sweeps over the grass of his own hills.

---

the view terminated by the distant horizon." Dunbar in October, 1834, also made notes describing this route ("Letters Concerning the Presbyterian Mission in the Pawnee Country," *Kansas Historical Society Collections*, Vol. XIV [1915–16], 597–98).

[CHAPTER XXX]

The Alarm

On the fifth night after our departure from the Otoe town, we encamped upon the banks of the Platte river.[1] The night was clear and cool, and the reflected stars sparkled in the neighbouring river.

The prevailing silence was now and then broken by the neigh of our horses who were pasturing at a short distance; or by the trumpet-toned cry of some wild goose, the leader of a flock, on their way to the north. Far to the south, a faint red light was reflected in the heaven; which one of the hunters attributed to the burning of a prairie, some twenty miles off.

A large fire of heavy logs had been built in front of the tent; and the party had gradually gathered round it. Two or three of our dusky companions, mingled with the group—grave, but observing spectators of the actions of the whites. Half of a large deer was roasting before the fire; and the Black Bear, with a face of vast importance, was busily engaged in concocting our evening's supply of coffee, in a large tin bucket, which swung from a pole, inclined over the fire. The interpreter was called upon for a story, and had just discharged a large roll of tobacco from his mouth to make room for the full play of his tongue. "Ugh!" exclaimed one of the Indians.

---

[1] If they had left the Otoe village on October 4, it would now be the night of October 8, but this date seems unlikely. Dodge's expedition took only a bit over three days to cover these eighty miles (Ford, "Journal," *Mississippi Valley Historical Review*, Vol. XII [1925–26], 555–56); Dunbar, traveling with the Pawnees, arrived at the Grand Pawnee village on the third day ("Letters Concerning the Presbyterian Mission in the Pawnee Country," *Kansas Historical Society Collections*, Vol. XIV [1915–16], 597–98). Furthermore, Ellsworth concluded his treaty with the Pawnees on October 9 (Kappler, *Indian Affairs, Laws and Treaties*, II, 416).

"What's the matter now, *Hah-che-kah-sug-hah?*"[2] asked the doctor, addressing the Indian by his native name. The Indian glanced his eye towards the speaker as he heard his name uttered; but after standing for a moment, he walked off a few steps, and placed his hand behind his ear, in the attitude of one engaged in earnest listening.

"What does he hear, D[ougherty]?" said the doctor, turning to the Indian agent.

"We will know presently," returned the other quietly, without evincing more curiosity than the red companion with whom he had so long taken up his residence.

For a moment the Indian stood with his brows knit; his eyes bent to the ground; his head inclining a little forward; his nostrils expanded; and every sense, apparently on the *qui vive.* He remained so for a few seconds; then throwing himself upon the ground, pressed his ear against the sod.

"What do you hear, Hah-che-kah-sug-hah?" asked the agent, in the Otoe tongue.

"There are Indians on the prairie," was the answer.

This annunciation being interpreted, drew forth loud expressions of surprise from the whites; but the Indians were perfectly quiet; they asked no questions and made no remarks. They appeared to have the greatest reliance upon the Indian, whose keen hearing had been first attracted by the sound. They watched him earnestly, but calmly, as he lay upon the ground. After continuing in this position for some time, he slowly rose up, and

---

2 This Indian was one of the principal braves of the Otoe nation, and has since become a chief. The name Hah-che-kah-sug-hah was given to him on account of his deadly success in the war parties against the Osages. It signifies, *the man who slays the Osages.* Though distinguished for ferocity in battle, yet in private life he was one of the most joyous, pleasant fellows I ever met with.—JTI. Catlin identified that man as the "aged chief of the Missouries" (*North American Indians,* II, 27) and painted him. Was he the O-ah-ha-che-gi-sug-a who signed the Otoe treaty (Kappler, *Indian Affairs, Laws and Treaties,* II, 401)? At the articles of peace signed at Fort Leavenworth, November 12, 1833, he was listed as an Otoe and his name was set down as "Ah-che-kah-sucker, He that strikes the Osages" (*Sen. Doc. 512,* IV, 729).

placed his hand again behind his ear—the very image of the most intense attention. Then taking up a pouch and rifle, belonging to one of the hunters, he stole off until he was lost in the gloom which hung over the prairie.

The contrast between the whites and Indians was now clearly observable. The former immediately commenced a conversation, teeming with suppositions, suggestions, and all that outpouring of confused ideas, usual, when a dozen persons altogether ignorant of a subject, attempt to throw a little light upon it, for the benefit of their neighbours. The Indians, on the contrary, remained perfectly cool; so much so, that one of them, quietly turned the attention of the cook, to a large piece of meat, which he was frying to a cinder, in his eagerness to listen to the comments of the party. They appeared to take the matter with as much quietness as if they had been in the heart of their own town, instead of a large prairie, infested by bands of hostile tribes.

Nearly ten minutes had elapsed, when a loud, shrill cry arose in the prairie from two different quarters.

"Ugh! Otoe!" repeated several of the Indians, but without moving.

At that moment another long quavering whoop sounded in the air.

"Hah-che-kah-sug-hah!" ejaculated one of the Otoes.

A few moments elapsed, and two strange Otoes appeared in the camp, followed by the dusky form of our Indian friend.

In a few words they told their story. They had been to the Pawnee village, which was about ten miles off, and had left it that evening. About an hour previous they had been espied by a party of Sioux Indians; who had pursued them. Seeing a light, they fled for it. Their enemies followed, and they believed that even now, they were lurking in the prairie, at but a short distance from the camp.

In an instant all was uproar. Some ran for their guns; some loaded; others filled their powder-horns; others swore at their comrades, on account of the loss of some article of equipment; but all were busily employed in suggesting to their neighbours what was best to be done in the present emergency, and all followed their own inclinations. "Raise the flag!" at last cried one, "and let them see that there are whites in the party, the fear of their rifles may keep them off."

This was no sooner proposed than executed. A tall pole with a striped flag floating from the end of it, was reared in front of the tent, in the full light of the fire.

The old Iotan saw the flag hoisted, and though he did not exactly understand why it was done; still, he supposed that there was some meaning in it. So he followed the example of the whites, and erected a pole among a pile of kettles, marking his place of encampment. He then decorated the end with a striped flag, which he had hitherto used as a wrapper on state occasions.

"But Major," said one [soldier?], looking rather wild, and walking up to the Indian Agent, "we are representatives of government—will the Sioux dare to fire on the United States?"

"If all the people of the United States were *all* assembled, I presume they would not," was the quiet answer. "But you had better get back from the fire. The Otoes have done so already. They know that an Indian can pick a man off easier, if he stands in the light of the blaze than if he keeps in the shade. You had better join them in the grass yonder,—there is no chance for running, for there's no place to run to."

This was satisfactory, and in another moment the questioner had followed the example of the savages.

The confusion lasted for a short time; but at length, each man had prepared himself. When this was completed, there was nothing more that could be done. There might be an enemy within a few yards, and they might be at the distance of many miles. The darkness was so great, that it was impossible to see more than ten yards beyond the fire. Our foes, on the other hand, if any there were, would be able to catch sight of our forms moving between them and the flame, at twenty times that dis-

From a lithograph after Carl Bodmer, in the atlas accompanying Maximilian, Prince of Wied, Travels in the Interior of North America.

A Buffalo Dance

"They were fantastically dressed, in buffalo skins, so as to bear a strong resemblance to that beast. They retained the head, beard, and legs of the animal entire; and were so well disguised, that several of them at a distance, might have been mistaken for the brute itself. . . . The chorus commenced with a low, mournful ditty, which set the whole herd of dancers in motion. . . . as the chant grew more and more animated, the vivacity of the herd increased."

tance. At length a young Indian rose up, and moving swiftly past the fire, threw himself on the ground beyond. For a moment he remained stationary; and then raising his head, commenced worming his way through the long grass, until he was lost in the darkness. He returned after an absence of nearly half an hour. He had made a long circuit round the camp, but had discovered nothing. He had seen no signs of an enemy; and he gave it as his opinion, that they had abandoned the pursuit, and that no other human beings besides ourselves were in the neighbourhood. As he concluded, he took his seat at the fire, with the confident air of a person who felt that there was nothing to be apprehended from this exposure. He was soon followed by the rest, and in a short time the camp was as merry and noisy as if nothing had taken place to excite their fears.

[CHAPTER XXXI][1]

Preparations for Reception—Reception by Grand Pawnees

During the evening previous to our arrival, several half-breeds, who had been sent out by the Commissioner to gain information of the probable reception which awaited us, came dropping in, all bearing promises of a friendly welcome, from the Pawnee chiefs. At sunrise the next morning, the tents were struck, and placed in the heavy baggage wagons; and a more than usual bustle and note of preparation was heard in the camp. The soldiers seated themselves upon the grass, to examine and prepare their arms; and the Otoe Indians, were busily engaged in ornamenting themselves for the meeting. Some had spread their blankets upon the prairie, and were anxiously employed in tracing various figures in vermilion, upon their woolly surfaces. Some, eagerly bending over the small pools of still water left in the dry

[1] In the original edition Vol. II began here; in the present edition succeeding chapters have been renumbered.

bed of the river, were painting their faces with vermilion, manifesting as much interest and anxiety in the choice of their ornaments, as a young belle preparing for her first ball. Paint was placed on and rubbed off. Faces were striped first in one direction, then in another; and the advice of those who were sitting round, was asked and given, with all the gravity befitting so important an operation. In the meantime, two or three finished their toilets, and seated themselves at a short distance to serve as models for the rest. Several who had acquired some reputation for skill in this art, were busily engaged in painting up the less gifted of their companions. Whilst this was going on in one quarter, in another, five or six Indians, who either had no paint, or cared not about the opinion of those they intended to visit, lay stretched at full length in the grass. Here they kept up an incessant drumming upon their breasts with their fists, in exact time to a chant, which they were letting out at the top of their lungs, and which always wound up with a loud yell, by way of chorus.

But there must be an end of all things, and in due time there was an end of the preparations. The tents were packed; the Indians were painted and striped to resemble any thing but men; the soldiers had adjusted their arms; the horses were saddled; the oxen were secured before the heavy baggage wagons, and the party commenced slowly moving towards the village.

It was a fine sunny morning; the clumps of trees which clustered on the low banks of the river, and the numberless islands which dotted its broad, shallow waters,[2] were alive with woodpeckers of every size and hue. In every direction, they darted among the tall dead trees which overhung the muddy stream,

2 "Any one on approaching it [the Platte] would suppose it to be as large, or larger than the Missouri or Mississippi. In many places it is from a mile to a mile and a half in width, with a current which is even stronger than the Missouri. At other points it presents nothing but one cluster of islands, from the size of six or eight feet square, to sixty miles in length. . . . All these islands are covered with a thick and heavy growth of timber . . ." (Ford, "A Summer on the Prairie," *Army and Navy Chronicle,* Vol. II [May and June, 1836], 321).

making the trunks resound with the incessant hammering of their small but powerful beaks. Large flocks of gaily plumed parroquets, whirled screaming past us, with a surprising velocity.

At ten o'clock the party had travelled several miles across the prairie, and our vicinity to the village was becoming more perceptible. Mounted Indians, sent out to watch for our approach, were seen here and there flying across the hills in the direction of the village, to give notice of the arrival to their chiefs. At a distance we could perceive several bands of Indians in pursuit of large droves of their wild and fiery horses, which they were urging at a headlong speed in the direction of the town. In another quarter, on the top of a ridge of small hills, groups of five or six were standing, intently watching the motions of the party, which, from the jaded state of the oxen, were necessarily slow. The soldiers who had been lazily lounging across the prairie, were now called in, and formed in a compact body round the baggage wagons. An hour more brought us in sight of the village.

Upon our near approach, we could perceive that the hills surrounding it were black with masses of mounted warriors. Though they swarmed upon their tops, to the number of several thousands, yet they stood motionless and in silence, watching the approach of the mission. At length a single horseman detached himself from the mass, and came galloping down the hill and over the prairie to meet us. As he approached there was a wild, free air about him, and he governed his gigantic black horse with the greatest ease. I could not but think that if the rest of these warriors were of the same mould, any resistance of our band, however desperate, would avail but little against an attack of these proud rulers of the prairie.

Upon reaching the party, he sprang from his horse, and shook hands with Mr. E[llsworth]. He then gave directions through the interpreter, that the band should be drawn up in as small a compass as possible, to avoid all contact with his warriors. After

[1 2 1]

spending some time in completing his arrangements, he galloped back, and gave the signal to the rest. In an instant the hills
were deserted, and the whole mass of warriors were rushing
towards us, across the broad bosom of the prairie. It was a moment of intense and fearful expectation. On they came; each
mad horse, with erect mane and blazing eye, urged forward by
the bloody spur of an Indian master. They had reached within
two hundred yards of the party, but still the speed of their horses
was unchecked, and the powerful tramp of their hoofs rang like
thunder upon the sod of the prairie. At a signal, however, from
the chief, the band separated to the right and left, and commenced circling round us, in one dark, dense flood. Their whoops
and yells, and the furious and menacing manner in which they
brandished their bows and tomahawks, would have led a person
unacquainted with their habits, to have looked upon this reception as any thing but friendly. There is something in the fierce,
shrill scream of a band of Indian warriors, which rings through
the brain, and sends the blood curdling back to the heart. Their
ornaments, though wild, were many of them beautiful. The
closely shaved heads of some were adorned with the plumage of
different birds. Others wore an ornament of deer's hair, bound
up in a form resembling the crest of an ancient helmet, and a
plume of the bald eagle floated from the long scalp-locks of the
principal warriors.[3]

Some few wore necklaces of the claws of the grisly bear, hanging down upon their breasts. The bodies of some were wrapped
in buffalo robes, or the skin of the white wolf; but the most of
them wore no covering, save a thick coat of paint.[4] This they

[3] Compare the reception of Dodge's expedition two years later: Kingsbury,
"Journal of the March of a Detachment of Dragoons under Dodge," *American
State Papers, Military Affairs,* Vol. VI, 133; Ford, "Journal," *Mississippi Valley
Historical Review,* Vol. XII (1925–26), 556; Ford, "A Summer on the Prairie,"
Army and Navy Chronicle, Vol. II (May and June, 1836), 312.

[4] Murray in July, 1834, observed at Fort Leavenworth: "The dress of these
Indians consisted of a belt of deer-skin round the middle, with a flap passing
between the legs, and fastened again to the belt behind. Their legs were covered
by tight leggins of deer-skin, and their feet by mocassins; while their shoulders

had profusely smeared over their bodies and arms, and many had even bestowed it upon the heads and limbs of their horses. After dashing round us for some time, the chief waved his hand, and the turmoil ceased. The warriors sprang from their horses, and seating themselves round in a large circle, waited for the arrival of the chief of the Grand Pawnees.[5] In a few moments he advanced to meet Mr. E[llsworth], accompanied by the different chiefs of Tappage Pawnee, Pawnee Republican, and Pawnee Loup villages. He was a tall, powerful Indian. A fillet of the skin of the grisly bear, ornamented with feathers, was bound round his head. Over his shoulder was thrown a large mantle of white wolf-skin, also adorned with feathers. His legs were cased in black leggings of dressed buffalo hide, worked with beads, and fringed with long locks of human hair. These were taken from scalps won in his various war expeditions, and hung down over his knees, trailing upon the ground as he walked. He first advanced and welcomed Mr. E[llsworth], and afterwards the rest. The chiefs of the three different villages were then introduced, and repeated the words of welcome uttered by the first.[6]

were loosely and gracefully covered, or half covered, by a blanket or buffalo-skin" (*Travels in North America*, I, 253–54).

[5] Sharitarish (Characterish, Sa-re-cher-ish, Sa-ni-tsa-rish, Shah-re-tah-riche, Sa-re-cher-ish, etc.), the Angry Man, the Ill-Natured Man, Loup Blanche, White Wolf. "For the Grand Pawnees this treaty [October 9, 1833] was signed by Sharitarish, seemingly the third chief of that name since 1806, with Big Horse (*Asah-kuchu*) signing below him; but everyone seems to be agreed that Big Horse was the head-chief and Sharitarish, the second chief or principal war-chief" (George E. Hyde, *Pawnee Indians*, 136). "Everyone" probably did not include Irving, who did not put a name on the chief, but did give a clue when he described the white wolf skin he wore. Furthermore, in 1835, Colonel Dodge, who was accompanied by Major Dougherty, agent for the Pawnees, recognized Angry Man as principal chief of the Grand Pawnees (Kingsbury, "Journal of the March of a Detachment of Dragoons under Dodge," *American State Papers, Military Affairs*, Vol. VI, 133–34). There he was described as "a shrewd, intelligent old fellow, and very talkative for an Indian. . . . In explaining the relations he stood in to the neighboring tribes, he appeared to possess all the ingenuity of a modern politician." He was first signer for the Grand Pawnees to the articles of peace drawn up at Fort Leavenworth, November 12, 1833 (*Sen. Doc. 512*, IV, 730).

[6] Little Chief of the Tappages, Blue Coat of the Republicans, and Big Axe of the Loups. They will be noticed later.

This ceremony was scarcely finished, when a movement was observed among the crowd, and a powerful roan horse, mounted by an armed Indian, bounded forward to the middle of the circle, where the rider sprang from his back. He was a stranger among the tribe, and spoke not their language—a Kioway[7] Indian, from the borders of Mexico—a member of those wild tribes, who like the Arabs rove the immense plains of the west, and carry destruction to all who are not strong enough to resist them. After pausing and looking around him for a moment, with a glance that seemed to challenge opposition from the assembled warriors, he walked up to Mr. E[llsworth]. He was slight and beautifully formed; but there was a fire in his eye; a swell of the nostril; and a proud curve of the lip, which showed a spirit that brooked no opposition; shunned no danger; and could only be quenched by the chill of the grave. His long black hair, which trailed behind him on the ground, was plaited together, and ornamented with about twenty plates of massive silver. A band of silver was fastened round his throat, and several large medals of the same metal hung upon his breast. Upon his arms were several bands of silver, and rings of the same upon his fingers. His leggings, though more finely wrought, like those of the chiefs, were fringed with scalps. A scalp consisting of the entire upper part of a human head, hung from the bit of his fiery horse. Upon coming up he offered his hand to Mr. E[llsworth], and in succession to the rest; and after pausing and gazing upon us for a short time, with some curiosity, he sprang upon his horse, and riding through the circle, was lost behind the more distant crowd of warriors.

For a short time after the introduction of the various chiefs, the mass of grim beings hemmed us in, sitting upon the ground like so many dark forms of statuary, without voice or motion.

---

[7] We afterwards learned that this Indian had become enamoured of a young girl of his own tribe, the wife of another; but her husband having gone upon some expedition, she had taken advantage of his absence to leave her nation with her lover; and together they had fled to the Pawnee village, which they reached a week previous to our arrival.—JTI.

Several at length arose, and coming towards Mr. E[llsworth], and Major D[ougherty], (the United States agent for the Pawnee Indians,) extended the stem of their pipes to the lips of each, then, instantly retiring, resumed their station in the crowd. By this action, we afterwards learned, that each pledged himself to present a horse to the person to whom he extended his pipe. In the meanwhile, two old men, who had no horses to lose by the free indulgence of liberal feelings, rose up, and by loud and vehement harangues, endeavoured to pique the liberality of the rest. They boasted of the number they would bestow, *if they but had them,* and recounted as examples the acts of generosity which they had performed in their youth. As that youth ran far back, beyond the memory of the oldest inhabitant, there was little probability of their being contradicted.

After they had finished, the Wild Horse, (I do not recollect his Indian name) the principal warrior of the nation, stood up and harangued the assembled multitude.[8] He launched out in a long panegyric upon the whites, which was delivered with a warmth of expression no doubt greatly increased by the sight of the wagons laden with presents. This warrior was one of the most singular as well as ferocious of the tribe; and many were the tales of his war expeditions, afterwards related to us by the trappers, as we lay stretched around our night-fires. His height could have been but little short of seven feet, and every limb was in proportion. Unlike the rest of his tribe, his hair remained unshaven, and hung in long tangled locks, which reached nearly to his waist, and were profusely smeared with red ochre. His low, retreating forehead was almost buried in wrinkles; and his eyes, deep set in his head, glowed like living coals. His nose was large

8 By principal warrior, Irving probably meant principal war-chief. It is unfortunate that Irving did not discover his Indian name. One of the signers of the articles of peace at Fort Leavenworth, November 12, was Ah-sah-ron-kah-re, Wild Stud Horse (*Sen. Doc. 512*, IV, 730); Irving's Wild Horse did accompany the Ellsworth party back to the fort. Is this the Asahkuchu (Big Horse) whom Hyde named as chief of the Grand Pawnees (*Pawnee Indians*, 126)? Is this the Ah-sha-kah-tah-kho who was fourth signer to the treaty of October 9?

and prominent; and the size of an enormous mouth was not at all diminished by two streaks of vermilion, which he had drawn from each corner, to his ears. He wore neither covering nor ornament, unless the profusion of black clay and red ochre which covered his body, deserved that name. He stood out in his naked proportions a giant among those who surrounded him; and the wild energy of his gesticulation as he delivered his harangue, showed the prodigious strength hidden in his form, and which only required an occasion to bring it into action. From his youth upward he had been the leading warrior in the nation, and his deeds had spread a terror of his name through all the hostile tribes. Though no chief, his influence in the village was equal to theirs, rendering him as much an object of jealousy to them as of dread to their enemies.

When he had finished his address, the chief rose and spoke to his men. After this the circle opened, and forming into two lines, one on each side, the warriors prepared to escort us into their village.

[CHAPTER XXXII]

Journey to the Grand Pawnee Village—Old Indian Female—Chief's Lodge—Indian Feasts—Kioway Female

As soon as we emerged from the crowd that had surrounded us, we perceived the plain between us and the village swarming with the rest of its inhabitants. It appeared as if every man, woman, and child had looked upon the day of our arrival, as one of jubilee. The boys had thrown aside their bows and arrows, the females had abandoned their drudgery, and the old men had ceased their songs of former victories, to paint themselves up for the festival. The reception was over, and all the requisite awe of their nation had been impressed upon us. They now threw aside the stern, unbending character of the Indian warrior, and pressed round us with all the kind hospitality of hosts, in receiving their most welcome guests.

Small bands of young men amused themselves by dashing around the party, at the full speed of their horses, and attempting to oust each other from their saddles by the violent collision of their animals. Occasionally a few would start off in a race across the plain, whooping and screaming, and clattering their arms in the ears of their steeds, to excite them even beyond the mad rate at which they were careering.

Others of the young men hung round the party, making their remarks on its different members, and occasionally exciting loud peals of laughter from their comrades. These however were frequently cut short by a stern word from one of the chiefs.

The whole road from the plain to the village, was lined with women and children. They had not dared to approach during the formalities of our reception, but now eagerly pressed forward to gaze upon so unwonted a sight as that of a white stranger entering freely into their village. Besides this they were all anxious to gratify that curiosity which is peculiarly strong in the bosom of an Indian—especially a female.

They were nearly all mounted upon little stiff-maned drudge horses of the village, sometimes singly, but generally in clusters of two or three.

In particular, one withered, gray-headed old squaw, with a family of four children under her charge, attracted our attention. She was mounted upon a little wall-eyed, cream-coloured pony, with a roach mane and a bob-tail. There was a lurking devil looking out of his half-closed eye, the very antipodes of his rider, who sat upon his back like the picture of Patience. Her charge she had arranged, as well as could be expected from a person in her situation. One little fellow, whose eyes gleamed like sparks of fire, from beneath the long tangled hair, which nearly covered his face, was striding almost upon the neck of the horse, armed with a heavy Indian whip. One little one was dozing in her arms, another was clinging tightly to her back. The face of a fourth, like the head of a caterpillar, just ready to emerge from a cocoon, was peering from the mouth of a leather bag, fastened between her shoulders.

But though the woman thus scrupulously divided the burden with her steed, he seemed far from satisfied with his situation, and at last determined to rid himself of his encumbrance.

Tossing his head in the air, he commenced waltzing, and capering round upon his hind feet, to the great discomfiture of the squaw. In great tribulation she reached out both hands, and clung with might and main to the high pommel of the Indian pack-saddle, while two of the children, left to their own guidance, clung like monkeys round her body.

The horse, finding that the first experiment had not succeeded to his satisfaction, altered his plan of action. He planted his fore feet firmly upon the sod, and flourished his heels as high in the air as his head was the moment before. Still his rider continued to cling to the saddle, making use of every expression of Indian objurgation and soothing, in a vain appeal to the sensibilities of the restive animal. There was one, however, evidently delighted with his capers; this was the naked little elf perched upon his neck, who evidently aided and abetted the mutiny by a sudden switch of his whip—occasionally casting back his sly, laughing black eye upon the chattering old lady and her screaming brood.

At last the animal finding that no physical force of his could free his back from the burden, came to the conclusion that the less time he spent in accomplishing his journey the shorter would be his ordeal. So he started off at a full gallop for the village, and we caught our last glimpse of him as he dashed between the lodges, urged on by the lash of his imp-like little rider.

When the party had once commenced its march, it was not long before they reached the point of destination; for though the Indians crowded forward to satisfy their curiosity, they remained at such a distance as to offer no obstacle to our progress. This rule of etiquette was, however, occasionally transgressed by troops of untrimmed, goblin-looking little urchins who hung upon the heels of the party. They crowded around the baggage wagons, and gazed with a mixture of terror and wild delight upon the oxen, who, with lolling tongues and reeling steps, were, almost inch by inch, winning their way to the village.

Several times when a circle of little curious faces, anxious to see, but ready to run, had formed around the team, a sharp, shrill scream from some more mischievous of the gang, would in an instant disperse all their rallied courage, and send them scampering at full speed over the prairie.

Another grand object of attraction was *the Black Bear,* who trudged in front, surrounded by a rabble crowd of women and children. From the first moment of our arrival he had been an object of intense curiosity, and had been gazed at with a mixture of fear and astonishment by the whole nation. But there is an old saying that "too much familiarity breeds contempt;" and in this case it was verified. By degrees, the circle which formed around him at a respectful distance, became more and more compressed. It was in vain that he attempted to rid himself of their company; they swarmed around him like ants. If he quickened his pace, they did the same; if he lingered, they were equally slow; and if he turned upon them, they scattered in every direction. But after a while, even this wore off, and they finally hemmed him in, so that it was almost impossible to move for the crowd. When they had thus closed upon him, the lurking spirit of mischief began to show itself. They tugged at his coat tail, they pulled his pantaloons, and they jostled him until the perspiration, the effect of fear and exertion, poured in streams down his face. At length one toothless, gray-headed old crone, attracted by the glistening appearance of his black leather cap, made a violent snatch, and seized hold of it. A hot scramble ensued for the prize, which, after much derangement to the wardrobe of the negro, was obtained by the rightful owner. He had no sooner regained his property, than he opened his shirt, and placed it next his bosom. He then buttoned his coat over it up to the chin, evincing his respect to the nation by performing the rest of his journey *uncovered.*

We found that the Pawnee village had been rebuilt since it was burnt by the Delawares.[1] It is situate in the open prairie, at the foot of a long range of hills, and within about fifty yards of the Platte. The river at this place is about two miles broad, and very shallow, being constantly forded by the squaws, who visit the different islands, and obtain from them the only fuel and building materials, to be found in this part of the country.

The lodges are numerous, and stand close together, without the least regard to regularity. They are built in the same way as those in the Otoe village.[2]

On account of the scarcity of wood, several families congregate together in the same lodge. The male portion pass the whole day, lounging and sleeping around, or gorging themselves from the large kettle filled with buffalo flesh, which is perpetually over the fire.[3]

[1] "One of their villages containing 2,500 inhabitants, has been burnt last summer by the Delawares, who at the same time destroyed the corn and other vegetables" (Ellsworth to Herring, Fort Leavenworth, November 6, 1833). This punitive raid, of course, had taken place while the Pawnees were away on their summer hunt. See also n. 1, p. 6.

[2] Two years later Kingsbury wrote: "The Pawnee village is built after the same plan with that of the Ottoes, but it is not so neat in appearance. The space between their lodges is occupied by horse-pens, where they confine their horses every night to prevent their being stolen by the neighboring tribes, with whom they are at war" ("Journal of the March of a Detachment of Dragoons under Dodge," *American State Papers, Military Affairs,* Vol. VI, 133). Ford ("Journal," *Mississippi Valley Historical Review,* Vol. XII [1925–26], 556) estimated the village at one hundred lodges. Dunbar in 1834 figured the inhabitants at two thousand and described the construction of lodges at length ("Letters Concerning the Presbyterian Mission in the Pawnee Country," *Kansas Historical Society Collections,* Vol. XIV [1915–16], 599–600). Another detailed description of the Pawnee lodges (1844) will be found in J. Henry Carleton, *The Prairie Logbooks,* 66–69.

[3] Allis "Letters Concerning the Presbyterian Mission in the Pawnee Country," *Kansas Historical Society Collections,* Vol. XIV [1915–16], 699) gives a vivid picture of life in such a lodge: "There is generally not much regulation in a Pawnee lodge, while some of the men are singing, others are talking, others sleeping, others smoking, others eating, at the same time, the women are engaged in cooking, pounding corn, makeing moccasons, dressing robes, etc. they are also talking, & scholding, the children playing, & fighting, among the whole I often get confused. some of the largest of there lodges, contain 4 or 5 families, my chief has

As we entered the village, the tops of the lodges were completely covered with women and children, and the area in front of the chief's dwelling was equally crowded. When we reached the front, the chief, who had ridden in advance of the party, stepped from the dark passage which formed the entrance to his abode, to meet us. He was completely enveloped in a robe of white wolf skin, upon which was painted a hieroglyphic account of his warlike achievements.[4] Upon the approach of Mr. E[llsworth], he advanced towards him, and taking the robe from his shoulders, presented it to him, requesting him (through the interpreter) to keep it for his sake. He then ushered the party into his dwelling, and pointed out the place allotted for the reception of the contents of the wagons. After this he called together a number of Indians, and gave them directions to assist in unloading. He stood at the door, watching their movements, to prevent any attempt at purloining—a crime too common among the lower classes of an Indian village.

Nearly half an hour elapsed in this way, during which time the lodge was becoming more and more crowded. One dusky form after another glided with a noiseless step over the threshold, moving across to the darkest corners of the lodge. Here they seated themselves upon the ground, and shrouded their shaggy robes around them, so as completely to screen the lower part of their faces. As they fixed their unwavering gaze upon us from the dark parts of the building their eyes seemed to shine out like glowing balls of phosphorus.

Not a word was spoken—no undertoned conversation was carried on—all was silence, save the hurried footsteps of those who were busied according to the directions of the chief. No jests were uttered, for we were now under the roof of their leader, and any word spoken in derogation of his guests would have called down instant punishment.

30 persons in his lodge." Ford noted that sometimes as many as ten or twelve families lived in one lodge ("Journal," *Mississippi Valley Historical Review*, Vol. XII [1925–26], 556).

4 Sharitarish (White Wolf).

Upon our entrance into the lodge, a large kettle had been filled with buffalo flesh and hard corn, and placed over the fire. When we were fairly settled in our abode, and the bustle of unloading had in a measure passed away, the wife of the chief (by-the-by he had five of them[5]) poured the whole of its contents into a large wooden bowl. She then armed each of us with a black dipper made of buffalo horn, and made signs for us to commence.

We did not wait for a second invitation, but immediately, with both fingers and dippers, attacked the mountain of food before us. We had not eaten since daylight; it was now late in the day; and the appetites of the party, never particularly delicate, having increased in proportion to the length of their fast, the devastation was enormous. But every excess brings with it its own punishment; and our case was not an exception to the general rule. Scarce had we finished, when a little Indian boy, half covered with a tattered buffalo skin, forced his way into the lodge, elbowing in among the warriors with all that transient air of consequence worn by *little* characters when charged with some mission of importance. He came to the side of the chief, who was sitting near us, with his legs doubled under him, after the Turkish fashion, and whispered in his ear. The chief rose, and announced that the Long Hair, the second warrior of the village, had prepared a feast in honour of our arrival, and was waiting for us to come and partake.[6] There was some demurring as to the acceptance of this invitation. The Interpreter,[7] however, informed us that there was no resource, as eating your way into the good will of the savages, is necessary to the success of an Indian treaty. It was useless to plead that we had already

[5] Murray gives a glimpse of the wives and children of this chief on the summer hunt (*Travels in North America*, I, 279–80).

[6] Hyde makes clear that the several chiefs of the names of Sharitarish and Long Hair were rivals for the hereditary chieftainship of the Grand Pawnees and alternated in possession of that office (*Pawnee Indians*, 102–107, 112, 118–23).

[7] Louis La Chapelle was interpreter to all the Pawnees at this time. It is very likely, however, that Irving means Dougherty here.

eaten sufficient, for that is a thing incredible to an Indian, who always carries with him an appetite proportioned to the quantity to be eaten, and the opportunity of doing so. Let the latter come as often as it may, it invariably finds him prepared.[8]

After some consultation, seeing no remedy, we left the lodge, and followed our little guide through the intricacies of the village, to the dwelling of the Long Hair. When we entered he was sitting upon the ground, and motioned us to a seat upon some dirty cushions of undressed hides. He was a stern, gloomy looking man, with an anxious, wrinkled brow, a mouth like iron, and an eye like fire. He evidently made efforts to be sociable; but it was not in his nature; and during the whole feast, the stern, unbending character of the Indian warrior, was continually peering out from beneath the show of hospitality. He urged us to eat, and he even attempted to smile; but it more resembled the angry snarl of a wildcat, than the evidence of any pleasurable emotion. In short, we liked him not, and hurried through our feast as soon as possible. When we had finished, and while a number of the party were smoking, in turn, from a large red stone pipe, which he passed round, the Doctor rose and slowly sauntered round the lodge. He at length observed a small bundle of bones, and skin, which hung from a pole crossing the centre of the lodge. Curious to know what it might contain, he reached out his hand to take hold of it. From the moment that he had left his seat, the brow of the chief had darkened, but he said nothing; contenting himself by narrowly watching the motions of his guest;—but no sooner had he touched the bundle, than the effect upon the frame of the Indian was like an electric shock.

8 Every traveler talked about this custom. On the day after his arrival at the Grand Pawnee village, Dunbar was invited to eat at six lodges before noon: "When a person is invited to a feast, he does not please, unless he eats as if he loved what is set before him" ("Letters Concerning the Presbyterian Mission in the Pawnee Country," *Kansas Historical Society Collection*, Vol. XIV [1915–16], 599, 609–10). When he arrived at the Grand Pawnee village during the summer hunt, Murray had buffalo bull meat "as hard, tough, and stringy as ever fell to the human jaw to masticate" (*Travels in North America*, I, 280–81, 341–49). See also n. 3, p. 81.

He half started from his seat; the veins on his forehead swelled like whipcord; and his eyes shot fire.—With clenched fists and extended arms, he shrieked out something between a yell and an imprecation. The secret was soon explained by the frightened Interpreter. The bundle that had attracted the curiosity of the Doctor, was the medicine bag[9] of the lodge. To disturb this is one of the greatest outrages that can be inflicted upon the superstitious feelings of an Indian. At another time, the Doctor might have paid dearly for his rashness. As it was, at the earnest solicitations of the Interpreter, he resumed his seat, and the anger of the chief passed away. Shortly after this, another courier arrived to invite us to a third feast; and taking our leave, we followed him. This feast was exactly the same as the former. Before we had finished, invitation after invitation came pouring in upon us, until we had visited about ten or fifteen lodges. One after another, the different members of the party then gave out, and returned to the abode of the chief.

Upon our return, Mr. E[llsworth] assembled the different warriors, and after some consultation, the following day was appointed for holding a council, to agree upon the terms of the treaty.

When this was settled, the chief turned and spoke a few words to the heralds.[10] They immediately started through the village, proclaiming the time appointed for the council.

[9] Every lodge in an Indian village contains what is called its Medicine Bag, which is hung up in the most conspicuous place, and regarded with the greatest veneration, not only by the inhabitants of that individual lodge, but by the whole tribe. Little is known of their contents, as they are seldom opened, and always with the greatest formalities. On these occasions, all possible care is taken to exclude strangers, whose presence or interference is regarded as a certain source of future misfortune.—JTI. Murray noted that "the medicine-bag[s], wherein are contained arrow-heads, with which their fathers have killed a foe, scalps, and any other similarly precious ancestral relics" were carried on the hunt and suspended in the moveable lodges (*Travels in North America*, I, 285–86). George Bird Grinnell declared that the Pawnee medicine bundles hung on the west side of the lodge opposite the door, and discussed their legendary origin (*Pawnee Hero Stories and Folk-Tales*, 351–53). George A. Dorsey (*Traditions of the Skidi Pawnee* [*Memoirs of the American Folklore Society*, VIII], 339) described the warrior bundles or bags.

From George Catlin, North American Indians, I, *Plate* 101.

Scalps and Scalping

While Mr. E[llsworth] was thus engaged, the rest of the party drew round the fire, to discuss the different events of the day. The bearskin, forming the inner door of the lodge, was slowly raised, and a female stepped timidly in, and moved rapidly, and evidently with a desire to escape observation, into the darkest part of the lodge. Her whole appearance bespoke her a stranger. She was beautiful; and though a timid being, moved with the step of a queen. She was the wife of the Kioway Indian, and her dress was of a richness corresponding with his. A bright band of silver was fastened round her neck; a small jacket of scarlet cloth, the spoil of some pillaged caravan, edged with silver lace and beads, was secured round her waist and breast, with scarlet ribands, and a long garment of blue cloth enveloped the rest of her form. Like her husband, she wore medals of silver upon her breast, and bracelets of the same upon her wrists. Her mocassins, also, were more finely ornamented than those of the Pawnee women, who were seated around.

From the moment of her entrance, she became the object of attraction to all eyes. Observing this, she withdrew into one of the berths, and dropping in front of her a screen of grass matting, remained there for the rest of the day.[11]

10 These heralds are self-elected, and are composed of the oldest men in the village, who run through the town to spread the orders of the chief. When no such service is required, they amuse themselves by stalking round the village, yelling out advice to the young men, with voices which may be heard at the dis- tance of a mile, but which, as far as I was able to judge, was but little attended to.—JTI. An interesting description of the function of the heralds or criers among the Omahas is given in James, *Account of the Expedition under Long*, XIV, 290–93. Dorsey distinguished between the criers of the chiefs and those of the priests (*Traditions of the Skidi Pawnee*, 336).

11 "Within these buildings the earth is beat down hard, and forms the floor. In the center a circular place is dug about 8 inches deep, and 3 feet in diameter. This is the fireplace. The earth that is taken from this place is spatted down around it, and forms the hearth. Near the fireplace a stake is firmly fixed in the earth in an inclined position, and serves all the purposes of a crane. Mats made of rushes are spread down round the fire on which they sit. Back next the walls are the sleeping apartments. A frame work is raised about two feet from the floor, on this are placed small rods, interwoven with slips of elm bark. On these rods a rush mat is spread. At proper distances partitions are set up, com- posed of small willow rods interwoven with slip of bark. In front of these apart-

CHAPTER XXXIII

Grand Pawnee Village—The Council

The second day after our arrival was appointed for holding the council.[1] It was a fine frosty morning. The sun rose like a huge ball of crimson over the low hills; pouring a flood of lurid light upon the dancing waters of the Platte, and gemming with a thousand tints, the frost beads that glittered upon the tall withering grass of the prairie.

A number of us left the lodge early in the morning, and strolled towards the banks of the Platte. A few gaunt, sinewy wolf-dogs were prowling about the silent village, in search of food. The savages had not yet left their lairs, except one or two solitary individuals, muffled in their robes, who at sight of us, hurried to their abodes to give information that the strangers were stirring. Occasionally, as we passed the dark funnel-like mouth of the dwellings, the half of a face would be seen, cautiously looking out, and after staring at us for an instant, would vanish into the interior to call out the rest of the inhabitants.

We had not proceeded far, before about a dozen half-starved Indian wolf-dogs collected at our heels. Here they followed, raising their nostrils, baring their long white fangs, and uttering deep growls. Their green flashing eyes; their long bristling hair; and their tails stiffly extended as they slowly stalked after us, convinced us that they waited only for the slightest appearance of fear on our part, to commence an attack. It also plainly showed

---

ments, either a partition of willow rods is erected, or rush mats are hung up as curtains. But this is not always the case. In some lodges the simple platform alone is to be seen, without either partitions, or curtains. In others there is not even the platform, and the inmates sleep on the ground" (Dunbar, in "Letters Concerning the Presbyterian Mission in the Pawnee Country," *Kansas Historical Society Collection*, Vol. XIV [1915–16], 600).

1 The council was held on October 9.

that however welcome our appearance might be to the Indians, there were some members of the village who did not participate in the general feeling of joy.

In spite, however, of this show of ill will, we continued our walk until we reached the Platte. Here we seated ourselves upon the trunk of a tree lying prostrate on the bank of the river.

In the meantime, the Indians had received intelligence of our movements, and began to edge towards the stream. The children came running openly and in droves. The old men and warriors carelessly sauntered along towards the water, and came down upon us as if by accident. Others more modest, crouched down in the long grass, creeping stealthily forward, until every stump concealed a painted form, and every bush was alive with curious faces.

Nearest to us was a tall, thin Indian, clad in an old, worn-out buffalo-robe. There was a "gallows-bird" look about him,—no doubt some prodigal son, disinherited by a crusty old curmudgeon father. He was standing with his back half towards us, and his face turned away, apparently gazing up the river; the very attitude to "give the lie" to his eyes, which were convulsively straining towards us, from the corner of their sockets, and scanning our every movement with an intense and eager curiosity.

At length one of the party wishing to inquire about our horses, beckoned him forward. This was a signal for all the rest. They came trooping up from every quarter, under the pretence of giving information; and upon every sign made by us, about twenty tongues gabbled unintelligible answers. After spending about half an hour upon the banks, and finding that nothing was to be gained in the way of information, we turned off in the direction of the village.

It was now humming with life. The warriors were collected in small knots of five or six, and, by their vehement gestures, were apparently engaged in earnest conversation. The children were rolling and tumbling in the dirt; the squaws were busily engaged. Some were bringing from their lodges large leather sacks of shelled corn; others were spreading it out to dry, upon the leather of their buffalo-skin tents, which had been stretched out upon the ground. Others were cleansing from it the decayed kernels and packing it up in small sacks of a whitish undressed leather, resembling parchment. These were then deposited in cache-holes[2] for a winter's store.

At a distance from the village, a band of females were slowly wending along the top of one of the low prairie ridges, to their daily labour in small plantations of corn. These are scattered in every direction round the village, wherever a spot of rich, black soil, gives promise of a bountiful harvest. Some of them are as much as eight miles distant from the town.

There is a fearful uncertainty hanging round the lives of these females. At the rising of the sun they depart to their toil, often never to return. They are constantly exposed to the attacks of lurking foes, who steal down upon their villages, to cut off stragglers. They come and disappear with equal silence and celerity. Their presence is unknown, until the long absence of a friend, or a mutilated body, found sometimes after the lapse of several days, conveys to their friends a thrilling token, that the hand of the destroyer has been busied among them, and the hour of vengeance has passed.[3]

As we proceeded, we were again waited upon by a committee of the dogs of the town. They formed in a train behind us, with the same expression of ill feeling that had been manifested by their predecessors. But this last display of rancour was of short

2 The *Cache*, is a large hole dug in the ground like a cistern. It is narrow at the top (about four feet in diameter) but wider as it descends, until its form somewhat resembles that of a jug. It will contain about an hundred bushels of corn. Upon leaving their villages, the Indians deposit the corn which is to serve for their winter's store in granaries of this description, and cover the apertures with earth, so that it is impossible, for a person unacquainted with their exact position, to discover the entrance. The name *Cache* is given by the French traders who derive it from the word *cacher* (to conceal).—JTI. See also the variants cited in McDermott, *Glossary of Mississippi Valley French*, 37.

3 Dunbar described at considerable length the work of Pawnee women ("Letters Concerning the Presbyterian Mission in the Pawnee Country," *Kansas Historical Society Collections*, Vol. XIV [1915–16], 610–12, 613–14).

duration; for a stout, tattered Indian, who looked as if his last ablution had been performed during his infancy, rushed out from one of the lodges, and with a few vigorous applications of his foot changed the aspect of affairs. In an instant the glistening eyes of the curs sank from fury to meekness; the hair which bristled boldly up was sleeked quietly down to their backs; the tails which had stood out as erect as bars of iron, were tucked snugly away between their legs, and the snarls were converted into yells. In short, the canine committee were unmercifully beaten, and fled yelping and howling in every direction.

Our attention was now called to the long, lean, wiry old heralds, who were stalking through the town, calling forth the warriors, and exhorting them to prepare for the council. Occasionally they stopped to gossip with some gray-headed crony, who stood blinking like an owl at the entrance of his dwelling. At other times they paused to bestow a little wholesome advice upon some wild urchin, guilty of some breach of decorum towards their guests.

Upon reaching the lodge of the chief, we found that active preparations had been made for holding the council. The goods and presents which had been received hastily into the building, were now piled up carefully. The lodge had been swept clean; a large cheery fire was crackling in the centre. The rabble crowd of loungers and hangers-on had been routed; and besides the family of the chief, we were the only occupants of the spacious building.

At mid-day the chiefs and braves began to assemble. They were full dressed; many of the young warriors had spent the whole morning in preparation, and now presented themselves, fully ornamented for the meeting.

As the hour for the opening of the council grew nearer, the tall, muffled warriors poured in, in one continuous stream. They moved quietly to the places allotted them, seating themselves in silence round the chief, according to their rank. There was no wrangling, or bustle for precedence; each knew his station,

[1 3 9]

and if perchance one of them occupied the place of some more distinguished warrior, upon his appearance he immediately rose and resigned him his seat.

The crowd continued flowing in until the lodge was filled almost to suffocation. As they came in, they seated themselves, until five or six circles were formed, one beyond the other, the last ranging against the wall of the building. In the ring nearest the chiefs, sat the principal braves, or those warriors whose deeds of blood entitled them to a high rank in the councils of the nation. The more distant circles were filled by such young men of the village as were admitted to its councils. The passage leading to the open air, was completely blocked up with a tight wedged mass of women and children, who dared venture no nearer to the deliberations of the tribe.

In the course of half an hour, nearly all the principal warriors had assembled. The chief then filled a large stone pipe and lighting it, drew a few puffs, inhaling the smoke into his lungs, and blowing it out in long blasts through his nostrils. He then passed it to the whites, who, each having inhaled a few whiffs in their turn, handed it to their neighbours. These again passed it on, until it had made the circuit of the whole assembly. While this was going on our attention was attracted by a violent commotion in the passage. In a moment afterwards the naked head and shoulders of the Wild Horse towered above the crowd. He forced his way through them, and burst naked into the building. Here he seated himself in the inner ring, leaning his back against one of the pillars which supported the roof. The chief scowled grimly at the disturbance caused by his entrance. The Wild Horse, however, was a giant, whose wrath was not to be courted, and the matter passed off in silence. After a short time Mr. E[llsworth] rose and addressed the council, stating the views of the United States, and at the same time, the conditions of the treaty.[4]

4 The speeches as reported by Edward Ellsworth are in *Sen. Doc. 512*, IV, 601–604. The treaty is in Kappler, *Indian Affairs, Laws and Treaties*, II, 416–18.

During the whole of the address, every sound was hushed into a deep and thrilling silence. Not a form stirred; but all sat with their eyes steadily fixed upon his countenance. There was not even a long-drawn breath to break in upon the voice of the speaker; though now and then, some proposal, which met with peculiar approbation, would elicit a loud grunt of approval, from the deep, sonorous chests of the whole assemblage.

When Mr. E[llsworth] had finished his address, the chief of the Grand Pawnees rose and folded his heavy buffalo-robe round his body. His right arm and breast were left bare. The other hand and lower part of his body, were completely hid by the dark folds of his shaggy mantle. For a few moments he stood facing Mr. E[llsworth] in silence; then stepping forward, his chest seemed to swell out,—he threw back his head, and raised his arm, with one of the fingers slightly extended, as if to command attention. He then paused and gazed with a hawk eye upon the iron faces of his warriors. The pause and glance were momentary; and without moving the position of his arm, he commenced his harangue. It was short, energetic, and abounding with all the high-wrought figures of Indian oratory. As he proceeded he grew more and more animated; his chest rose and fell; his finely modulated voice, which at first had stolen like music over the stillness, grew louder and louder, until its deep, fierce tones rang like thunder through the building. He threw his robe from his shoulders, leaving bare his almost convulsed frame. He fixed his eagle eye upon us; he extended his bare arms towards us, he waved them over our heads, with a wild fury of gesticulation. Had it not been for his words of friendship, our fancies would have led us to imagine him some demon, pouring out the most fearful threats of vengeance. For about ten minutes his voice rolled through the lodge. Suddenly he fell from his loud, energetic language to the silvery, guttural tones natural to him, and in a short time finished his harangue.[5]

5 When Edward Ellsworth wrote to Irving from Fayetteville, Arkansas, May 22, 1835, on hearing that his friend was turning author, he volunteered: "Should

After him, his son, the second chief of the tribe, rose and commenced an address.[6] While he was proceeding, a noise of voices arose at the extreme part of the lodge, near the passage. At first they were low and smothered; but at last they broke out into loud and angry altercation. The Wild Horse was crouching

---

you wish to get the speeches of the Indians I will bring on the Companies [commissioners?] Book which I took them down in." But this was much too late, for *Indian Sketches* was coming off the press. Had it not been, the young author probably would have quoted the eloquent, polite, and politic speech of the head chief of the Grand Pawnees: "My father: I accede to what you ask; I am glad to accept the proposition; I am glad that our great father knows where we live, and pities us, and is going to help us. For my part, I am not only willing but glad to accept the proposition. My father, I am in hopes things will now be changed; that the whites will not do as they have done. They go *around* us to get to the mountains and Mexico, because they fear us; but now I hope they will come to us as to a *home*. All the Pawnee chiefs have heard what you say. I now speak for all those young men you see crowding the door. They desire peace, and will eat out of the same bowl with all nations. My father, we have been, as it were, like men travelling, sick, weary, and dying; but your arrival and the words spoken to us have resuscitated all. We are all glad at what you say, and hope you will make it good. What I have said to you is true. I thank you, my father, for what you do for us, and hope you will send the proferred aid as soon as possible. We view your promises as certain truth; as much so as if we had the substance of them now in our hands. At present we look like persons who have passed through a burning prairie. We are black, our robes are dirty; but I hope we shall soon dress like other people. We are poor, and in great need of what you offer. All the chiefs and braves on this side I have conversed with, and I believe they think as I do, and will be under great obligations to you. Let us know, my father, what you will do for us. All are anxious to see the treaty. You have come a great ways, and have come to do us good. We would be glad could you commence giving us some of those good things next spring. Look at these dirty and greasy people, my father; they surely need your help. Blacksmiths, my father, we should like near at hand. It is a great distance to go to Missouri for little things. I am glad, of course, to have a shop anywhere, but would like it nearer. I thank you, my father; all the squaws and children thank you; it is a great day of rejoicing among them. I speak for my village; all its inhabitants are glad; and though we never saw you before, we love you at first sight. You desire of us exactly what we wish ourselves. You cannot want peace more than we do. My father, I find nothing more to say. I am so glad that I have forgotten half what I had laid up to tell you."

6 Kingsbury also mentioned a son of Angry Man: "We were met two or three miles from the town by the son of the principal chief in full dress. He had on a scarlet-colored coat, trimmed with silver lace, a hat decorated with bands of tin and red feathers, with leggings and moccasins ornamented with different colored beads" ("Journal of the March of a Detachment of Dragoons under Dodge," *American State Papers, Military Affairs,* Vol. VI, 133). Edward Ellsworth did not record any speech by this young man.

at the foot of one of the pillars, with his hands interlocked with each other, his arms encompassing his legs, and his body nearly hid by the long matted hair which hung over it. He was roused by the disturbance; but at first contented himself by an occasional sharp word addressed to the crowd. This silenced it for a few moments; but at last the brawling voices broke out into open clamour. The savage started to his feet, stalked among them, shook his brawny arms over their heads, and thundered a few stern words in their ears. This had the effect of magic in soothing the angry passions of the disputants. The voices sank into silence, and the noise was hushed. For a few moments he maintained his menacing attitude over them; and then resuming his station at the foot of the pillar, the chief proceeded in his harangue.

When he concluded, several chiefs rose and addressed the party, welcoming them to their homes, with the kindest expressions of hospitality.[7] At the same time they expressed their entire acquiescence in the terms of the treaty. After them several of the braves and warriors rose, and spoke to the same effect. When they had concluded, the following day was appointed for signing the treaty. The pipe was again passed round, and the council breaking up, the warriors left the lodge.[8]

During the whole of the deliberation, which lasted about six hours, the interior of the building was excessively hot. The instant it was cleared, we strolled out into the open prairie. A large crowd was gathered at a distance. We went towards it, and found it assembled to witness the slaughter of one of our oxen—

[7] The only other speeches recorded by Edward Ellsworth were very brief remarks by Little Chief of the Tappages and Mole-in-the-Face of the Republicans, and a rather longer one by the Pawnee Loup chief, to whom he gave the name Spitfire (*Sen. Doc. 512*, IV, 603).

[8] Although the treaty was officially dated October 9 (Kappler, *Indian Affairs, Laws and Treaties*, II, 416), the concluding remarks of the commissioner at the council make clear it was signed on October 10: "A treaty will be ready for you to sign in the morning. In the meantime, let me say, this is a happy day, and an ox will be killed to give you a feast. To-morrow, also, some goods will be delivered to *this* village; and then I will proceed to the other villages, and carry them their portion" (*Sen. Doc. 512*, IV, 604).

the destined victim for the ratification of the treaty. The hunter who was to enact the part of butcher, had loaded his rifle, and now moved forward. The crowd spread off on each side, leaving the animal exposed to view. The beast, then for the first time seemed to have a suspicion of the fate that awaited him, raised his head, and gazed steadily at his butcher. The hunter took a few steps—the gun was to his cheek—the trigger clicked—we heard the bullet strike—the ox reared his heavy frame, and fell forward on the ground; but the ball had merely fractured the skull without being fatal. By degrees the animal raised himself from the ground upon his haunches. His head hung heavily forward, and a thin streak of blood trickled down from the bullet hole in his forehead. Still he feebly supported his form upon his fore feet. His huge body rocked to and fro in the last extremity of anguish, and deep bellowings burst from his heaving lungs, resembling the tortured cries of a human sufferer. A second time the hunter advanced and fired; the ball was fatal; it crushed through the bone of the skull, and the beast fell forward with a deep groan. The crowd, raising a loud cry of exultation and delight, closed round him. The exhibition was sickening; we turned away and left the Indian butchers to their work.

[CHAPTER XXXIV]

Receiving Horses—Departure from Grand Pawnees—Crossing the Platte—The Iotan's Wife

The morning at length arrived upon which we were to take our leave of the Grand Pawnees, and shape our course for the village of the Pawnee Republicans. It is situated upon the Loup fork of the Platte river, about twenty miles distant.

The couriers appointed to carry the tidings of our approach to the nation, had left the village the night before. We were now drawn out in the area in front of the lodge, awaiting the movements of the soldiers who were scattered around, some driving in, and others searching for, the horses, on the small islands of the Platte.

The chief of the Pawnee Republican village, after lingering with us till the last moment, started forward across the river. In the dim distance we could perceive his flake-white horse skimming like a bird over the crests of the hills. Now he disappeared in their deep, undulating hollows, now he again flashed for an instant on the eye as he passed over the brow of some more distant ridge. He was pushing forward to reach his village, and marshal his warriors.

In about half an hour, the soldiers returned, driving in the horses, and commenced saddling them for the march.

In the meantime, those Indians who had promised horses on the first day of our meeting, brought them up. A young Indian first came forward, and led up a bright, jet-black mare—after him followed another, holding in his hand a long buffalo tug, or halter, which restrained the wild motions of a two years' old colt. His colour was snowy white, here and there broken with spots of brown. He had been caught wild from the prairies but a few weeks before. He was a slave, but he had never been mounted—his back had never bent to a burden. They led him up in his own native wildness—his tail stood out—his ears were pricked up—his eyes starting—his nostrils expanded—and every hair of his long mane seemed almost erect with an undefinable feeling of terror. At one moment he dashed swiftly around at the full stretch of the long tug which secured him—then pausing, and shaking his long mane over his head, he fixed the gaze of his almost bursting eyes upon his captor. Then raising his head, and casting a long, lingering, and almost despairing gaze upon the hills of the prairie, which till then had been his home, he made a desperate leap forward, dragging to the ground the Indian who held the end of his halter. Others, however, rushed to his assistance, and held him in. The crowd then attempted to close round him, but he reared upon his hind legs, and kept them at bay, with rapid and powerful blows of his fore feet. At length a young Indian who was standing near, threw off his robe and crept cautiously towards the animal from behind. With a sudden leap he bounded upon his back, and seized the tug, which was secured in his mouth. Before this, the efforts of the animal had been violent; but when he felt the burden upon his back— when he felt the curbing hand of his rider—he sent up a shrill and almost frantic scream—he bounded in the air like a wild cat —he reared, he plunged, but in vain; his rider was a master hand, and retained his seat as unmoved as if he had constituted part of the animal itself. He curbed him in—he lashed him with his heavy whip, until he crouched like a dog upon the prairie. His spirit was crushed; and the last spark of freedom was extinguished. Shortly after, one of the hunters came up and tied a pack upon his back. He made no resistance, and they led him off with the rest, to finish his days in drudgery and toil.

In the meantime the other Indians led up their horses. It was evident that many of them had made their promises in the excitement of the moment. They were now fulfilling them as matters of conscience, not of inclination; and their horses were valuable in proportion. One was lame, another blind; one had large patches of skin galled upon his back, and the ears of another were cropped close to his head. In fine it was evident that they had selected the very worst of their animals for the fulfillment of their promises. Our *stud* was a collection of the maimed, the halt, and the blind. One after another they came lingering up, until one Indian alone lagged behind. The chief inquired for him, and was told that he had gone out to search for his animal. Ten minutes elapsed. At last there was a movement in the crowd, and a sly-looking, old white-headed Indian made his way through it. In his hand he held the end of a long buffalo tug: the other was secured to his horse. Such a horse! he was blind of both eyes; his tail had been cut off short to his rump; his ribs stood out in bold relief; and his very joints creaked, as he walked stiffly after his leader. As for his age there was no mode of telling it, as his teeth had long since dropped out; but it must have been in-calculable.

There was a smothered giggling among the women, and a downright squall of laughter among the children, as the horse stalked forwards towards its future owner. The old Indian moved towards Mr. E[llsworth], and without raising his head placed the end of the halter in the hand of one of the soldiers. There was a deal of mischief in his look, and I could hear a smothered chuckle rattling beneath the folds of his robe, as he drew it up over his face, and disappeared among the crowd.

We now mounted and started at a rapid pace for the banks of the river. The heavy lumbering wagons followed more slowly, and a train of about half the village brought up the rear.

Upon reaching the banks we found that the Otoes were al-ready on their way through the river. Some were wading up to their arm-pits; others, had missed the ford, and were swept down the stream, holding their blankets high over their heads to keep them dry, as they struggled across the rushing current. Others, mounted on horses which they had trafficked for with the Paw-nees, were dashing and spattering through the shallow parts of the river, or clinging to the manes of their steeds, as they ploughed their way through the deep current.

The river at this place was nearly two miles broad, here and there interspersed with small islands. The depth was ever vary-ing; in some places it was but a few inches, in others it must have been from ten to twenty feet. At one moment, the water scarce reached the fetlocks of your horse—the next step sent him floun-dering up to the holsters.

After reaching the banks of the river, a short consultation was held. The heavy baggage wagons were then sent forward, with two Indians to guide them over the ford. After them fol-lowed the dearborn wagons. One was driven by an old soldier, who kept steadily in the wake of the teams. Two mules drew the other. They were driven by our half-French, half-devil Joe, who was seated upon the dash-board of the wagon, swearing in broken

English, sometimes at the animals, and at others, at the slow pace of the oxen which dragged the wagons in front. For some time, he followed steadily in their train; but at length his patience became exhausted, and he determined to drive forward at all hazards. He plied his whip upon the flanks of the mules. At the first application they stopped short—at the second they kicked up—but at the third they commenced moving forward—for they had learnt by long experience, that the patience and perseverance of their driver in the application of the lash, were sufficient to overcome even their own almost inexhaustible fund of obstinacy, and ill nature. Half a dozen steps brought the water up to the bottom of the wagon. The mules doubted, but the driver whipped on. Another half a dozen steps, and the water gushed over the sides into the wagon—still the lash was busy. The next moment the beasts were swimming, with only the tips of their noses and ears, visible above the surface. The wagon had disappeared beneath the water, and the head of the driver, shaded by a broad-brimmed hat, went skimming along the surface, pouring out a steady stream of French and English oaths, jumbled into one common mass. Occasionally an arm was flourished above the water, inflicting a little chastisement upon the nose and ears of the animals, which caused them to dip under the water, with a prodigious increase of snorting, but not much acceleration of speed. At length, however, the deep water was passed, and after drifting about a hundred yards down the river, the wagon gradually rose above the surface, and travelled slowly up the opposite bank.

The rest of the party then commenced their march in Indian file across the ford, keeping in a line with a tall Indian, who led the way. Most of the party followed the guide; but some of our horses were restive, and missing the ford, drifted us a short distance down the stream, where we reached a small island, and scrambling up its bank, galloped across to the opposite side.

Here we found a wife of the Iotan chief, standing on the edge of the water.[1] She had accompanied him from his village. She was young, tall, and finely formed; her face, next to that of the wife of the Kioway Indian, was the most beautiful we had met with. Her hair was parted across her forehead, and hung down upon her shoulders. A small jacket of blue cloth, was fastened round her shoulders and breast, and a mantle of the same, was wrapped around her body. They had been presented to her by the commissioner, but a few days before. She was standing upon a small sand-bar, and the water was gurgling around her feet; a short distance in front of her, a deep channel was rushing with a powerful current. She looked at the water, and then at her dress, with an expression of almost childish sorrow, for, to swim the river would ruin her finery. The Indians had all reached the opposite bank, and were waiting for the rest to come up, so that no assistance could be expected from them.

Just then the hunters dashed by her, into the deep channel, but did not even notice her. I was the last of the party, and she knew it; for though we could not speak the same language, there was an imploring expression in her large dark eye as she fixed it upon me, that told every thing. Still I hesitated: I thought of pushing on; there was a powerful struggle between selfishness and a desire to assist her; she saw it, and speaking a few words in her own silvery tongue, she at the same time pointed to her new dress.

There was something so sorrowful in the tone and gesture, that I could not resist it. I took my rifle in my left hand, and reached out my right, she seized it; she placed her foot on mine, and, with a sudden bound, was upon the back of my horse, stooping behind me, with her arms round my neck. The horse had so long been accustomed to have his own way in every thing, that he grew very indignant at this new imposition—but a lunge of the spurs subdued his wrath, and he bounded forward into the rushing river. He was a powerful animal, and took to

1 Perhaps this is the wife "of not more than twenty-five years of age" mentioned by Merrill in 1834 ("Diary," *Nebraska Historical Society Transactions,* Vol. IV [1892], 164).

the water like a sea-fowl. The river rushed and roared around us, and we could feel the strong nervous quivering of his limbs, as he bore up against it. But occasionally as he went snorting along, he cast back spiteful glances at his riders. I expected mischief, and it came to pass. We felt his hoofs touch the bottom —three leaps—he was up the bank—his heels flew in the air— the arms of the squaw were jerked violently from my neck, and I saw her describing a somerset through the air; she landed upon her feet and received no injury. The Indians raised a shout of laughter, and the horse, satisfied with being relieved from his extra burden, jogged quietly on towards the Republican village.

[CHAPTER XXXV]

Journey to the Republican Village, and Reception

In about half an hour, our whole troop were safely landed on the bank of the Platte, opposite the town of the Grand Pawnees. In the faint distance we could perceive the inhabitants, still standing upon the tops of the lodges, and watching our movements. A few who had lingered in our train, and crossed the river with us, now prepared to return. After sunning themselves for a short time on the dry grass, to take off the chill they had received in swimming across the cold current, they again plunged into the river. Their dark heads and bodies, were seen scattered over its whole breadth; until shut out from our view by one of the hills of the prairie.

The distance between the Grand Pawnee, and the Pawnee Republican Village, is about twenty miles. The last is situated upon what is called the Loup Fork of the Platte river, and is about the same in size, as that of the Grand Pawnees. The different portions of the tribe who live upon this river, were formerly united. In the course of time, however, as their numbers increased, the difficulty of obtaining timber for fuel and building, also increased, until at last they divided into four distinct bands,

From a sketch (1841) by Father Nicolas Point, S.J., in Father Pierre-Jean De Smet,
Letters and Sketches. *Courtesy the St. Louis Mercantile Library.*

Fording the River Platte

*"Some were wading up to their arm pits; others, had missed the ford,
and were swept downstream. . . . Others, mounted on horses which
they had trafficked for with the Pawnees, were dashing and spattering
through the shallow parts of the river, or clinging to the manes of
their steeds, as they ploughed their way through the deep current."*

each under a separate chief. The first seated itself upon the Republican Fork of the Platte, and is known by the name of the Grand Pawnee tribe. The other three located themselves upon the Loup Fork of the same river, and are distinguished by the names of the Republican Pawnees, the Tappage Pawnees, and the Pawnee Loups.[1] They are altogether distinct from the Pawnee Picks, and speak not the same tongue. During our stay among the Grand Pawnees, we found a Pawnee Pick residing among them, but his language was unintelligible to the whole nation, with the exception of one Indian, who had resided among his people.[2]

Our journey now lay across the prairie. An advance guard of about twenty Pawnees took the lead, conducting a number of loaded mules. Sometimes they were only ten or fifteen rods ahead, and then would push forward until we nearly lost sight of them. Behind us straggled our little band of Otoes; all on

---

[1] Irving called these tribes by the names then current: Ethnologists designate them now as Chaui (Grand Pawnees), Kitkehahki (Republicans), Pitahauerat (Tappages), and Skidi (Wolf Pawnees, Loups, Panimahas). Location of the three villages on the Loup Fork in 1833 is not entirely certain. Irving, though he confused the identity of the Tappage and Republican villages (see n. 2, p. 159), placed the three in a Tappage-Republican—Little Republican—Loup sequence, as did Dunbar and Allis in 1835 ("Letters Concerning the Presbyterian Mission in the Pawnee Country," *Kansas Historical Society Collections*, Vol. XIV [1915–16], 617, 700). This upstream direction from lowest to highest seems to have been the normal travel route. It was also, according to Grinnell (*Pawnee Hero Stories*, 216) and Hodge (*Handbook of American Indians*, II, 214), the traditional alignment of these villages. Waldo R. Wedel (*An Introduction to Pawnee Archeology* [Bureau of American Ethnology *Bulletin 112*], 23–38), however, on archeological grounds, placed the villages in a (Little) Republican—Tappage—Loup sequence, which, if I interpret Irving correctly, would mean that the Ellsworth party would have gone first to the central one of these three towns, then downstream to the lowest of them, and *then* back upstream, passing once more through the Tappage village, to the Loup. The Irving-Dunbar-Allis alignment appears more reasonable. For the general history of the Pawnees, consult Wedel, *Pawnee Archeology;* Grinnell, *Pawnee Hero Stories;* John B. Dunbar, "The Pawnee Indians; Their History and Ethnology, Their Habits and Customs," *Magazine of American History*, Vol. IV (April, 1880), 241–81; Vol. V (November, 1880), 341–42; Vol. VIII (November, 1882), 734–54; Hyde, *Pawnee Indians*.

[2] The Pawnee Picts (Pani Piqué or Tattooed Pawnees) lived on the Red River. They were, according to Hyde, really Wichitas.

foot, except the wife of the Iotan chief. She had contrived by her winning arts, to soften the flinty nature of the old iron-sided soldier who drove one of the wagons, so as to get a seat upon a pile of bear-skins, composing our bedding. Here she exerted herself, to maintain her hold in the good will of the veteran Jehu, by narrating to him by gestures, an account of her passage over the Platte.

The soldier listened to her patiently, and occasionally condescended to smile, when by her gesticulation, the story appeared to warrant it the most. At length one of his comrades rode up and asked:

"What are you and the wife of Iotan laughing at, Mack?"

"Curse me if I know," retorted the other. "The squaw keeps up such a *bloody* cackling, I suppose there must be some joke, and so I laughed."

After travelling a few hours over the prairie, we passed a single tree. It stood like a solitary sentinel, to guard the waters of a small spring, which gushed out at its foot; the source of the only brook, which had crossed our path, during the whole route. The tree was an aged one; short, and sturdy. If aught might be judged from its gnarled and fantastically twisted limbs, it had maintained its station for centuries, contending against the fierce storms and tornados, which had swept the prairie. We felt a kind of companionship with this "veteran of the storms;" and as if by common consent, the party, both Indians and whites, came to a halt, to rest under its branches, and drink of the water which gurgled along at its roots.

In a quarter of an hour we again pushed forward. After an hour more of laborious travel, through long waving grass, we descried large droves of horses, with uplifted heads and erect manes, gazing at us from the different eminences. We perceived also the flying forms of mounted Indians, in the distance, and groups of others clad in flowing robes, and standing like statues upon the heights. This showed us that the town was not distant, and that its warriors were on the watch for our coming. Intervening hills, however, still shut it out from our sight. As we proceeded, the groups disappeared one after another, and as we mounted the eminences where they had stood, we could perceive them, dashing forward, until they sank behind the brow of a high ridge, which still hid the town.

In half an hour, we ascended this ridge, and halted upon its top. A large plain, of about two miles in extent, lay at its foot. It was bounded by the waters of the Loup Fork, glittering through the verdant foliage which fringed its borders. On the opposite side of the river, was a high bluff, on which was situated the dingy lodges of the Republican village.

The plain in front of us, was alive with Indians. We had come upon them before they were prepared for our reception. Large troops were scouring the plain, apparently without an object. Single Indians were galloping in different directions; some up the banks of the river, and others towards the village. The tall form of the chief, mounted on his white horse, was seen dashing to and fro among the bands, giving his orders, and assigning to all their several stations. In a few moments, a torrent of warriors poured down the steep bank, which led from the village. They plunged into the river, forced a foaming path through its water, broke their way through the thicket on its brink, and bounded over the plain, to the spot where the chief awaited their coming. A second confusion now seemed to take place, and all the different squads of horsemen congregated together, as if awaiting directions. This continued for a short time. The chief then detached himself from the crowd and galloped a few yards in front, and calling out a single warrior sent him towards us. The whole scene at our feet, was like the distant perspective of a panorama. The approaching warrior seemed at first to crawl along at a snail's pace. But when he drew nearer, we could hear the heavy tramp of his horse's hoofs, and see that his speed was furious.

He plied the lash, and kept at full stretch, until within a few paces of us. Then by a powerful effort, the horse was drawn almost erect in the air, and stopped in his mad career, as suddenly as if converted into stone. His rider sprang from him, and advanced to the Interpreter. He bore a request from the chief, that the party would descend into the plain, where his warriors could receive them in better style.

The request was obeyed, and in about twenty minutes, upon receiving a second message from the chief, we drew up to await the coming of his warriors.

The leader, who still maintained his stand in front of the mass, then waved his arm. At this motion the band separated. A large body remained stationary, while an equal number galloped several hundred yards, to the right and left of the main division, and halted with their horses heading towards the party.

For a short time the chief stood watching the actions of both. It was not until he saw that every man was at his post, and every form as unmoved as stone, that he gave the signal. Then raising his arm, he wheeled his horse round, and sent up a long quavering whoop. Before it died away, a thousand throats had echoed back its ringing tones, and a thousand voices lent their aid in raising a cry, which almost shook the prairie. Although accustomed to its sound, and although we knew, that there was not a hand in that band, but would be extended towards us in friendship, yet its wild fierceness fairly caused us to shiver. At the same time the impulse was given to the horses. At first their movements were regular, but before a hundred yards had been passed, each man sent up his shrillest cry, urged his steed forward to the utmost stretch of his speed, and the whole band came dashing forward in wild confusion. At the distance of about a hundred yards in front of us, the three divisions met, but for a moment; then separating, the torrent whirled in a circle round us at the same mad gait. Through the whole mass, we could perceive the powerful form of the chief. He was urging his steed round in the innermost circle; and above the loud din of whoops and yells, we could hear the tones of his trumpet voice, cheering his warriors onward in their wild course.

[1 5 4]

After this had continued for a short time, he made another signal, and one after another the whole band checked their horses, and became motionless. Then dismounting, a great number of them loosed the tugs from their beasts, and cast them loose to career at will over the prairie. The chiefs, however, and the principal men of the nation, still remained on horseback to escort the party into the village.

When the band had seated themselves around, the same ceremony of presenting horses was repeated, which had taken place at the arrival of the party at the village of the Grand Pawnees.

About the same number were given as on the preceding occasion. As before, the old men who had nothing to offer, made up for it in speeches, exhorting others to munificence. They possessed in a high degree that generosity which is indulged at the expense of one's neighbours, and gains great applause from the world.

When this ceremony was finished, the circle opened, and our troop again mounting, prepared for their journey to the village.

[CHAPTER XXXVI]

Indian Mischief—Crossing the Loup Fork of the Platte— Entrance in the Republican Village

No sooner had the chief signalled by his movements his intention that the party should set out, than the dark ring round us was broken, and the whole mass of Indians flooded the prairie— pouring in the direction of their village. It was a scene of vast confusion. The horses which had been cast loose by their owners, careered wildly around the crowd. The mounted horsemen dashed about with a mad fury almost equal to that of the masterless beasts. If any thing could give to an inexperienced person an idea of a field of battle, where man and horse are alike urged on by a reckless disregard of life, it is a scene like this.

[155]

There was a striking contrast between the conduct of the older and more influential chiefs, and that of the younger warriors. The first rode gravely by the side of the party. There was something stern, and even savage, in the fixed repose of their painted faces.

Every forehead was wrinkled with the thousand lines that seam an Indian brow; and, but for the tell-tale eyes which glittered in their deep-sunk sockets with a startling brilliancy, you would not have known that boiling blood, and hearts which could nourish passions like fire, were beating in the bosoms of those iron warriors.

These were the chiefs and older men of the tribe; the young men rode at a distance. There was nothing to restrain *them;* they took no part in the councils. Their chiefs had ordered them to receive the party as friends, and they had obeyed their orders. They knew that a treaty of peace was to be made with the whites. They knew that in future the axe and scalping knife were to lie idle, and that war was to be at an end. But they did *not* know, that they were thus removing the only barrier which insured their own safety, and were forming the first link of the chain, which always has ended, and always will end in fetters to the free spirit of the Indian.

During the whole way from the plain to the bank of the river, the party kept compactly together. At length, however, one of the soldiers, mounted upon a powerful horse, gradually edged away, until he was about fifty yards distant from the main body. It was done without thought, and probably for the sake of gaining space that his horse might move more freely. He had reached some distance, and gained a point, beyond the observation of the chief. Here the spirit of waggery and mischief, which flourishes with rich growth in the bosom of a young Indian, began to display itself in the various pranks which they attempted to play upon him. Frequently they would flit their horses across his path, and in passing, dashed their heavy robes across the eyes of the animal causing him to rear, and plunge. This was a source of

[1 5 6]

great annoyance to the rider, who was not the best horseman in the world, and had been mounted that day more for the sake of show, than for any desire which he had for the station. He did well enough as long as his steed travelled at a walk. He was most sorely puzzled when his speed was accelerated, and completely driven to his wit's end, when the horse grew restive under the annoyances of the Indians. *They*, however, always took especial care to be quick in their movements, and keep beyond the reach of his brawny arm; for there was something in the grave, worried features, and giant form of the veteran, which spoke a man not to be trifled with. For some time this continued, and he bore it with exemplary patience. At last a little, old wiry Indian, half covered with a buffalo robe, which from long use retained but little of its woolly covering, determined to come in for his share of the sport. He was mounted upon a little horse, of as lean and sinewy a make as himself, with an eye as fiery as a coal. He had no hair upon his tail, but at the successful accomplishment of any of his mischievous feats, he wagged the naked stump with an expression of keen satisfaction and relish.

At first the old fellow contented himself by whirling his beast round and round the powerful horse, which bore the veteran; and so near as almost to touch him at every circuit. The soldier did not appear to relish this, but still took no active measure in the defensive. Finding that this was borne with patience, the old fellow grew bolder. In making one of his circuits, he ran his steed violently against the flank of the horse which bore the soldier, casting the rider from his precarious seat, almost on the neck of his beast, and causing a furious discharge of heels of the aggrieved animal. At last the old Indian came to still closer quarters, and galloped full tilt against the horse, while a loud laugh was raised among the young Indians. The soldier recovered his seat, but began to lose his temper, and when the old man repeated his manoeuvre he became downright angry. The most of the Indians saw that there was mischief in his eye, and drew off. The old man, however, was too much delighted with the success of his pranks to think of stopping. In the meantime the soldier made preparation to retaliate. The horse upon which he was mounted was of a very large size. He had relished as little as his rider, the rigs that his tormentors had run upon him. The soldier knew this, and acted accordingly. As the Indian came again at full sweep, to run aboard of him, he suddenly drew in the powerful curb bridle, with a strong jerk, and at the same time buried his spurs in the flanks of his horse. The animal planted his fore feet into the sod, and his heels were discharged from behind as if thrown from a catapult. They came in contact with the ribs of his opponent's horse, at the moment that he was about to close with him. The nag was driven to the distance of several yards, and the rider hurled from his back, and sent rolling in the grass.

Though the Indians had relished the pranks played by their comrade, their enjoyment of the retaliation was greater; and they hooted, and jeered him, not so much for his breach of hospitality as for his want of success. To get rid of them, he plied the lash upon his little steed, and together they went scampering to the village. The soldier in the meantime, taking advantage of the diversion in his favour, returned to the party.

A short time only elapsed, before we were at the brink of the river.[1] Here the chief led the way across the shoalest fording place. The rest of the Indians, however, regardless of the depth, plunged in, and in a few moments, its whole surface was black with them.

It was a scene of great hubbub and confusion. Some were mounted upon powerful, and sinewy horses, which sped through the water like sea-birds. Others floundered, half drowning through the deep channel, frightening the more timid by their snorting and splashing. Some of the Indians threw themselves from their steeds, and boldly stemmed the current, half swimming, and half wading; while the relieved horses, scattering in

[1] The Loup. They probably crossed about eight or ten miles above Fullerton, Nebraska.

[158]

every direction, ploughed their way through the bubbling stream, and made for the nearest land. The baggage wagons toiled slowly along in the rear, keeping closely upon the trail of the chief.

After some time the whole party reached the opposite shore, at the foot of the high bluff, upon which stood the Republican village.[2] The bank was steep, and almost precipitous. There was a pause of some length, before the arduous task of dragging the heavy vehicles up the hill, was imposed upon the jaded oxen. At length, however, a string of twelve were fastened before a single wagon, and united their strength to draw it up. The Indians stood by, with looks of wondering curiosity; but when they saw the lash inflicted, and the nervous efforts of the beasts, they shrank back with a feeling of fear, lest they should turn upon their persecutors. Even the older warriors showed signs of dread, and the children scampered in undisguised terror up the steep pathway. They paused, however, upon the top of the bluff, where they deemed that they might gaze in safety, upon the movements of their guests. After a sound drubbing, and much swearing on the part of the drivers, the jaded animals forced the wagons up the hill, and slowly proceeded through the village.

2 It is unfortunate that we do not have a record from any other member of the expedition for this portion of the travels. Irving apparently confused the names of two villages. The first town they came to would have been that inhabited by the Tappages and a portion of the Republicans; Kingsbury ("Journal of the March of a Detachment of Dragoons Under Dodge, *American State Papers, Military Affairs*, Vol. VI, 133) and Dunbar and Allis ("Letters Concerning the Presbyterian Mission in the Pawnee Country," *Kansas Historical Society Collections*, Vol. XIV [1915–16], 617, 700) all so describe it. The Little Republican village, which Irving next visited, is readily identifiable by reference to its size; see n. 3, p. 178.

[CHAPTER XXXVII]

Indian Females and Feasts

Many of the inhabitants of this town had been present at our arrival at the Grand Pawnee village, and to them the novelty of our appearance was over. To the rest, however, more particularly the women and children, all was new, and our day of entering into the town, was one of jubilee. We found the pathway lined with women and children, and the spaces between the lodges, crowded with them. Here and there were knots of wild-looking boys, with their bows and arrows tucked under their arms, staring with open mouths, upon the travelling lodges as they termed our heavy wagons. Groups too of females—the married women with troops of children—some on their backs and others at their heels, crowded round. Young and beautiful girls, also, wild as deer, were gazing at us with deep curiosity, but maintained a timid distance.

The most dauntless of the crowd, were two or three old crones, squalid and dirty in the extreme, and who, if aught might be judged from their looks, were the oldest women that ever lived. Every thing was withered about them, but their tongues, which still flourished with the vigour of former years. They were like racers; they had run against time, and gained the heat. Each of these beldames singled out her victim, from among the members of our party, and exerted herself to the utmost to render his situation agreeable, by dinning his ears with her garrulity.

Another worthy of this class, had been entrusted with the care of about a dozen children of all ages and sexes. These she had ranged upon the dome-like top of one of the lodges to see the spectacle, as we passed by. She stood in front of her elfish brood, keeping at bay by the violent exertions of both tongue and talons, the crowd, who, in their anxiety to obtain a view, were attempting to invade her sanctuary.

The persons who had placed their little goblin young ones in her charge, understood well her nature. Her tongue knew no rest. At one moment it was busy in bestowing a shower of wholesome advice, upon some refractory little urchin, whose curiosity would not permit him to sit easy; and at another it was waging a wordy war with the passers by. She fluttered, and ruffled round her bevy, with all the peevish irritability of an old wet-nurse hen, placed in charge of a family of graceless young ducks, who need all her advice and attention, to keep them from danger.

After winding our way through the town, we at length came to the lodge of Blue Coat,[1] the chief of this village. He had nothing of the stern coldness of the leader of the Grand Pawnees. He attended personally and assiduously to our comfort—assisting even in unloading, and bringing in our baggage. When this was finished, he seated himself and opened a conversation, through the interpreter. There was an intelligence in his re-

[1] The name of Blue Coat, is given to the chief of the Republican Pawnees on account of his wearing a blue camblet coat. He is proud of the title and prefers it to his Indian one. He is much more refined in his manners and ideas than the rest of his nation, and is considered by the traders, and his own people, the very *beau ideal* of the Indian warrior.—JTI. It is difficult to say whether Blue Coat was chief of all the Republicans or perhaps only of the Little Republican village. Irving gave him the place of first importance here at what must be the Tappage-Republican village. Murray (*Travels in North America*, I, 274) called Capot Bleu the "great chief of the Republicans," as did Cooke, who found him "remarkable for dignity and suavity of manner" (*Scenes and Adventures in the Army*, 110). Kingsbury ("Journal of the March of a Detachment of Dragoons under Dodge," *American State Papers, Military Affairs*, Vol. VI, 133) named Blue Coat chief of the Pawnee Republicans, but later (p. 135) set down Mole-in-the-Face as chief of the Republican village and Blue Coat as chief of the Little Republican village. When Catlin painted the Pawnee Republican Ah-sha-la-coots-ah, Mole-on-the-Forehead, he called him "chief of his band" (Thomas Donaldson, *The George Catlin Indian Gallery in the U. S. National Museum* [Smithsonian Institution Annual Report for *1885*], 68). Edward Ellsworth, in reporting the council of October 9, quoted a very brief speech by "Mole-in-the-face, Chief Repub. village" (*Sen. Doc. 512*, IV, 603). In none of these accounts is Blue Coat's Indian name given. He was killed June 27, 1843, in a Sioux attack on the Pawnee village near the Pawnee Mission (Carleton, *The Prairie Logbooks*, 107–10; Dunbar and Allis in "Letters Concerning the Presbyterian Mission in the Pawnee Country," *Kansas Historical Society Collections*, Vol. XIV [1915–16], 656–57, 730).

marks, and an ease in his manners, which almost made his guests forget they were conversing with a wild, untutored savage.

It was not long before the lodge became crowded. The old warriors, moved with a hushed step, across the building, and listened, to our conversation. Occasionally, some distinguished brave stalked in. There was a great difference between his manners, and those of the less noted warriors. The latter, stole quietly into the lodge, taking their stations in some remote and retired nook, as if they entertained a doubt of their privilege of entry. But as to the former, the bold and lofty carriage; the swelling chest; the uplifted head; the slightly expanded nostril; the keen searching eye, which flashed daringly around, showed him to be one who owned no ruler, and who knew that none in that assembly, would dare dispute his will. He would take his seat in the most conspicuous part of the lodge, and gaze calmly, and silently upon the strangers.

It was not long before messengers came from different lodges, inviting us to feasts, which had been prepared in honour of our arrival. We had learned by this time, that there was no escape from the invitations of an Indian host, so we followed the guide, who led us to the dwelling of the second chief.[2]

We found him seated upon a small leather mat. He was a fat, oily fellow, with a jolly, good-natured face. Still its expression was tempered by that gravity, which, from long habit, has become almost natural to the race, and proverbial among the whites.

Around him were lounging about a dozen Indians. Some, reclining with their backs against the pillars supporting the roof, with their eyes half closed, were smoking their stone pipes. Some were lying half asleep upon the clay floor, with their feet within a few inches of the fire; and others were keeping up a sleepy song.

2 The other Republican signers of the October treaty were Lay-shah-rho-lah-re-ho-rho, Ah-shah-lay-kah-sah-hah, and Lay-shah-ke-re-pahs-kay (Kappler, *Indian Affairs, Laws and Treaties*, II, 417). Could the second of these be Catlin's Ah-sha-la-coots-ah and the Ah-shah-lay-koh-she (The Dead Horse) who was the first Republican signer to the articles of peace at Fort Leavenworth, November 12, 1833?

At a short distance from the fire, half a dozen squaws were pounding corn, in large mortars,[3] and chattering vociferously at the same time. In the farther part of the building, about a dozen naked children, with faces almost hid by their bushy, tangled hair, were rolling and wrestling upon the floor, occasionally causing the lodge to echo to their childish glee. In the back ground, we could perceive some half a dozen shaggy, thievish-looking wolf-dogs, skulking among the hides and bundles, in search of food, and gliding about with the air of dogs, who knew that they had no business there.

Upon our entering, the lounging Indians roused themselves from the floor; the smokers woke from their reveries, and the dogs slunk out of sight. The women and children, however, went on as before, the former pounding and chattering, and the latter frolicking over the floor. When we had seated ourselves, a large bowl of boiled buffalo flesh was placed before us, and signs made for us to fall to. The chief himself acted as master of ceremonies. He thrust his hands into the bowl, and turned over and over the heap of smoking meat, selecting the best morsels [for us], and welcoming us with warmest expressions of friendship. Several times, appearing to be annoyed by the noise and clamour of his wives, he turned round, and let out a volley of angry words, which, however, they treated with no attention. There is but little doubt that he was a hen-pecked husband, for with all his jovial appearance, there was a cowering look about his eye, when he met the vinegar glance of one or two of his oldest wives.

Before we had finished with him, half a dozen different messengers had assembled in the lodge, waiting for us to follow them to the abode of some of the other chiefs. It is customary for the guest, when he is unable to dispose of the whole pro-

3 The mortar is in universal use among the uncivilized tribes, answering the purpose of a mill. The hollow is formed, by kindling a fire upon the top of a block of wood, into which it gradually sinks itself, until it forms a sort of bowl. The cavity is then cleaned from the coal-black, and is fit for use. These mortars are generally a foot in diameter, and about eight inches deep. Corn is pulverised in them, by using a billet of wood as a pestle.—JTI.

vision placed before him, to send what is left to his own quarters. The duty of carrying it, is generally entrusted to one of the junior members of the family, who when departing upon his errand, receives a particular caution from the squaws to be careful and bring back the bowl.

It was near sunset when we finished our visits. We had gone from lodge to lodge, followed by a crowd of men, women, and children, until we had visited nearly half the dwellings in the village. Our receptions were different, according to the dispositions of our hosts. Some were stern and solemn in their demeanour, and others as sociable, and even lively as the whites. In some of the lodges, the females were of an acid temper, and to these our presence was not as agreeable as we could have wished. They made no hesitation in speaking their minds to the half-breed interpreter, who in turn, with iron gravity, translated the whole to us, without abating an epithet, or softening a single peppery expression.

When we emerged, we found a small crowd collected in front, which drew back as we appeared. Curious as they were, there was nothing troublesome or forward in their mode of gratifying their curiosity. The children followed at a distance. The older Indians would mark the route which we must take, and then hurrying on, would seat themselves in some situation, where the whole party must pass in review before them. There was none of the prying, meddling spirit which is shown among the whites.

We had scarcely reached the lodge of the chief, and were congratulating ourselves that the eating part of the business was terminated, when the heavy bear-skin which hung over the mouth, was flapped back, and a boy came across to the place where the Interpreter was sitting. This immediately caused us to suspect that another feast was on foot, and we were making for the door, when we were arrested by the Interpreter, who was too much of an Indian not to relish these eating parties.[4]

4 Louis La Chapelle, according to Allis, was a Pawnee half-blood. He was killed in the Sioux attack on the Pawnee village near Willow Creek, June 27, 1843

He shouted out, that three of us had been invited to attend at the lodge of one of the older warriors, who had prepared something which he thought would be more acceptable than buffalo flesh and corn. Although but little inclined to attempt any thing in the way of eating, still we determined to accompany him, for we were curious to see what new article of food, could be raked up in the village, where every soul seemed to live on buffalo flesh and corn.

Following our guide, therefore, after a dark walk we reached the place of invitation.

The interior of the lodge was illumined by the light of a bright fire, burning cheerily in the centre. In front of it was seated the warrior who had invited us. He was an old man with a bottle nose, and a most ponderous corporation; and when seated behind it with his feet doubled under him after the Turkish fashion, he looked like a large sphere.

Upon our entrance, after sundry puffs and heaves, he rose to his feet, and welcomed us, pointing out seats upon several mats which had been placed for us, at his side. He then told his squaw, whose leanness was in proportion to his rotundity, to place before us the article to be disposed of. We watched her narrowly as she moved to a large kettle hanging over the fire. There was something in it of a reddish-yellow colour. What could it be? We had never fallen upon any article of that description before. The squaw seized upon a long, sharp-pointed stick, and commenced spearing into the pot; but at every attempt the active occupant contrived to dodge from her weapon, in spite of her efforts. However, it is an old adage, that "perseverance conquers all difficulties," and at length she struck the object of her search, and drew out, impaled upon the point of her weapon, a large boiled *pumpkin*. This she immediately commenced dividing in strips.

While the ceremony of spearing had been going on, we

("Letters Concerning the Presbyterian Mission in the Pawnee Country," *Kansas Historical Society Collections*, Vol. XIV [1915–16], 730).

watched with some curiosity, to see what all this trouble was to produce; but when the pumpkin made its appearance, the expression of countenances was most ruefully changed. I looked round towards my companions. Their eyes were fixed with silent agony upon the preparing feast. There was no retreat—it must be eaten; and we were the persons who were doomed to do it. I had hoped to derive a little comfort from them. I had hoped too, that they might relish a sodden and water-soaked pumpkin; and that under cover of their appetites, I might escape unobserved. The expression, however, of their faces forbade the idea, and I determined to perform my share of the mastication, in a manner creditable to a civilized man.

We fell to desperately, therefore, under the vigilant eye of our fat host, who was continually plying us with fresh pieces, according to the laws of Indian hospitality, and to refuse which would be regarded as a slight. How we managed to get through that vegetable feast, I can hardly say; it was one of the severest trials of the whole of our campaign; yet we did get through with it, and emerged from the lodge in safety.

When we returned to the abode of the chief we found it crowded. Groups were squatting in every direction, wrapped in their robes, indulging in a low, muttered conversation. This was occasionally broken by a deep, emphatic exclamation, which always bursts with a convulsive sound from the chest of an Indian, when engaged in a debate of some interest. But upon our return the conversation gradually flagged, and their sole occupation was to sit, with their eyes fastened upon us, as we were collected round the fire.

From an engraving after Seth Eastman, in Henry R. Schoolcraft,
The Indian Tribes of North America, I, Plate 46.

A Medicine Man Curing a Patient

"... he hummed a low chant, occasionally raising his voice until he
caused it to sound loudly ... and then again sinking it, until it reached
the ear of the listener, in low and almost inaudible murmurs. There
was something wild, and rather forbidding in the features of this
individual."

CHAPTER XXXVIII

The Doctor's Adventure—Indian Dirge

When we had at first collected together in the chief['s] lodge, we we found that one of the party, Dr. M[ay], was not present. There were many conjectures as to his absence, but after a while he made his appearance. He was considerably out of breath, and related to us an adventure which he had just met with, or rather which he had forced himself into. He had remained in the lodge after we left it, to attend at our last feast. Having nothing in particular to employ him, he slapped his white beaver, which turned up all around, upon the top his head, girded his deer-skin hunting shirt closely around him, and thrusting his hand into his breeches-pocket, set out upon a voyage of discovery. He had not travelled far before his attention was attracted by a low chanting song, proceeding from one of the lodges which stood a little apart from the others, and near the edge of the bluff, overlooking the river.

Without a moment's hesitation, he walked towards it, entered the low, funnel shaped mouth, and peeped over the bearskin which hung before the inner entrance, opening immediately into the lodge.

A large fire was burning cheerfully in the centre. Over it hung a kettle which was kept constantly stirred by an old Indian, dressed in a buffalo robe, whitened with chalk, and ornamented with hieroglyphic symbols. As he stirred he hummed a low chant, occasionally raising his voice until he caused it to sound loudly through the whole building, and then again sinking it, until it reached the ear of the listener, in low and almost inaudible murmurs. There was something wild, and rather forbidding in the features of this individual.

A few steps from the fire, lay two forms, completely covered by a heavy buffalo robe; and bending over these stood another

Indian, dressed similar to the first. He too, was humming a low song, at intervals dancing to a slow measure round the robe.

The doctor suspected that these were Medecin-Men,[1] and that they were performing some of the miraculous cures, which they boast of in the village, and which give them a reputation for superior sanctity among the credulous Indians, who believe them to hold communion with the Great Spirit. Their ability to perform these cures, arises frequently, from their superior knowledge, of the hidden medicinal virtues of different herbs. By jumbling with their healing art, an unintelligible species of mystic mummery, and by pretending to hold a direct intercourse with the Deity, the cure of their patients is attributed more to his immediate interferance, than to any virtue of the medicines which they have received.

After humming round them, the Medecin raised the edge of the robe, exposing the naked heads and shoulders of two old, shrivelled squaws. The person at the fire, then reached to the other a large dipper, filled with part of the contents of the kettle, which was greedily swallowed by the squaws. The robe was then thrown over them, and again the Medecin commenced his hum and dance.

Now the Doctor was a curious man, and although he saw

1 Every tribe of Indians has its Medecin-Men. They are a kind of priest or prophet. Their influence, however, is very variable, and depends upon the popularity which they may have acquired with the nation. As long as they confine their prophecies to those events, which they know will be agreeable, so long are they regarded with high veneration; but as soon as they commence predictions of evil—or attempt to reveal unpalatable truths, their influence wanes, themselves are shunned, and their predictions scorned. They are also skilled in the virtues of herbs, and act as physicians in healing the sick. From this they have derived the name of Medecin, (signifying in French, physician.)—JTI. Prince Paul of Württemberg had much better luck ten years earlier in being invited into a Pawnee medicine lodge, though he did not see the medicine man professionally engaged, either as priest or doctor (*First Journey to North America*, 437–40). Medical practice among the Pawnee—the treatment of a badly burned man, a sick child, a woman in childbirth—was described by Dunbar and Allis in "Letters Concerning the Presbyterian Mission in the Pawnee Country," *Kansas Historical Society Collections*, Vol. XIV (1915–16), 600–601, 703, 706. Murray (*Travels in North America*, I, 358–60) also reported the treatment of a sick child.

every thing that was going on in the inside of the lodge, as distinctly as if he had been there himself, still he was determined to see more. For a moment he paused to reflect, whether it would be prudent to intrude upon these mystic ceremonies, and risk incurring the anger of such influential persons, as he knew these Medecin-men to be. But prudence was a quality with which he was not much troubled; so without more hesitation he kicked up the bear-skin, and stepped boldly into the lodge, in front of the two priests.

For a moment they gazed at him, as if they doubted their senses. Their eyes flashed fire, and raising their voices, they made the lodge ring with their yells. At this unusual sound, the two old women raised the robe, peeped from under it, and seeing the white man, added their voices to the chorus.

After gazing for a moment, the Doctor attempted to approach the fire, but the Indians warned him back, ordering him with menacing gestures, to leave the lodge. These he pretended to misunderstand, at the same time attempting to enter into a parley with them, in order to gain as much time as possible for observation. Still they placed themselves before him, sternly ordering him to depart. He attempted to explain to them that he was a Medecin-Man in his own country, and wished to be acquainted with their secrets, and that in return he would communicate his. But it was useless; either they did not understand him, or they did not value his information, for they persisted in their ordering him to quit the lodge. The Doctor then determining, at all events, to obtain a look into the kettle, darted round them, and made for the fire.

There was now something of menace in their faces; and one of them rushing to the side of the lodge, seized a large club, resting against one of the pillars. The Doctor took to flight, and stopped not, until he arrived, most villanously out of wind, at the chief's lodge, where he narrated his adventure.

After this I strolled out with one of my companions. It was so late that there were few of the Indians stirring. Here and

[1 6 9]

there, we encountered individuals sitting upon the high bank, gazing upon the gliding waters of the Platte. It seemed as if they were engaged in a species of devotion, for they did not heed our approach, but sat humming a low, a very low muttered song. We passed them, and continued our course along the high bluff, looking down upon the Platte, which was dimly seen, reflecting the stars that twinkled upon its restless water. The prairie insects were piping their evening calls, and the creaking of the thousand creatures, who were hid in its long matted herbage, told that they were conscious their hour of song and revelry had come. Occasionally we heard the long howl of a wolf, softened by the distance, and now and then some serenading owl, would raise his voice from the dark fringe of trees, which drooped over the opposite bank of the river, and send forth a long quavering whoop.

We strolled along the bank for half a mile, glad to be free from the well-meant though tedious attentions of our hosts. At length, however, we turned for the purpose of retracing our steps, when our attention was attracted by a low, mournful cry, from the midst of a number of small mounds, at a short distance, the burial ground of the village. We approached the spot so cautiously, as not to disturb the person who was stationed there. Upon the top of one of the graves, a large mound covered with grass, was lying an Indian girl. Her buffalo robe had escaped from her shoulders, and her long dishevelled black hair, was mingled with the grass of the prairie. Her bosom was resting upon the sod, and her arms extended, as if embracing the form of the being who was mouldering beneath.

Believing that she was some female belonging to the tribe, singing a dirge over the grave of some departed friend, we listened attentively to her song. At one moment, it would rise in the air with a plaintive sound, as if she was dwelling with mournful tenderness, upon the virtues of the deceased. At times, she would seem to speak of the feelings of his heart; at others, the note would seem to be one of war, of battle; and then her song would burst from her, with the startling energy of a person, who was in the midst of the scene itself, and was acting over the feats of the silent dead. At these moments, she raised her head, and her whole frame seemed swelling with the inspiration of her theme; but in the very midst of this energetic burst of enthusiasm, the chord of some more mournful recollection would be touched, and the song would sink from its high, and ardent tone, to a note of wo, so despairing, that it appeared as if the sluices of her heart were opened, and the deep-hidden stream of her affection, was flowing out in the mournful melody.

After a short time she rose from the ground, and wrapping her robe round her, walked slowly towards the village. It was not until she was completely lost to our sight, that we left our sheltering place, and followed in the direction which she had taken. We had heard the Indian dirge sung before by different females, of the tribe, but as we considered them mere pieces of formality, we had passed by, without heeding them. But in this lonely being, there was an air of deep desolation, as she lay upon the grave, and a hopeless, despairing tone, in her low, melodious voice, that laid bare the recesses of a withered heart.

We were so much interested in her, that we had accurately noted her appearance, and now hurried towards our lodge, with the intention of finding out her history from our interpreter— a matter of no great difficulty, as the history of every individual of the village is known to all. We found the half-breed interpreter sitting in front of the fire, wrapped in his blanket-coat, with his elbow resting upon his knee, and his hand supporting his chin. There was an air of iron gravity and even sternness in his deep-marked features that denoted a man not prone to yield to womanish emotion. We walked up to him, and by means of a Frenchman,[2] (for he spoke no English) inquired the history of the girl—at the same time narrating the scene in the prairie.

2 Possibly Alexander Laforce Papin, agent of the American Fur Company at the Pawnee villages. To assist him at this time, he had men named Bijou, Beby, Vincent, La Chapelle, and Claighorn (Joshua Pilcher to Pierre Chouteau Jr, Near the Bluffs, 15th Octr. 1833, Chouteau-Papin Collection). It is certain that Irving

If it had been in the nature of his face to wear a more scornful expression than it usually did, the smile of contempt which passed over his weather-beaten features, as we related our story, would have added to it. For a moment, he seemed surprised—then added, that she was a squaw, who resided in the adjoining lodge, and but a short time before, he had heard her say to her mother, that as she had nothing else to do, she believed she would go and take a *bawl* over her dead brother's grave. He had been killed five years before.

Here was a waste of sympathy. We were vexed that we had suffered our feelings to be enlisted in the mock misery of this girl, who was merely performing a customary mummery. There was an expression of enjoyment in the keen eye of the half-breed, as he watched the disappointed expression of our faces. A grim smile played over his reddish-brown face, and I believe if he had ever been guilty of such an action, he would have indulged in a loud explosion of merriment.

At that moment, the broad voice of our black cook, announced that the supper was ready. Discarding both the girl, and her griefs, from our minds, we seated ourselves upon the floor, preparatory to commencing the almost hopeless task, of masticating a supper of dried buffalo's flesh, which had been boiled for only two hours.

When we had finished, it was late in the evening—the Indians had ceased moving through the lodge, and wrapping themselves in their shaggy robes, had composed their forms upon the clay floor, for slumber.

The servants now busied themselves in spreading out our bear-skins. This completed, each retired to his couch, and in a short time a dead silence reigned throughout the building.

---

met Papin, for on October 12 this St. Louis Frenchman wrote from the Pawnee villages to his brother, Milicour, among the Osages, that he was sending "this letter" by the commissioner "who is a fine man" (in French, Chouteau-Papin Collection). Furthermore, Papin signed the treaty of October 9. The half-blood interpreter, of course, is Louis La Chapelle.

CHAPTER XXXIX

An Old Warrior—Indian Dogs—A Night Scene

About midnight I awoke; it was intensely cold, so I rose up and picked my way over prostrated forms to the fire. An old Indian was seated by it; his hair was snowy white, and hung in long locks upon his shoulders. There were several scars traced upon his face, and even by that faint light, the marks of deep wounds were visible upon his breast. His robe had fallen from his shoulders, leaving bare the withered wreck, of what must once have been an Herculean frame. I did not know him, nor could he have ranked among their chiefs. His cheek was resting in the palm of his hand; his eyes were intently fixed upon the burning brands which flickered up a dying, broken blaze. In his right hand he held a small piece of wood, with which he raked together the coals, though seemingly unconscious of what he was doing. In front of him lay an uncouth-looking tomahawk, made of wood, and across it his otter-skin pouch, and stone pipe: the symbols of war and peace thrown together, in a manner which seemed to denote that to their owner, the day of strife was past. His look was fixed upon the brands, but his mind, busied in its own wanderings, took no note of the things before his eyes. Could he be meditating upon the probable results of the coming of the white men among them? Could he be sitting there buried in his own musings, and prophet-like, looking through the dim vista of futurity? Could he see his own chivalric race, gradually withering at the approach of the whites, and the descendants of those, whose hearts now beat as free as the eagle's, crawling over the earth, a stigma to their name, and a curse to themselves? I could not prevent these thoughts from stealing over me, as I sat opposite to him, gazing upon his face, so noble and dignified, even in its ruin. Upon my first approach, he had not observed me, but after a short time, he raised his head, and perceiving me, reached out his hand, while a friendly smile played over his face. Then pointing to his scars, he endeavoured by signs to narrate to me an account of the different war expeditions, in which these had been received. Each wound had a tale of its own, and each scar told of a different battle. After spending some time in telling his story, he lighted his pipe, and first drawing a few puffs he passed it to me with the usual word of politeness, (Looah.)[1] I puffed for a few moments, and returned it to him, he then inhaled a few draughts of the smoke, and again reached it to me, and I, after again smoking, reached it to him. This operation of smoking and passing it to each other, continued until the pipe was empty; then knocking the ashes from its bowl, he raised himself upon his feet, and taking up his pouch and tomahawk, drew his buffalo robe over his head, and left the lodge. Upon being deserted by my companion, I looked around upon the muffled forms, thickly strewed over the clay floor, with that strange feeling of loneliness, which is experienced by a person, the only being awake, among a hundred sleeping forms, and which is peculiarly strong in a place where every individual is a stranger, perhaps an enemy. The lodge was about sixty feet in diameter, and seen by the flickering, uncertain light of the fire, it had a wild appearance. The stern, silent countenances of the sleeping warriors, as they reclined with their backs resting against the pillars which supported the lodge, reminded me of the eastern tale, in which a whole city of living beings, were converted into statues. Their features were at rest, they were not now the mirrors which reflected the passions of their hearts.

---

[1] This is a word more frequently used than any other in the language. As far as I was able to learn, it had no particular meaning, but signified—almost any thing.—In fact it comprises about half of the language.—JTI. Murray, describing a feast in a lodge, wrote: "I found a vacant place near the owner. . . . A bowl, either of Indian corn or buffalo meat, was then placed in the centre; the guests sitting cross-legged, like tailors, around it. There was a horn-spoon for each person; and at the word "Lô,' or 'Lô-wa,' we all fell to work. This word comprises their whole vocabulary of 'assent,' 'satisfaction,' and 'compliment': it invariably begins and concludes a feast, each guest saying it as he enters and leaves the tent" (*Travels in North America*, I, 305).

Even those passions were slumbering, but still, their heavy lines were left, with an enduring mark upon their brows. If those stone-like faces wore so savage a character, when nature had thrown her own calm over them, how truly fearful must they have been in the day of battle, when every frenzied feeling was at its height, and every demon passion was ruling with relentless sway. As to those who were lying upon the floor, their sleep was death-like—it seemed dreamless.

The gaunt Indian dogs were prowling stealthily through the building. They knew that their hour of freedom had come, and with every leaping blaze of the embers, I could see them scattered throughout the lodge. There must have been nearly fifty of them in full motion, yet there was not a sound to be heard.[2] They wound their way through the sleeping Indians, with the cautious and practised step of veteran burglars—too well acquainted with the wakeful habits of their masters, not to be silent in their doings; and too much in the habit of stealing, to be able to resist the temptation to plunder. Occasionally they paused, and cast a doubting look upon me, as I sat watching their movements. They however came to the conclusion that I was a stranger, and from my short stay, was not aware that it was the custom of every Indian, to bestow a bountiful share of wholesome kicks, upon every dog that came in his path, as a punishment for the thefts which he had already committed, and as payment in advance for his future transgressions. While I was watching their movements I was startled by a loud whine, which seemed to proceed from the roof of the lodge. At that sound there was a general scamper towards the mouth of the lodge, for they were certain, that the cry would awaken the savages, and that flight was their only safety. I had turned at the moment of the noise, to ascertain the

---

[2] According to Murray, the dogs were not always silent. He figured that on the summer hunt there were "upwards of four thousand dogs in the encampment. . . . In this nightly howl they all join (at least, of all those round our tent, I could not see one exception) . . . it is needless to suggest, even to the most sluggish imagination, the grand effect of a dog-chorus, at midnight, in the Pawnee village" (*Travels in North America*, 287–88).

cause of it. At the top of the lodge, and about ten feet from the ground, was a large dog, suspended by his teeth to a flitch of bacon, which had been hung up to the rafters to keep it in safety. Upon coming into the lodge, the animal had espied this, and mounting upon a high pile formed by our baggage, had sprung out at it, as it hung. He had been successful in his leap, and had buried his teeth in the meat. But this accomplished, he could do nothing more—he was dangling full ten feet from the ground; and his only supporters were his jaws, which were fastened into the end of the bacon. He dared not let loose his hold, and he was equally certain he could not maintain it. In his predicament, he raised his voice, in a long, low, plaintive howl. Scarce had the sound escaped him, before a dozen clubs were clattering against his ribs, and as many clamorous voices raised in the hue and cry against him. With a loud yell, relaxing his jaws, he landed upon the head of an old Indian, who was dozing beneath, in defiance of the howls of the dog, and the clamour of his foes. The animal did not pause, but gaining his feet, scampered across the building, and made his escape amidst a shower of missiles of all descriptions.

[CHAPTER XL]

Leaving Republican Village—Prairie between that and Tappage Village—Reception by Tappages—Departure—White Cranes—Black Chief of the Loups—Reception—Chief's Lodge—Soldier Chief's Feast

The next morning about ten o'clock, we set off for the village of the Tappage Pawnees, situated upon the Loup Fork of the Platte, about eleven miles farther up the river.[1] As we left the

1 For Tappage, read Republican (see n. 1, p. 151, and n. 2, p. 159). Dunbar

town, a crowd of men, women and children followed us, in the hope of obtaining presents. The chief too, escorted us out. He was a princely man. His head was shorn, excepting the scalp-lock; his face was free from paint; a long string of wampum, the only ornament he ever wore, hung from his neck; a blue blanket covered one shoulder, leaving bare his high, prominent chest, and the sinewy arm which curbed the restless movement of his fretted horse. He had been used to the saddle from childhood, and now governed his impatient animal, with the calm control of a practised rider.[2]

There is nothing upon which the Indians pride themselves, more than their horsemanship. Almost living in the saddle, they are as much at ease, when mounted, as when sitting upon the floor of their own lodge. Many a time, I have seen two or three village urchins, beset some unfortunate horse, while quietly dozing and ruminating, upon the prairie. After sundry coaxings and efforts, they would succeed in mounting upon his back, and then without saddle or bridle, and with a whoop and yell, that terrified the startled steed into a full gallop, they would scamper madly along, clinging to his mane, and to each other, with a tenacity which would have astonished any one but an Indian.

After accompanying us about a mile, the chief returned, followed by a number of his warriors. The rest joined our band, and travelled in company, for the purpose of witnessing our reception by their rival village. Our pace was slow, being regulated by that of the oxen, who toiled painfully along in the rear.

The prairie was beginning to show the effects of the autumn frost, and the grass wore a blighted, withered look. The sun shone red and lurid through the hazy atmosphere, denoting what at this season of the year, is called among the whites, Indian summer. Not a breeze rustled the dry grass, or rippled the swift,

placed this, the Little Republican village, four miles above the Tappage-Republican town, Allis six miles ("Letters Concerning the Presbyterian Mission in the Pawnee Country," *Kansas Historical Society Collections,* Vol. XIV [1915–16], 617, 700).

2 Capot Bleu once more?

glassy waters of the Platte. Every thing was quiet, except the loud voice of the teamster, expostulating with his oxen; or an occasional crack, from the whip of Joseph, as he urged forward his mules.

Now and then, we came upon large droves of horses, belonging to the Republican village. They were roving along the banks of the Platte, in bands of several hundred, prancing, and capering as wildly, as if they were still free, upon their own prairies. Upon our approach, they raised their heads, and gazed fearlessly upon us. Two or three of the largest, then left the herd, and slowly approached. For a moment they remained motionless, then with a loud snort, flinging their heels in the air, they dashed back to the drove, which sped off, with a sound like thunder. Occasionally too, we would pass a small hillock, upon which an Indian stood motionless, watching our movements. There is a classic air about them, when seen at a distance, with their robes flowing in graceful drapery round them, their forms drawn fully up, and their outstretched arms supported by their long spears. As these scouts thus gazed, so calm and motionless, I almost imagined they regarded us with the despair of persons, who knew that their fall was near, but that resistance was hopeless.

While we were yet several miles distant from the village, we observed mounted Indians, driving before them large droves of horses, to be ready for service in the wild ceremony of our reception.

The town of the Tappage Pawnees is situated upon a broad plain overlooking the Platte. It is the smallest of all the Pawnee villages, and contains about a thousand inhabitants.[3] The most of them were now poured out upon the prairie, where we could

[3] Kingsbury reported the "Little Republican village [as] much smaller than the others, containing only a part of the Pawnee Republics, the others living with the Pawnee Tappeiges" ("Journal of the Movement of a Detachment of Dragoons under Dodge," *American State Papers, Military Affairs*, Vol. VI, 133). Dunbar noted that "the little Republican village, at which a part of that band reside . . . is also situated on the high bluff near the stream" ("Letters Concerning the Presbyterian Mission in the Pawnee Country," *Kansas Historical Society Collections*, Vol. XIV [1915–16], 617).

distinguish them in the distance, drawn up in a motionless body, waiting for the signal to dash forward to meet us.

When we approached sufficiently near, it was given. Once more, we beheld them coming surge-like upon us, and changing their course at the very moment when our ruin seemed inevitable. Again the dizzying evolutions of the troop passed before us. The wild neighing of the horses, mingled in confusion—with the thunder of their hoofs—with the yells and whoops of the Indians, and the clashing sound of their bows and tomahawks. When this was concluded, the ceremony of presenting horses was performed. Half an hour brought us to the town, where as before we found every being on the look out for our coming, and every preparation made, to receive us in a manner worthy of the nation. There is a sameness in Indian customs and habits, which render description tedious. Suffice it to say, that we were received by the chief and his people with all the kindness and hospitality which their means afforded.[4]

About ten o'clock on the next morning we mounted our horses and clattered through the village on our route for the town of the Pawnee Loups, situated about five miles farther up the river.[5] This is the wildest of the four villages, owing perhaps to the savage nature of its chief.

We rode in a straggling string along the low, irregular prairie. The Otoe Indians skirted along the bank of the river. Those of the soldiers, who were not engaged with the teams, reconnoitered the different pools of water, in hopes of coming unawares upon

4 The Republican chiefs have already been named in n. 1, p. 161, and n. 2, p. 162. The Tappage chiefs, who have rather been squeezed out of the picture, were Little Chief, Lah-ho-pah-go-lah-lay-shah-rho, Ah-ke-tah-we-he-kah-he-gay, and Skah-lah-lay-shah-rho (Kappler, *Indian Affairs, Laws and Treaties*, II, 417). Little Chief was one of the speakers recorded by Edward Ellsworth at the council of October 9 (*Sen. Doc. 512*, IV, 603). Murray knew Little Chief, whose Indian name he gave as Tarawicadi-à: "He was the head chief of the Tapage tribe, and a man of considerable influence and ability" (*Travels in North America*, I, 302).

5 Dunbar and Allis both placed the Loup village three miles above the Little Republican ("Letters Concerning the Presbyterian Mission in the Pawnee Country," *Kansas Historical Society Collections*, Vol. XIV [1915–16], 617, 700).

some pensive duck, who might be dozing upon the surface. Here and there we observed a broken patch of corn, at the bottom of some ravine, where the washed earth was of so soft a texture as to require but little trouble in cultivation. Occasionally too, we passed a clump of dwarf trees, closely grouped together over the brink of a spring, or run of water. Otherwise the prairie was bare of forest, and covered only with long withered grass.

When we had ridden about half the distance, a number of Otoes came scampering up, to tell us that there were about a dozen white cranes, standing upon a sand-bar in the Platte. This incident, trivial as it may seem, created quite an excitement among the troop. Half a dozen loaded rifles were handed from the wagons, and as many soldiers[6] started off followed by a troop of Indians, with their arrows ready fitted to their bows, in case the fire-arms of the whites should fail. But all this preparation was useless, for when they arrived within about three hundred yards of the bank, one of the birds, who, like an old man, on a cold day, was standing with his head closely snugged up against his breast, and gazing in moralizing mood upon the swift water, suddenly shot out a neck, three feet long, and turned a quick and steady eye upon the approaching hunters. He gazed a moment, then taking a step, and slowly raising his wings until their tips nearly met over his back, he rose from the earth, as if by mere volition, uttering a shrill cry which brought after him, his startled comrades. As they rose, a shower of bullets whistled after them, without disturbing their flight. They slowly mounted in air floating like a snow-flake over the silver Platte. For a few moments they lingered over its shining bosom, as if loth to leave their resting place; but after wheeling in several widely extended circles, they soared to an immense height, and then took a steady course to the eastward and were lost to the sight.

It was not long before we reached a high bluff in the prairie,

---

[6] On leaving the Otoe village, the commissioner had sent back four of the seven soldiers who had accompanied him from Fort Leavenworth; perhaps Irving merely used the term for members of the traveling party.

from whence we descried the village of the Pawnee Loups, about half a mile distant, but we saw no signs of preparation to receive us. A single Indian alone appeared, galloping at full speed over the prairies. His horse was of a dark cream colour, fierce, and powerful. To his bit was attached a scalp, consisting of the whole upper part of a human head, the hair of which must have been full two feet in length, nearly reaching the ground. The horse-man proved to be the Black Chief of the Loups.[7] When he had come within a few yards of us, he sprang from his horse, and reached out the bridle to one of our soldiers to hold.

His face was far more swarthy than that of any Indian we had ever seen; but it was not more dark than the nature of the man. He was perfectly naked, with the exception of a pair of leggings of dressed buffalo hide, worn apparently for the sake of display-ing a profusion of scalp-locks, with which they were heavily fringed. His frame was not large, but muscular and finely formed. His high chest looked as hard as rock, and the tread of his mocas-sined foot, was as firm as iron. His whole figure was one, which for fine proportion, and strength, might have served a sculptor, but his scowling face marred the beauty of his person. Yet he had his virtues. He was true to his word, and faithful to his friends; but upon his enemies he let loose every evil passion. The old and the young; the defenceless mother, and the harmless child, alike fell beneath his war-club.

7 The name Black Chief does not figure among the signers of the treaty of October 9 or the Fort Leavenworth articles of peace of November 12. In Edward Ellsworth's report of the Pawnee council on October 9, Spitfire was given as the name of the chief of the Loups (*Sen. Doc. 512*, IV, 603); and in a letter from Fayetteville, Arkansas, May 22, 1835, young Ellsworth wrote to Irving: "Give old 'Spit Fire' a kind remembrance [in your book]." The first Loup signature to the treaty was that of Big Axe (Kappler, *Indian Affairs, Laws and Treaties*, II, 417) and Kingsbury two years later reported that The Axe was chief of the Pawnee Loups ("Journal of the March of a Detachment of Dragoons under Dodge," *American State Papers, Military Affairs*, Vol. VI, 133). Prince Paul of Württem-berg reported that in 1823 "Ta-rare-kak-scha which means Ax" was one of the leaders of the tribe (*First Journey to North America*, 437). Big Axe died in the spring of 1840 (Allis, in "Letters Concerning the Presbyterian Mission in the Pawnee Country," *Kansas Historical Society Collections*, Vol. XIV [1915–16], 723).

He advanced towards us, and grasped our hands with a grip which would have done credit to a vice; then turning round, he awaited the coming of his warriors, who had now assembled in the prairie.

Minute after minute passed, but still there were no signs of approach. The brow of the Black Chief grew troubled, and his eye darkened, at the delay. Still the minutes passed on, and the band remained motionless. The eye of the chief was nearly hid beneath his scowling brow, and he gnawed at his under lip, with a species of savage calmness. After a moment he called one of the Pawnees, who had accompanied us from the last village, and sent him forward with some instructions to his warriors. The Indian bounded towards the band, but before he had gone more than one quarter of the distance, a loud yell burst from them, and with a heavy, resistless motion, they bore down upon us. The Indian who had started, fled back to the party. At the moment that the cry sounded from the Pawnee Loups, the chief raised his head, and sent up a long, shrill scream in answer; then springing on his horse, he sat motionless, watching with a keen eye, their every movement. They had approached within a hundred yards of the party, when he again raised his voice in a loud whoop, and waving his arm, they separated and rushed to right and left, round us.

But few horses were presented by this village, as a party of Sioux Indians had stolen down upon them but a few weeks before, and swept off nearly one-third of the horses belonging to the town. The chief gave as an excuse, that he had gambled away nearly all that he possessed.[8] This was in fact the truth; for we

[8] One of the principal games of the Pawnees, and the one on which the most gambling is carried on, is played by means of a small ring and a long javelin. This ring is about four inches in diameter; and the object of the player, is to hurl his javelin through the ring, while it is sent rolling over the ground, with great speed, by one of his companions in the game. The javelin is filled with barbs nearly the whole length, so that when it has once passed partly through the ring, it cannot slide back. This is done to ascertain how far it went before it struck the edges of the ring, and the farther the cast the more it counts in favour of the one who hurled it. It is practised by the children, young men, and chiefs. The

From George Catlin, North American Indians, I, *Plate* 59.

The Ring and Javelin Game (Hoop and Pole)

"This ring is about four inches in diameter; and the object of the player, is to hurl his javelin through the ring, while it is sent rolling over the ground, with great speed, by one of his companions in the game. The javelin is filled with barbs nearly the whole length, so that when it has once passed partly through the ring, it cannot slide back. This is done to ascertain how far it went before it struck the edges of the ring, and the farther the cast the more it counts in favour of the one who hurled it."

afterwards learned that the horse which bore him, was the only one left, of a large number that he owned but a short time before. Upon reaching the village we found, as usual, crowds of women and children, curious to see us, though they did not press round us as in the other villages.[9] This was owing to the presence of the chief, who rode by our side, and who, in fierce tones, ordered the crowd of gazers to a distance. A concourse had assembled, too, around the entrance of his lodge; but upon our approach, they drew back, and permitted us to pass freely. In the inside we found a few of the principal warriors, who alone had been admitted; the women and the rabble had been prohibited from entering, and they dared not disobey orders. There was a feast, as usual, but we ate little, as we knew what was to follow. Scarce had we finished, before a little urchin was in attendance, to conduct us to the lodge of the Soldier Chief, the second brave in the village.[10] We found him seated at a little distance from the fire, awaiting our arrival. As we entered, he rose, and presented to Mr. E[llsworth] a large buffalo robe, upon which was painted a hieroglyphic account of his warlike deeds. After this he seated himself, and commenced describing the different fights, and explaining the meaning of the various symbols.

He was a tall, thin man, with a sharp muscular face, and a

first gamble for single arrows—the second for a bow and quiver—and the last for horses.—JTI. Murray declared the Pawnees would play sometimes "for five and six hours, in the mid-heat of an August day, without intermission. It is made subservient to their taste for gambling; and I have seen them lose guns, blankets, and even one or two horses, in a morning" (*Travels in North America*, I, 321–22). Stewart Culin says "The game of hoop and pole . . . was played throughout the entire continent north of Mexico" (*Games of the North American Indians*, [Bureau of American Ethnology *24th Annual Report;* 1902–1903], 420–527). For the mythological origin of this game, originally played for the direct purpose of calling the buffalo, consult Dorsey, *Traditions of the Skidi Pawnee*, 254–59, 344.

9 Allis (1834) reported that the Loup village contained about seventy-five lodges; Dunbar a few months later estimated seventy ("Letters Concerning the Presbyterian Mission in the Pawnee Country," *Kansas Historical Society Collections*, Vol. XIV [1915–16], 697, 618).

10 Irving's variation for Big Soldier, one of the signers of the treaty of October 9 (Kappler, *Indian Affairs, Laws and Treaties*, II, 417). According to Hyde (*Pawnee Indians*, 157), he had become head chief of his village by 1844.

deep-sunk eye, which glittered in its socket like that of a basilisk. There was no spare flesh about his frame, but all was brawn, and sinew. His look was that of a person formed for the endurance of great, and continued toil, and his hardened face showed that he had weathered exposures of all descriptions.

He apologised to the commissioner for not having come out with the rest of the tribe to welcome him—being at bitter enmity with the chief, and refusing on all occasions to act in concert with him.

A large bowl of boiled corn was then placed before us, and each of us furnished by the Soldier's wife with a small dipper of buffalo horn. Having partaken of the mess as sparingly as the laws of Indian politeness would permit, we took our leave. After we had left the lodge, the Indian agent [Dougherty] who accompanied us related the following account of a murder which had occurred but a few months previous, and which was the origin of the bitter feud between the Soldier and the Black Chief.

[CHAPTER XLI]

The Shian Captive

During the month of May previous, business had called Major Dougherty to the Otoe Agency, on the Missouri. One morning, while there, a wearied messenger made his appearance. He had been sent by a half-breed from the Pawnee village, with intelligence that the Loups had taken a Shian [Cheyenne] woman prisoner, and intended to burn her at the stake, in the course of a few days.[1]

[1] The Pawnee Loups are the only Pawnee tribe that yet retain this custom. They offer their victim to the Great Star, (the planet Venus.) The prisoner is, if possible, kept in ignorance of his intended fate, until led out to die. The sacrifices are generally offered in the spring of the year, to insure a bountiful harvest.—JTI. According to Hyde (*Pawnee Indians*, 154), "The Skidi priests kept a star chart, painted on a large piece of hide, which from astronomical evidence

The Agent determined if possible to save her. Having made a few hurried preparations, he set off with five companions. A journey of three days brought them to the village. The news of their visit and the object of it had preceded them, and they experienced an ungracious reception. No hand was extended in friendship; no voice uttered the words of welcome. As the little band passed through the village, the tops of the lodges were crowded with women and children, and an immense concourse was drawn up in front of the dwelling of the chief. They forced their way through the fierce and sullen mob, and cleared a passage to the entrance.

seems to date back to the 15th century; and since the human sacrifices were an integral part of the Skidi star worship, this practice must be of very early origin." A Loup medicine man in 1823 told Prince Paul of Württemberg (*First Journey to North America*, 439–40) "that human sacrifice had taken place among them, as among other neighboring nations. He said, however, that this difference obtained, that they selected only one of their captives, and treated the rest as prisoners. The one selected for sacrifice was kept in the house of the priest for a long time, and was well taken care of. On a day, when the morning star, which holds a high place in their religious observances, shone the longest, the victim was tied to a post, killed with arrows, and then burned with the customary ceremonies. In the ashes the priest read the future, for the Pawnees believe in pyromancy." Recorded attempted sacrifices occurred in 1817, when a Padouca (or Ietan) girl was rescued and carried to freedom by Pitalesharo, son of Old Knife, and for which in 1821 at Washington he was presented with a silver medal by the young ladies of Miss White's Seminary; in 1818, when a Spanish boy was "bought" at a forced sale by Alexander LaForce Papin and Old Knife and taken down to St. Louis by Manuel Lisa; in 1827, when Dougherty, with Captain G. H. Kennerly, Papin, and others attempted to rescue a Padouca woman who was killed in the attempt to carry her off after a purchase had been arranged; in 1833, as reported here by Irving; and in 1838 an actual sacrifice of a Dakota girl, as reported by Dunbar and De Smet (Jedidiah Morse, *Report to the Secretary of War . . . on Indian Affairs*, 247–49; James, *Account of the Expedition under Long*, XV, 153–55; Alphonso Wetmore, *Gazetteer of Missouri*, 341–50; "Letters Concerning the Presbyterian Mission in the Pawnee Country," *Kansas Historical Society Collections*, Vol. XIV [1915–16], 631; Hiram M. Chittenden and Alfred Talbot Richardson, *Life, Letters, and Travels of De Smet*, III, 976–88). Detailed descriptions of the sacrificial ceremony, apparently derived from eyewitnesses, are to be found in James, *Account of the Expedition under Long*, XV, 151–53; Dunbar, "Letters Concerning the Presbyterian Mission in the Pawnee Country," *Kansas Historical Society Collections*, Vol. XIV (1915–16), 631; and Grinnell, *Pawnee Hero Stories*, 362–69. Frances Densmore (*Pawnee Music* [Bureau of American Ethnology *Bulletin 93* (1927)], 18–23) gives an account of the morning star ceremony.

Here stood the chief.[2] *His* welcome, and *his* alone was cordial. He ushered the Agent into his dwelling, nor did he turn a deaf ear to his request, that the Shian female might be spared. He told him, however, that *he* had no power to free her, and that all he could do would be to assemble a council of the nation, and lay the matter before *them;* that he would use his influence; and that if they could be prevailed upon, the captive should be saved. He accordingly despatched messengers in every direction, to call a council of the chiefs and braves of the nation, and they assembled that very night. They took their seats around the lodge in silence, with faces which gave but little hope of a merciful result to their deliberations. In the centre sat the Agent and his companions; and near them the Shian captive. She had been led in passively, and made no appeal, for she had no hope. It seemed as if every sense and feeling had been paralyzed, by the horror of her approaching fate.

The Agent rose and stated his object to the meeting. He was a firm man; he had spent much of his life among the savages; but it needed all his resolution, and all his knowledge of the Indian character, to effect the desired object. As he spoke there was no friendly look returned; no sound of approbation uttered. They listened with a calm, cold air, and he finished his address, conscious that he had gained *no* point, nor enlisted the friendly feeling of a single breast, in the whole of the dark circles which surrounded him.

When he ended, the chief, who during the whole time had been seated quietly at the foot of a pillar, rose. He was in favour of releasing the captive, and of sending her off with the whites. He spoke with the wild energy, and vehement gesticulation customary among the Indians. During his speech there was a silence —a portentous silence in the lodge. But when he had finished, a hundred throats yelled out cries of anger, and a hundred eyes gleamed fiercely upon him. It was not, however, in his nature to yield. Incensed at the opposition to his will, he raised his voice,

2 Irving's Black Chief (Big Axe).

[1 8 6]

until it even drowned the noise of the whole assembly, and swore by the Great Spirit, that she should be delivered to the whites; and he dared any man of the whole assembly, to offer her the slightest injury.

All quailed before the master spirit, and bowed to the superior energy of his nature. One after another they left the lodge, until the chief, the captive, and the whites were its sole occupants. In a few moments the chief went out also. In an hour he returned, followed by two armed warriors, whom he stationed in the opposite part of the lodge, placing the squaw between them. Upon being asked the reason of this precaution, he mentioned that the Soldier Chief, instigated by one of the Medecin-men of the village, had created some disturbance, which caused him to fear for the life of the captive, and that these men were placed to protect her. He evaded all farther inquiries, and shortly after left the lodge.

The whites stretched themselves upon their bear-skins, but scarcely closed their eyes that night. The guards kept watch on each side of the captive; motionless, but sleepless. On the following morning, the horses were saddled in front of the lodge, and the party having armed themselves, prepared to mount. The chief led out the captive, and forcing back the angry crowd, he placed her upon a horse, between two of the whites; at the same time cautioning them to lose no time in leaving the village. They accordingly attempted to push forward; but the crowd hemmed them in so closely, that it was with difficulty they prevented their horses from trampling them down. This throng continued to press round them, until they reached the lodge of the Soldier Chief. As they passed it, a bow twanged from within, and an arrow whizzing through the air, was buried up to the feather in the side of the Shian captive. With a loud scream, she tossed her arms in the air, and fell forward upon the neck of the horse. At the same moment, a loud roar rose from the multitude; and two Indians seizing the bridle, jerked the horse onwards. The crowd opened to let them pass; but before the whites

[1 8 7]

could follow, it had again closed. At that moment, the Agent heard a loud whoop behind him, and turning, beheld the Black Chief, and the Soldier, grappled in a desperate conflict, while the followers of each, stood by, watching the result. They were both unarmed, and the issue was to depend upon their bodily strength alone. They were well matched, but the Black Chief had the advantage, for he had a deadly gripe upon the throat of his opponent.

The Agent knew, however, that whichever might be victorious, the conflict would terminate fatally to himself. He therefore sprang from his horse, and succeeded with the aid of several chiefs, in dragging them apart, and put an end to the contest. He then turned to look for the captive. She had been borne off by the crowd, who were rushing over the prairie with deafening yells.

Still determined if possible to save her, he sprang upon his horse and galloped after them. But he was too late. They had torn the wretched being to pieces, smeared themselves with her gore, and were whirling her head and quivering limbs in the air.[3]

From that time, there had been a settled hatred, between the Black Chief and the Soldier. They spoke not; they entered not the lodges of each other, and acted no more in concert than if they had been two leaders of separate villages.

[3] Dunbar confirmed this story: "The last . . . was shot from the horse on which she was sitting behind the agent. He had purchased her, and paid the full amount demanded for her, in goods, and when proceeding out of the village with her, the 'medicine men,' deeming that if they should let her go, their good fortune would depart with her, since she was devoted [to the morning star], shot her as before mentioned. A part of the village was ready and would immediately revenged the insult offered to their agent, had he not interposed to prevent bloodshed" ("Letters Concerning the Presbyterian Mission in the Pawnee Country," *Kansas Historical Society Collections*, Vol. XIV [1915–16], 631). Allis also reported this episode briefly (*ibid.*, 700–701). There are close parallels between the stories told by Wetmore and by Irving, possibly because they were both derived from Dougherty. Although Wetmore's book was published in 1837, his account was first printed in "a late Missouri paper" and from it reprinted in *Atkinson's Casket* (Philadelphia), in October, 1827 (Vol. I, 392–93).

[CHAPTER XLII]

Exploit of the Black Chief—Alarm in the Village

We were sitting late one evening, in the lodge of the chief, around the fire. There were about thirty Indians present, some were lying upon the floor, and others sitting huddled up, wrapped in their robes, with their unbending gaze fixed upon our faces. The servants were spreading our bear-skins and blankets, preparatory to our retiring for the night. While thus situated, the interpreter, after dwelling upon the desperate nature of our host, related to us the following anecdote, illustrative of his character.

About a year previous to this, the Black Chief had by some means or other fallen into disgrace with his people. They shunned him, and refused to admit him to their councils, until by some heroic action, he should wipe off the stain upon his name. He knew that there was no resource; that the blood of an enemy alone, would retrieve his fame. He determined, therefore, to shed it, in a manner which even the most desperate of his own tribe, would not have dreamed of, and which would strike a salutary terror of his name, into the hearts of his hostile neighbours.

Early one morning, taking his bow and quiver, he left his lodge, and started on foot for the Crow village, about two hundred miles distant. He set out upon his journey, without attendants, and singing his death-song. His tribe watched until he was out of sight; they knew not where he was going; he might return soon, in a day, in a month, and perhaps never. They knew his desperate character; they knew that his errand was one of blood; and they doubted not, that if he returned, he would bring home trophies, sufficient to place him once more, at the head of their councils.

On the evening of the fourth day, he reached the Crow village; but waited at a short distance, concealed in a prairie, until it was completely dark. He then entered the village, and passed through its very centre. Several of the inhabitants were stirring, but the darkness was so great that they did not regard him particularly, and he passed on, undetected. At length he came to a lodge, a little apart from the rest, with a horse standing at the door, tied by a halter of buffalo hair. Peering over the bear-skin, which hung before the inner entrance; he beheld two Indians reclining in front of a fire. A few feet from them, a squaw was pounding corn, in a large wooden mortar; and at a little distance, was a child sleeping on the floor. The backs of all were turned towards the warrior, and he hesitated not a moment how to act. Drawing forth his knife with his left hand, and grasping his tomahawk in his right, he dashed into the building. With two blows, he clove the skulls of the men; he sheathed his knife in the heart of the woman, and dashed out the brains of the child. Having scalped his victims he mounted the horse at the door, and started off. He had gone but a few paces, before he observed an Indian making for the lodge. He felt a strong hankering after his scalp also; but there were several other Indians at hand, and he feared detection. Resisting therefore the powerful temptation, he turned away and galloped for the prairie. Scarcely had he got clear of the village, when it rang with yells and screams; and in a few moments, he heard the clattering of hoofs, and the sound of voices in hot pursuit. In a night chase, however, the pursued has always the advantage; he has but to dash forward, while his foes, must either stop to keep his trace, or follow at random. So it was with the Black Chief; and long before morning his horse had borne him, far beyond the sound of pursuit.

He reached his village in safety; related his tale, and displayed his scalps. They hesitated not a moment, to believe him, for in recounting his exploits, an Indian never lies. He was received with honour; and once more resumed his seat in the councils of his nation.[1]

[1] The greatest achievement of a Plains Indian warrior was to "strike" an enemy in his own village and his own lodge.

This is a picture of Indian warfare—to steal like an assassin upon an unarmed enemy, and butcher him without the slightest chance of resistance. Blood is what he seeks—no matter whether from the veins of man or woman—infancy or age. A scalp is his trophy; and is alike glorious whether silvered with age, or torn from the reeking head of a youthful warrior. With the savage, a hankering for blood, is ambition—a relentless fury in shedding it, renown.

During the whole time of the narration, the chief, unconscious that he was the subject of discourse, sat gazing upon the fire. His face was as calm and quiet as if no evil passion had ever harboured in his bosom—as if his hand had never been stained with blood, or his ears rung to the wild screams of the dying.

The tale was scarcely finished, when we were startled by a loud outcry in the village. The next moment, the bear-skin was flung violently back; an armed Indian rushed into the lodge— shouted out a few words at the top of his lungs, and as quickly disappeared. Every savage sprang to his feet, and rushed to the door, and in an instant the lodge was deserted.

In a few moments the chief returned. Never had I seen such a change. His face which had lately been as unruffled as that of a sleeping infant, was hideously distorted. His eyes gleamed like fire, and his teeth were clenched with rage. One of the squaws spoke to him, but he heeded her not—snatching down from a shelf his bow and arrows, and catching up his heavy war-club, he again rushed out.

The tumult grew louder. The interpreter came in and informed us, that a party of Sioux Indians had stolen into the town—opened one of the large wicker pens, and carried off about

---

2 "Near each lodge is a pound, or fold, for the horses and mules of the inmates. These folds are made by planting pickets in the ground, the same as we do in building a stockade; are circular, with a hole on one side for the ingress and egress of the animals, which is securely fastened with bars tied by thongs" (Carleton, *The Prairie Logbooks*, 70). During the next decade, Sioux raids on the Pawnee became very serious; both Dunbar and Allis reported numerous attacks. This one, however, was merely a false alarm.

fifty Pawnee horses. They had nearly effected their retreat, when they were discovered by a young Indian, who gave the alarm, and the whole village was now in arms.[2]

On sallying forth, we found every thing in a state of uproar. Whoops and yells, mingled with the cries of women, sounded in every direction. Horsemen were clattering through the town; band after band dashed by yelling the war-whoop. The voices of the leaders were heard above all, giving orders and cheering their followers to the pursuit. At length they disappeared in the darkness, and the sounds of their voices died away as they galloped over the prairie.

In about an hour they returned, and the chief made his appearance, gloomy and morose. He had taken no scalps; he had seen no enemies; no horses had been stolen; and the whole tumult had been caused by a young Pawnee, who observing one of his own tribe busily engaged in collecting his horses at an unusual hour of the night, mistook him for an enemy and gave the alarm.

Nothing farther occurred to disturb us, and retiring to our couches, we slept soundly until morning.

[CHAPTER XLIII]

Departure from Grand Pawnees—Delegation— Death Song

Two days had elapsed, and we had again returned to the Grand Pawnee village. We now prepared for our return to the white settlements.[1] Nearly two months had elapsed since the prairie had become our home, and its wild sons our fellows. We had

1 It is impossible to date this; at a guess it would now be about October 18. Since Ellsworth's letter covering the Pawnee treaty of October 9 is dated "Fort Leavenworth, October, 1833," it is clear that the party had returned to the fort before the close of that month (*Sen. Doc. 512*, IV, 601).

lived in the land of the savage; we had seen, in his real character, the man of nature. We had seen him in his moments of joy, and pain; in his moments of pride and humility; in his paroxysms of excitement, when urged on by his impetuous nature; and in his hours of relaxation, when a calm was upon his burning bosom, and his passions were asleep. We had seen him, in his home, in the midst of his family, where the gushes of his heart were unrestrained; when the feelings of the husband, and father, and all the kind impulses of nature had burst the iron fetters of habit, and resumed their empire. The illusions thrown around him by the exaggerated reports of travellers, and the fictions of poets, had been removed; and we had beheld him, as he really was; an untutored, generous, yet savage man. He had lost much of the romance with which imagination had clothed him. His faults, his vices, his crimes, now stood out in glaring colours, and threw into the shade, many of his higher qualities. Still with all his imperfections, we had learned to admire his chivalrous nature; and to look upon him while uncontaminated by communion with the whites, as among the noblest works of his Maker.

The sun rose cheerily on the morning of our departure. A crowd had assembled in front of the chief's lodge, to take a last look at the band of pilgrims, who had ventured among them.

Many of the most distinguished warriors stood proudly drawn up, with their robes muffled round their folden arms, and their heads thrown back. They watched us silently, and with countenances as fixed as marble. The females were in groups; some in the area in front of the chief's abode; and others on the domelike tops of the lodges. The voice of childish glee was ringing among the crowd; and their merry games were going forward. Occasionally they would pause to watch the process of harnessing the horses before the wagons; and the next instant would resume their gambols.

A delegation of Pawnees, four from each village, had been selected to accompany us to the garrison, in order if possible,

to concert a general peace, among various tribes.² This delegation was joined by many volunteers, until at length, nearly
eighty were prepared to accompany us, to the terra incognita
of the white man.

A smile of kindness illumined the grim face of our savage
host, as he bade us farewell. The horses were saddled; the oxen
were yoked, and had commenced moving onward. We were preparing to mount, when our attention was attracted by a low,
and not inharmonious cry, which rose from the distant part of
the village. It came nearer and nearer, sinking into a long wailing
moan, in which many voices were united. At length a train of
Indians emerged from behind one of the lodges. They were
dressed in white buffalo robes.³ They approached us slowly, still
wailing out their mournful chant; and we recognized them for
our party of delegates, and their fellow travelers.

They were in fact singing their death-song, as is customary
with all the Indian tribes, before setting out, upon any perilous
expedition. It is merely a recounting of their different exploits
in battle, and winds up, by taking leave of their friends and fellow townsmen. Although it is sung with an air of vast resigna-
tion, by all; and although you would think, that after it, the

2 The official delegates presumably were those who signed the articles of
peace at Fort Leavenworth on November 12. For the Grand Pawnees, these were:
Shah-re-tah-rich, Ill-natured Man; Lah-pah-con-rah-coble-sha, The Mouth Chief;
Ah-sah-ron-kah-re, Wild Stud Horse; and Tay-loo-kah, Buffalo Bull. For the
Tappage: Ska-lah-lay-shah-rho, The Only Chief; Ta-rah-she-tap-potch, The Con-
tinual Mover; Kish-kay, He That Strikes the Bones; and Te-le-la-loo-li-ah-rho,
He That Makes Himself Chief. For the Republicans: Ah-shah-lay-koh-she, The
Dead Horse; To-lah-le-rah, The Medicine Buffalo; Tah-kish-ne-rah-koo, The Man
That Kills Many; and Tah-lak-kah-wah-ho, The Name of a Chief. For the Loups:
Kah-tah-rah-te-koo-tush, The Big Axe (by error listed among the Republicans),
Pah-kah-le-koo, Big Voice; Pah-shoo-she, The Brave; Kah-kah-la-le-shah, The
Carrion Crow (*Sen. Doc. 512*, IV, 730). Variant spellings of the Indian names of
these chiefs will be found in the commissioners' report of February 10, 1834, in
H. Rep. 474, p. 109.

3 The white buffalo robe is so called, merely from one of its sides being
whitened with chalk, in dressing it. The wool is of the same colour as that of
all others, (a dark brown.)—JTI. Irving may have been right about the buffalo
robes worn this day, but there were white buffalo robes which figured in religious
rites; consult, for instance, Fletcher and La Flesche, *The Omaha Tribe*, 283 ff.

songster, would go to the grave, "like a lamb to the slaughter;" yet from all that I could ever learn, there are no people that have a greater antipathy to dying, than the savages, or take more trouble to keep out of harm's way.

The melancholy dirge swelled loudly as the long train moved past us; but it gradually became fainter, and fainter, as they wound their way among the distant lodges, and disappeared.

In a few moments, we were galloping over the prairie, to overtake some of the party who had preceded us. A train of Indians followed us, and the tops of the lodges were crowded.

After travelling a mile, we at last crossed the top of a ridge, and lost sight of the town.

[CHAPTER XLIV]

Storm—Dog Feast

A heavy storm of mingled snow and rain set in, on the day after our departure from the Pawnee village.

If there is any thing truly comfortless, it is a camp upon a rainy day. Every thing combined to add to its gloomy character. The fly of the tent, which might have afforded us protection, had been torn to tatters; and the roof of our canvas house, settled down into a bag. Through this a steady stream of water distilled, upon the centre of a board, which we had honoured with the appellation of a breakfast table. The blankets were rolled up, and piled in the middle of the tent, covered by a large bear-skin. This was nearly saturated with the drizzling moisture. A large pile of green logs, heaped up in front of the tent, refused to burn, but yielded a bountiful supply of smoke, which the wind occasionally wafted in clouds into our canvas habitation.

The thorough drenching which they had received, seemed to have soaked all pride and dignity, out of our Indian companions. They crouched like wet poultry round the fire, shutting their eyes, and holding their breath, determined to receive some of its warmth, in defiance of the clouds of smoke which it threw into their faces. Here and there, were small groups squatting out in the prairie; each man was huddled up into a knot, with the rain pouring in streams down his shaggy robe, and dripping off into the grass. The paint was drenched from his face, and his whole demeanour so utterly changed, that it was almost impossible to recognize the proud, haughty warrior, in the dripping, bedraggled being, then crouching in the grass, beneath the pelting storm. Once or twice, some poor, half-drowned fellow, with a desperate attempt at joviality, struck up a song, with a come-let's-be-jolly kind of an air, which was intended to set the weather and fortune at defiance; but it was a failure. At the commencement one or two voices struck in with valorous spirit, but finding that they were not supported, they gradually sunk into silence, leaving the person who had commenced the strain, to finish it as well as he might.

Drip—drip—drip—pattered the rain into a tin bucket, placed in the tent to receive it. At length a large puddle which had collected in the rear, overflowed its banks, and stole in a small rivulet through the centre of the tent. A smothered oath from one of the party, who was seated in the very track of the water, announced its intrusion. Several of the soldiers were then sent out, with pails and shovels, and in a short time succeeded in draining a part of the pond, and digging a different outlet for its waters.

Just then the yelping of a cur was heard at a little distance, in a clump of bushes, which the Wild Horse[1] had chosen for his residence.

"So! the dog too is a sufferer on account of the inclemency of the weather. No doubt the Wild Horse is completely drenched, and in a terrible fume."

Another hour passed, but still the rain continued. Just then the entrance of the tent was darkened, and the Wild Horse en-

[1] See n. 8, p. 125.

tered. He held in his hand a large wooden bowl, filled with boiled flesh, which he placed smoking before us. We were informed that it was dog flesh, and invited to try it. The soldiers had also received a share, but without being told what it was. "What is it," said one, taking up a small morsel, and holding it to his nose, "is it venison?"

"It tastes odd," said another, biting in two a large piece. Several of them then commenced an attack upon the contents of their bowl.

"I don't exactly *know* what animal this belongs to," said one of them, who was eating heartily; "and to tell the truth, I don't altogether like the *strangeish* taste, there is about it."

"Poh! what should it be," repeated another, "but venison? and mighty tender too. I wish there was more of it; fresh meat don't come every day upon these prairies, for the deer are getting powerful shy."

Just then the canvas opening of the tent was pulled back, and the iron face of the interpreter was thrust in to say, that the Wild Horse wished to know, if the commissioner was pleased with the *dog's* flesh. The soldiers overheard it, and in an instant the dish was hurled from the fire, and the gourmands made for the water, writhing and twisting their faces, as if they had been stricken by St. Vitus. The Wild Horse gazed upon them with amazement, mingled with anger; but when the interpreter explained the cause of the tumult, his displeasure vanished, and a grim smile lighted up his hard, weather-beaten face. Then turning to his wife, (for he was attended by his better half) he called for a fresh supply of the viand, and collecting round him a group of the vagabond-looking beings, who were nestling in the grass, they soon left little else but clean bones in the bowl.[2]

2 "If a Pawnee honours you with a feast, you must expect to be regaled on dog meat as a matter of course, besides you must eat out of the same ladle with all the other guests—taking a mouthful of meat and a drink of broth, and then passing it around on the same principle as the pipe—Dog Soup is the favourite dish of the Pawnees, Sioux, Crows, Blackfeet, and Cheyennes" (Carleton, *The Prairie Logbooks*, 70). See also n. 3, p. 81.

We lay for a whole day upon the banks of the Platte river, but towards sunset a bright blue streak appeared in the west, and the dark misty clouds began to drive off towards the south. The sun at length showed itself upon the distant hills, and before it had completely sunk in the west, the sky was as pure and cloudless as in one of the happy days of June. This was hailed with joy by the whole band, both Indians and whites, and preparations were made for an early start on the following morning.

[CHAPTER XLV]

Deer Hunt—Encampment—Indian Night Fires— Lost Horses—Doctor's Mule

On the third morning after leaving the village, I started out to hunt on foot in company with three Indians: two Otoes, who had borrowed rifles from the soldiers, and a Pawnee. The party, and the train of accompanying delegates, were journeying in a long line, over the prairie, at some miles distance. We had hunted for several hours, up and down the deep ravines, which intersected the prairie. My two companions had become separated from me; but a sturdy Pawnee lingered with me, and trudged lustily along at my heels, with the hope of coming in for a share of any game that I should kill during the day. We travelled up one ravine, and down another, but nothing was to be found.

"Ugh!" burst from the lips of the Pawnee. I looked round; he was crouching flat to the ground, and made signs to me to get my rifle in readiness. Vague suspicions of danger flashed across my mind; we had heard that there was a band of Sioux Indians lurking round our party. Could we have come unawares upon them? These ideas flashed momentarily upon me, but they as quickly subsided, and cocking my gun, I stole cautiously

[198]

From an engraving after Seth Eastman, in Henry R. Schoolcraft,
The Indian Tribes of North America, v, *Plate* 6.

Pawnees Torturing a Female Captive
(The Morning Star Sacrifice)

"The Pawnee Loups are the only Pawnee tribe that yet retain this custom. They offer their victim to the Great Star, (the planet Venus.) The prisoner is, if possible, kept in ignorance of his intended fate, until led out to die. The sacrifices are generally offered in the spring of the year, to insure a bountiful harvest."

towards him. He was crouching in some bushes, near the jagged
top of a small ridge, which looked down into a deep ravine. As
I approached him, he shrank still closer into his hiding place,
and made signs to me to pass to the top of the ridge. I crept
up slowly, and peered above its level; at the instant, I caught
sight of an Indian, as he squatted quickly behind a bush. My
fears seemed realized. We had fallen into the snare! I looked
back towards the Pawnee; he was still maintaining his position,
and keenly watching my movements. As he caught my eye he
urged me by his gestures to fire: I hesitated. At that instant the
dark form in front of me, rose slowly up from behind the bush;
and I recognised the stern, proud features of one of my Otoe
companions. The next moment, I caught sight of a large buck
lying lazily beneath the shade of a bush. The mystery was explained in an instant. The Pawnee had seen the animal; and it
was the deer, and not the Indian, whom he wished to be shot.
As I rose to fire the Otoe again crouched behind the bush; the
bullet missed, and the beast leaping up, sprang towards the spot
where his foe lay hid. He had scarcely taken three leaps, before
a shot whistled from a clump of bushes, at some distance, and
in a different quarter. The deer changed his course, and springing forward, made for the opposite side of the ravine. He dashed
through the bushes, and bounded like lightning up the ragged
steep. At that moment the Otoe, who had first secreted himself,
had a fair view of him; he must have been about a hundred yards
distant, and was dashing furiously up the craggy hill. The Indian
fired, and the deer fell on one knee, but regained his feet. In
front of him, was a steep bank, covered with shrubbery. He made
a desperate effort to gain it, but failed; and rolled headlong
down, until he splashed in the brook at the bottom. A loud
whoop burst from the three Indians, and the two youngest sprang
forward to the spot; while the third, who was a cautious old
fellow, stopped to reload his rifle.

When they arrived at the place where the buck had fallen,
they found that he was not dead, neither was his wound mortal;

one of his fore legs was shivered by the bullet, but he had gained his feet, and now stood at bay. His head was bent to the ground, and he dashed his antlers furiously in every direction; his eyes flared with a wild, menacing expression; and the white foam slavered from his mouth. The Indians made several attempts to thrust their knives into him, but were as often balked by his fiercely-brandished antlers. They hovered around him like wolves; now threatening him in one quarter; now in another; but his horns ever met them. They then both attacked him at once, and succeeded in inflicting a slight wound. It served only to increase his fury; he leaped towards them, with a ferocity that caused them in turn to take to flight. Just then, the Indian who had remained behind to load his rifle, came up. The buck faced towards him and again brandished his antlers; but a bullet hurled him to the ground, and the next moment a tomahawk was buried between his eyes. A sharp convulsive shudder passed over his frame, he made a desperate effort to gain his feet, but in vain, a second shudder concluded his mortal struggle, and falling over upon his side, he expired.

An Indian is a quick butcher, and not more than ten minutes had elapsed, before the animal was skinned, and cut up. Each of us took a quarter upon our backs and set off for the encampment; which we reached about an hour after night fall.

The party had encamped in a small isolated grove. It was completely clear of underwood, except here and there a tall bush; and there was not another tree in sight. A spring gushed out at the foot of a hill at a short distance, and flowed in a pure but scanty stream through the grove.

When we came in we found that the Indians had divided into squads, and that every ten or a dozen had kindled their own night fires. All the arrangements, preparatory to remaining quiet, were not yet completed. The soldiers were felling dead trees, for fuel. Joseph was busily employed, in hobbling and swearing at his mules; while Mordecai with the air of a connoiseur, stood by, assisting him with his advice.

Some of the Pawnees, and Otoes, were scattered through the grove in search of fuel. Some breaking dead limbs from off the trees, and others collecting what was already strewed upon the ground. Two or three were erecting shantees to keep off the dews of the night. And several young Otoes were employed in weaving a shed of boughs, to shelter the wife of the Iotan, who had been unwell for several days past; and whose disease always grew worse towards evening, when she would have been obliged to assist in the labour, if she had been in good health.

In the course of an hour, the Indians completed their arrangements, and kindled a string of fires along the dry bed of a stream. As I had never seen them when encamped, except upon the Platte, where all vivacity had been soaked out of them, I strolled among the different groups. They were all in high glee. I came to the fire, occupied by the Wild Horse's family and a few of his dependents. The old warrior was in the keen enjoyment of some witticism just uttered by a little shrivelled fellow, a hanger on, who was evidently trying to make himself agreeable; that he might be invited to partake of a racoon that was cooking over the fire, under the superintendence of the squaw of his host. The Wild Horse made room for me by his side, so I seated myself, nor was I permitted to leave until I had partaken of his viands. From his fire I went to that of the Long Hair, who was huddled up, with his whole soul apparently engaged, in roasting a small piece of venison, upon the point of a green stick. He looked up for a moment, and then turned his attention to the roasting meat. I soon left him and strolled off to the fire of the Otoes. Here I found the Doctor very cosily seated between the Iotan, and his wife, prescribing for *her*, and taking care of himself, by occasionally cutting a rib from a large piece of venison standing in front of the fire, impaled upon a stake of green wood.

Early the next morning the tents were struck, when Mordecai made his appearance with a very lugubrious face, informing us that two horses had disappeared, and that the mule belonging to the Doctor was also missing. The Doctor was in a fever. He ran down to the place where the animals pastured; he examined the bushes, and beat through all the long grass; but his mule, Kitty Keero, was not to be found. He then seated himself upon the stump of a tree, and thrusting his hands in his breeches-pockets, shouted the name of his mule at the top of his lungs; but no Kitty Keero answered him. At last the Interpreter pointed to a savage-looking Pawnee, leaning against a tree, with his hair matted and twisted in every direction, and a few long elf locks reaching down to his naked waist. He advised the Commissioner to send him in search of the horses; as he was a first rate fellow to track a hoof. A blanket was accordingly promised the Indian in case of success, and after hovering around the grove for a short time, in search of the hoof mark, he hit upon it, and started off like a hound.

In an hour he returned, bringing with him the vagrant animals. Kitty Keero gave utterance to a long apologetic bray, as she entered the grove. This was well received by her master, who was so much overjoyed at once more seeing her, that two or three reproachful repetitions of her name, were all the chidings she received.

The wagons then drove out of the grove, followed by the Indians; the rear being brought up by the horsemen. In front of them rode the Doctor mounted upon Kitty; and as they jogged slowly along, I could not help thinking, that they would have formed no inapt illustration of Sancho Panza and his beloved Dapple.[1]

1 "The Jolly Fallstaff Doctor May ought surely to come in   also his 'Kitty Koèroo'," Edward Ellsworth wrote to Irving from Fayetteville, Arkansas, May 22, 1835, on hearing that his friend was turning author.

[CHAPTER XLVI]

Elk Chase—Wandering from Party—Herd of Elk— Night Camp—Hill of Bones—Racoon—Indian— Return to Party—Wild Horse

On the morning of the fifth day of our journey, an Otoe Indian, who was on the look-out, came running to us with the intelligence of a large *gang* of elk.[1] All was excitement. The soldiers snatched their yagers; the Otoes their rifles; the Pawnees strung their bows, drew their arrows from their quivers, and all hurried after the Indian guide, over the prairie which had been burnt before us. In ten minutes we reached the top of a hill, looking down into a deep ravine, about three hundred yards distant. It was thronged with elk. Some were gamboling about; some resting amid the high luxuriant grass, which here had escaped the fire. Others browzing upon the foliage of the vines, which hung in long and graceful festoons from the dwarf bushes; and some were slaking their thirst at a limpid brook. But even in these, their moments of greatest security, their instinctive vigilance was not at rest. For while most of the herd were frolicking, several, who from their enormous size, and the unwieldly length of their antlers, appeared to be the oldest in the gang, had stationed themselves as sentinels, on jutting rocks in the elevated banks, which commanded an extensive view. There they stood on the look-out, their heads high in the air, their nostrils expanded to catch the tainted breeze.

Scarcely had our band paused on the top of the hill, before the eyes of the watchful sentinels were turned upon them, and a loud snort gave the signal for a general flight. The bushes and

---

[1] *Gang* in such a context had been current in America as early as 1660; Zebulon M. Pike, Patrick Gass, and William Clark all used it for a herd of elk or buffalo early in the nineteenth century. By the time Irving wrote, it was a common locution (See *Dictionary of American English*).

shrubs, snapped and crashed beneath their rush, as they rolled together in a heavy mass. Their branching antlers tore through the wild vines; and the whole herd dashed across the ravine and thundered up the opposite steep. Large stones and fragments of rock, gave way beneath the tread of the leaders, and fell bounding among the hindmost. Those in front broke off large masses of sandy soil from the edge of the banks, and losing their footing, were whirled back among their companions. Notwithstanding the confusion, however, half a minute had not elapsed, before the whole herd had surmounted the steep, and were flying over the prairie, with the swiftness of a whirlwind.

"No elk meat to-day," said Rash,[2] (one of the soldiers,) leaning on the end of his yager, and watching the herd as they swept behind a distant skirt of trees.

"Ugh!" ejaculated an Otoe, in answer.

"Ugh!" ejaculated half a dozen Pawnees, unstringing their bows, and turning off towards the camp.

"Ugh! nin-gah om-pah," (no elk) said Hah-che-kah-sug-hah,[3] shouldering his rifle and preparing to continue his journey.

I had been in the habit of hunting in company with this Indian, and when he started forward, instead of returning to the camp with the rest, I followed him. The deer were abundant in this section of the country, and our object was game. We commenced a keen search in the hollows, but for a long time were unsuccessful. At last the guttural "ugh!" from the Indian, informed me that he saw something: and the next moment he pointed out a large buck, reclining in a distant hollow. He immediately made for it, while I seated myself in the grass, to watch his success. After stealing along several hollows, and keep-

2 Wilburn Rash, a private in Captain W. N. Wickliffe's Company F, Sixth Infantry. He had enlisted at Fort Leavenworth June 10, 1830, deserted May 4, 1832, was apprehended June 30, 1832, and was in confinement under court-martial sentence in the spring of 1833. By the close of April he had been returned to duty (Muster Rolls, February 28–April 30, April 30–June 30, 1833, Richard Graham Papers).

3 For this Missouri chief, see n. 2, p. 116.

ing among the tall grass, he at last came upon the animal and
fired. The buck started up, staggered a few paces, then scoured
away over the top of a hill. The Indian, after pausing to reload,
followed, and also disappeared. I waited in hopes of hearing
the *whoop!* which usually followed a successful shot; but all was
silent; so I sauntered slowly along, expecting him to return.
Nearly half an hour had elapsed, when I caught sight of him,
standing upon the top of a high peak, at several miles' distance.
Supposing that he had been led off by game, I no longer delayed
for him, but struck forward, selecting a route for myself. I had
been in the habit of leaving the party at sunrise, previously as-
certaining the direction which they intended to take; then coming upon their trail during the day, by following it I had always
reached the camp by nightfall. From never failing in this, I
had grown self-confident, and this morning, I had not even inquired their intended course.

I travelled for many hours; following the hollows, and beating the tall grass, in hopes of starting a deer; but with the exception of a few grouse, I met with nothing. I had continued
thus unsuccessful till afternoon, and was sauntering along a high
ridge, looking round to see if I could perceive any trace of the
party, when suddenly turning my head, I caught sight of a number of objects, stringing slowly along the top of a ridge. At first
I was surprised; for I mistook them for a train of pack-horses;
but the next moment undeceived me, and I discovered that I
had come unaware, upon a herd of elk. There were about a dozen
of them. They were as quick-sighted as myself; for at the very
moment that my eye rested upon them, they also detected me.
They halted and snuffed the air; but I was too far off to taint it.
So they turned away, and slowly loitered on. I immediately made
for a thicket of brushwood, and beneath this shelter, rushed
swiftly towards them. I had not gone far, however, when, upon
rounding a small point of bushes, I came directly upon another
herd. There must have been more than a hundred in it. Many
were lying upon the ground; some were gamboling and frisking;

two or three were butting each other with their horns; and several wary old fellows were stationed round as sentinels. I was within a hundred yards of them, so I fired at a full-grown buck. The bullet struck one of his fore legs, and he fell. In an instant the whole herd were on their feet, and huddling together like frightened sheep, they fled over the hills.

I sprang from my hiding place, and drawing my knife, ran towards the wounded animal; but before I could reach him, he gained his feet, and hobbled off, at a rate which kept me at full stretch of my speed. I then stopped to reload my rifle, and followed expecting every moment to see him drop. He led me a long chase, over hill and dale, and across runs of water; until I gave out; and seating myself, saw him hobble out of sight.

It was now time to look out for the party; a thing which I had totally forgotten, in the heat of the chase; nor had I taken any note of the course I was pursuing; so that when my race was ended, I was completely bewildered. I was within a short distance of a well-wooded stream, and I suspected that the party would encamp, somewhere upon its banks. I knew too, that they must be to the westward of me, so I followed the course of the river.

I travelled till sunset, examining every ridge in the prairie; every bend in the thicket; but there was no human being to be seen, nor a trail, or foot print, on the burnt sod, except the hoof marks, where the herd of elk had passed. I then clambered to the top of a high-peaked hill, which overlooked the prairie for miles; but all was deserted. I determined, then to encamp for the night, in the neighbouring piece of wood, and in the morning to renew my search. At the same time, resolving like most persons who are in trouble, that if I got safely out of this scrape, I would take better care when next I hunted alone. I went down into the woods and built a fire. The night was cold, and bleak. There was no grass to make a bed; the wolves howled incessantly; and to judge from their snarling, and yelping at the foot of a tree, a little distance off, I imagined, that they had pursued some animal, which had taken refuge in its branches. The night passed away drearily, and with a joyous feeling, I once more saw the east streaked with the light of dawn.

Before the day had fairly broken, I left the grove, and pursued my course to the westward, until I again came to a ridge in the prairie. This I ascended and looked in every direction; but could see nothing. I raised my voice and gave an Indian hunting whoop, which might have been heard for a mile. The woods echoed it; but there was no other answer. I wished to discharge my rifle, in hopes that it might reach the ears of the party; but I had only a single charge of powder, left in my horn; and if I should be obliged to journey to the settlements alone, I thought that this would be too precious to be wasted. So in silence, and with drooping spirits, I continued my journey along the line of timber. The sun rose, and gradually ascended in the heavens. A vague doubt began to steal across my mind; that I had, perhaps, crossed the trail, in the obscurity of the morning twilight; for I was now much farther to the west, than I thought it possible, the party could have gone. About a mile in front of me a long arm of timber jutted out into the prairie. I made for it, determining if I did not then come upon their trail, that I would retrace my steps and carefully examine that portion which I had crossed before daybreak. I reached the timber; but saw no track. I again whooped; but as before, the echoing forests alone answered me; and with a sensation of utter loneliness, I turned round and retraced my steps. It was near mid-day when I reached my last encamping place. I had carefully noted every mark upon the black sod; I saw my own foot-prints, where I had struck out into the prairie in the morning; but nothing else. I then kept on for an hour longer, but my mind was constantly vascillating— whether to follow my own foot-prints until they guided me to the camping ground where I had left the party on the day previous, or to keep on to the eastward until I should reach the Missouri; or once more to return over the ground which I had just passed.

I remember well the spot where I paused to settle my purpose. It was a high swell, which commanded a view over miles of prairie, and even overlooked the top of the lofty trees in the thicket. It was strewed with bones. For several hundred yards, the whole hill was literally covered with them. It looked like some deserted charnel house; and I recollect even in the midst of my perplexity, taking up one and examining it—wondering whether it belonged to man or beast. The place might have been the scene of a battle; for the bones were so small that they could scarcely be those of animals. There were no skulls, either of man or brutes, to solve the mystery; and even the bones were covered with a greenish mould, from many years' exposure.

After some consideration, I resolved to retrace my steps, and accordingly turned down the hill, and once more proceeded on my journey. I now was growing hungry, and for once felt the miseries of a keen appetite. In the midst of these cogitations, I caught sight of the head of a racoon, who was reconnoitering me from behind the stump of a tree; I shot him, and skinned him; and kindling a fire, cooked part of him on the spot. The cinders from my fire, caught in a small patch of dry grass, which had escaped the general burning of the prairie; and in a moment it was in a blaze—filling the air with a cloud of black smoke. When I finished my meal, I slung the residue of my prize upon my back, and struck out into the prairie. I had scarcely done so before I caught sight of an Indian, standing upon the top of a ridge at some distance. In a moment after he perceived me, and waved his blanket over his head, to attract my attention. I raised the Otoe hunting-whoop, and his shout, faint, from the distance, answered me. I then started for the hill, and the Indian, seating himself, waited till I came up. He was one of the Otoes who accompanied us. His Indian name I do not recollect; but when translated it signified, *"the man that drags his heels."* It was given him on account of his shuffling gait, which it was said that he possessed, but which I could never discover.

We started together, and about a mile beyond the arm of

timber where I had turned back in the morning, we came upon the trail of the party.

Night closed in upon us, long before we reached their camping ground. I was nearly exhausted; the light racoon, which I carried upon my back, seemed to grow almost as heavy as a deer. My thirst grew intense; I stopped to drink at every pool; and kept constantly breaking off the tops of the rosin weed, and chewing its pitchy sap to keep my mouth moist. Still the Indian kept on with unwearied steps, sometimes pausing to listen as a cry sounded through the night air, or turning to point out the light of a prairie on fire at a distance. He did not slacken his pace, until with a deep ugh! he pointed out to me the night-fires of our party, glimmering in a thick grove, on the borders of a brawling stream.

A loud shout, followed by a genuine Indian yell, burst from the lips of the doctor, when he first caught sight of me. This was followed by a hearty shake of the hand, and warm congratulations from the commissioner, and the whole party.

I was afterwards informed, that the Indian who discovered me, had crossed my track on the day previous; and, upon being told that I had not made my appearance, he had been induced by the promise of a blanket to set out in search of me.

I had not been long seated before our fire, when the Wild Horse, dressed in a pair of white corduroy pantaloons, with the rest of his body naked, came stalking up to shake hands with me. His object evidently was to display this new article of dress; which had been presented to him by the doctor. Although highly delighted, he walked in them, as if in fetters; for though the doctor had a rotundity of abdomen, which completely out-measured that of the Indian, yet the other far exceeded him in the size and length of his lower extremities; and the garment sat so tight to his legs, that at a little distance he had the appearance of having been white-washed. He kept about us during the whole evening. I imagine, however, that in this short space of time he grew completely tired of his new garb, for the next morning, I saw his son scampering through the bushes, dressed in the same pair of breeches—though they were as much too large for him, as they were too small for his father. He, too, soon wearied of them; and after having once or twice tripped up his own heels in wearing them, he abandoned them to the wife of the Wild Horse, who, I believe, from that period "wore the breeches."

CHAPTER XLVII

The False Alarm

The sun was glowing with a mellow warmth, upon the prairie; when our train, slowly ascended one of the black, undulating swells, which traverse the whole face of the country. At our feet, lay a great prairie, intersected by a waving thread of timber, which extended for many miles, and was now tinted with the bright and variegated hues of autumn.

The Pawnees stood for a moment upon the top, casting their eyes about them. A shriek rang through the air; so wild, and shrill, that it caused even the most stern to start convulsively, and clutch their bows, while the deep guttural "Ugh" burst from every chest, as they turned towards the Indian, who sent up the cry.

He was standing a little in advance of the party; his slender but muscular frame, bent slightly forward; his form resting firmly upon one foot, while the ball of the other alone touched the ground, as if he had been arrested, in the act of stepping forward. His nostrils were expanded; his teeth slightly bared; his eyes intently fixed in the direction indicated by the extended forefinger of his outstretched arm. The eyes of the whole dusky troop were instantly turned in that direction. They gazed for an instant, and then the prairie sounded with their shrill, appalling yells.

At the foot of the hills, at the distance of about five hundred yards, a small band of Indians were emerging from a wood; their white blankets and glittering gun-barrels, contrasting strongly with the dusky forms, and savage weapons, of our Pawnee companions. For a short space, there was silence, and then arose the second wild shout of the Pawnees, while the hated name of "Konza! Konza! Konza!" burst in a howl from every lip.

The little band in the glen, sent up an answering shout, which though it sounded less loudly, on account of the smallness of their numbers, and the distance which intervened, was still replete with defiance. As they raised their yell, they snatched their rifles from their shoulders, and prepared for the encounter.

Just then a loud whoop was heard, and Wild Horse came rushing up the hill-side which we had just ascended. His long hair streamed in the wind. In his hand, he grasped his bow, and about a dozen arrows. He had heard the answering cry of the Konza, and had snuffed a fight in the wind, with the keen relish of a veteran warrior. His small black eye glittered with joy, as he looked down upon the handful, who had dared to send up a note of defiance. He uttered a wild, exulting laugh, and shaking his war-club with a fierce motion, towards the distant foes, he raised a war-whoop, and waved his men onward.

And now the loud voice of the Iotan chief rose amid the din, calling away his band of Otoes, and summoning them to the top of a neighbouring hill. He was at peace with the Konzas, and had nothing to do in the present strife; it was all the same to him which gained the day; so he coolly drew off his men, and waited to see the result. On an eminence at a short distance, stood the Apollo-like form, and snarling, tiger face of the Long Hair. His robe was thrown over his left arm, while his right, grasping his bow, waved his warriors fiercely forward.

For a very short space, the cloud of Indians hung upon the hill, and then, with one wild cry they swept down upon the devoted band. There was no order of battle; each rushed forward goaded by his own impulses. They raised no farther shout; every feeling seemed now absorbed in the deep, burning thirst for blood. Their adversaries displayed equal alacrity. A loud, fierce shout had answered the war-cry of the Pawnees; then all was silent; they leaped forward, prepared to give cold lead in answer to the feathered shafts of their ruder foes. As they advanced they separated, and extended their front, to prevent their being outflanked. They had now reached within about two hundred yards of each other, when a hesitation was visible in the Pawnee band. They moved slower and slower. One or two stopped, and gazed steadily at their approaching enemies: then they collected in groups, and seemed to consult. Even the Wild Horse, a savage who had revelled in blood from his infancy, dropped his uplifted war-club, and pausing, leaned upon his bow. The Long Hair drew up his haughty form, and, swinging upon his back his quiver, which had before hung in front, folded his arms, and appeared to wait passively for the approach of the opposite band.

A grim smile of scorn had curled the lip of the old Iotan chief, when he first beheld the hesitation in the Pawnee ranks. For, like the chiefs of most of the neighbouring tribes, though he feared the immense hordes which belonged to that nation, yet he most heartily despised every individual of the four villages. There was an apparent acknowledgment of inferiority in this numerous band, thus hesitating to attack the handful, who challenged them to the conflict, which pleased the veteran chief; for in war, his own nation and the Konza, had always been looked upon as equals.

In a moment, however, a like hesitation was observed in the ranks of the foe. They drew up and shouldered their rifles, and then moved frankly forward to meet the Pawnee warriors.

The old chief was perplexed. He held his hand anxiously over his eyes, to penetrate the mystery. Suddenly a new light seemed to flash over his countenance. Waving his hand in the air, he shouted the name of his own tribe, and rushed down the hill, followed by his band. It was a party of Otoes, instead of Konzas, and the recognition which had fortunately taken place, had prevented the effusion of blood, which otherwise would have followed.

The parties now drew off, keeping coldly aloof, and eyeing each other with those proud and haughty glances, which are apt to pass between rival people even when friendly.

The Iotan conversed a short time with a tall, thin Indian, who appeared to have command of the hunting party, and, after leaving with him, a worn-out horse which he had brought from the Pawnee village, resumed his journey, in which he was followed by the whites, and the long train of disappointed Pawnees.

For a short time, the Otoes watched the movements of the party, then turning off, they crossed the prairie, and disappeared in a piece of forest.

[CHAPTER XLVIII]

Elk Chase—Indian Sagacity—Indian Camp

On the following day we were traversing a valley between two black prairie hills, when the crack of a rifle sounded from a distant hollow, and was followed by a loud shout. The Indians stopped short, and listened, but the shout was not repeated. At length a young Pawnee, impatient, sprang upon a horse and galloped over a hill, beyond which the shout had arisen. As he disappeared over its top, a second shout was heard. After the lapse of a few moments a loud whoop rose from the same quarter, and suddenly a powerful buck elk, with branching antlers, and enormous tynes, dashed with mad leaps to the summit of the hill. He stopped short at the sight of our band and glared wildly around. He was wounded in the shoulder, and the Pawnee was in hot pursuit. Casting a quick glance round at his foe, and throwing back his head, he bounded along the ridge. The wound in his shoulder, lessened his speed. The Pawnee plied his lash. The heavy hoofs of his horse, struck with a jarring sound upon the burnt prairie; and a whirl of black ashes was raised in a light cloud around him. His long hair streamed in the air, and his

[213]

dark, heavy robe, fluttered from his shoulders, as he dashed forward. A great interest in the result was evinced. The Pawnees were anxious that their hunter should acquit himself well, in the presence of a foreign tribe, who watched his movements with a jealous eye. The Otoes lost their usual cold character, in the earnest interest, excited by the headlong chase; and the Indian hunter who had wounded the elk, stood upon the top of the hill, leaning upon the muzzle of his rifle, and watching the success of his ally.

The elk reached the end of the ridge, and sprang down its sloping declivity. The Pawnee horseman followed. In a moment after the elk was seen bounding up an opposite ridge, and leaping along its verge. His pursuer pressed on, about fifty yards in the rear. Here the chase was again in full sight, and continued so for a few moments. The elk was growing weaker and weaker. He came to the end of a ridge which was cragged and almost perpendicular. He paused for a moment on the brink; looked down the steep; cast a glance behind; then gathering his feet he made a desperate bound down the rugged bank, and in a moment's time dashed up to the top of a succeeding ridge. Almost at the same time, the Pawnee was at the end of the hill; he looked for a moment down the steep—he half urged forward his foaming horse, then reining him in, turned away, and commenced his return towards the party. As he was leaving the summit of the eminence, he looked around for the animal which had escaped him, but he had disappeared in a clump of shrubbery. Seeing the pursuit was ended, the Pawnees folded their robes around them, the Otoes shouldered their guns, and the whole party resumed its journey.

In the company with *Hah-che-kah-sug-hah* I soon after left the party and commenced a hunt over the prairie. We were overtaken by a young Otoe called "the Buffalo Chief."[1] He was armed with a rifle; and was a keen and generally a successful

[1] Chak-wong-guh-he-gah, The Buffalo Chief, was one of the Otoe signers of the articles of peace at Fort Leavenworth on November 12 (*Sen. Doc. 512*, IV, 729).

GEORGE CATLIN   *Courtesy the Smithsonian Institution*

He Who Kills the Osages, a Missouri Chief

"The name Hah-che-kah-sug-hah was given to him on account of his deadly success in the war parties against the Osages. It signifies, the man who slays the Osages. *Though distinguished for ferocity in battle, yet in private life he was one of the most joyous, pleasant fellows I ever met with."*

hunter. Several Pawnees also came loitering up, for they always hang in the wake of hunters, in hopes of obtaining a portion of what is killed.

We directed our course towards a lofty skirt of forest, fringed with brushwood. Here we thought that we might hunt success-fully; but the night closed in, and still we were empty handed. So we were obliged to set out in search of the spot, which we supposed would be the site of our night encampment. The In-dians moved forward with a swift, unwearied step. They seemed to glide along. Their blankets fluttered in the slight current produced by the rapidity of their motions, and I was obliged to hurry swiftly on, lest I should lose sight of them. An hour passed; they still pushed forward; they spoke not a word; not a sign of intelligence passed between them; they moved on rapidly through the dark, as if they guided their course by instinct.

"Ugh!" ejaculated Hah-che-kah-sug-hah, stopping short, and looking earnestly at some object upon the black sod.

"Ugh! ugh! ugh!" burst from the chests of several of the Paw-nees, as they gathered round the suspicious object, and bent down to examine it more closely. I came up to them, but could see nothing. The Indian pointed to the ground, and after much difficulty. I descried the faint impression of a mocassin upon the ashes of the burnt grass, though it would have escaped any, save the keen and ever-observing eye of an Indian.

A few words passed between two of the Otoes; then turning off they followed steadily upon the unknown track. They ap-peared to trace it without difficulty, though to me it was totally invisible.

In about ten minutes, there was another burst from the In-dians, and a broad gray line, traced across the black prairie, and visible in the darkness, announced that we had at length come upon the trail of our party. Here the Indians turned off in the direction indicated by the line, and passing down a deep hollow, we ascended a hill. From its summit we perceived at a short dis-tance, a dusky uncertain outline of timber, in a hollow; and the blazes of fires glimmering, and flickering among the trees, assured us that we had at last reached the resting place of the party. The camp lay nestled in a large grove of trees. Within a few yards of it, the Nemahaw river brawled over a stony bottom, with wild, and not unpleasant murmurings.[2]

The Indians had distributed themselves about the open woodland, in groups of five or six. Each group had its own night-fire, and a rough shed of boughs, to protect it from the dew. In the centre of the grove, and strongly reflecting the light of the fire, stood the canvas tents of the whites, and reposing before a pile of blazing logs, were the uncouth forms of the soldiers; their appearance at present being little less wild, than that of the Indians. At one end of the heavy logs, was stretched the demi-savage, half-breed interpreter,[3] reposing after the labours of the day, and gazing sleepily upon the fire, which blazed high amid the gathered timber. One or two Otoes were mingled with the whites; but the rest of the trusty band with the old Iotan, as master of ceremonies, were collected round a large fire, which burnt brightly at a few yards' distance. The graceful form of the Iotan's wife, was reclining upon a pile of dried grass, beneath a canopy of green boughs, which had been formed for her, by the young men of the Otoe party. Notwithstanding the assurances of the doctor, that she was recovering, she persisted in her resolution of remaining an invalid; for as long as she travelled in this character, the soft heart of the soldier who drove the wagon, prevented his refusing her a seat in the vehicle; and the fiery-tempered old Iotan still insisted, that the young Indians should perform her share of the drudgery.

There was something wildly noble, about this little band of Otoes. They were adorned with all the coxcombry of Indians, before they have degenerated from savage men, to civilized beasts. There was a frank, gallant bearing about them; a native

2 Probably the Big Nemaha.
3 Louis La Chapelle, the interpreter for all the Pawnees, was traveling with them to take part in the peace council on November 12.

chivalry, which caused us almost unconsciously to place more confidence in them, than in their fierce, untamed associates. Behind them, resting against the trees, were their borrowed rifles, glittering beneath the blaze of the fire. Around us in every direction, were the rough wicker sheds of the Pawnees, their fires gleaming with an uncertain, lurid light, among the tall, straight trunks of the overhanging grove.

The Indians in their shaggy robes, were flitting to and fro like troubled spirits; now hid in the gloom of the night, and now their dark eyes glittering, and their painted faces glaring, as they moved in the light of some blazing pile. Some had wrapped their robes closely round them, and sat buried in a gloomy reverie, with their scowling eyes fixed upon the burning logs, taking no part in the conversation of their comrades, nor any note of what was going on around them.

At length one of the young warriors struck up a wild song, which made the woods re-echo. Another joined it, and another, until the whole of the group round that fire, were engrossed in the theme. A single voice from a distant pile then struck in, another followed. Another fire then added its voice, and gradually it spread from one group to another, until every throat in the whole Pawnee troop, had united in it. It sung of war, and well did the gestures, and wildly energetic tones of the singers, express the meaning of the words. In parts, the blended voices swelled on the night air, with a mournfully melodious sound; but when the howl, with which they ended every verse, burst from the throats of the whole band, it was thrilling and fearful. The Otoes caught the wild enthusiasm of the moment, and they too added their voices to the savage concert, until it almost seemed to rend the black canopy above us.[4]

[4] Carleton, at the Loup village in 1844, also found such singing impressive: "After 'tattoo,' we heard the Indians coming toward our camp from their village. It was a still, calm, beautiful moonlight night, and, as the procession advanced, the war-song, chanted by hundreds of voices, swelled gradually upon the ear, with its wild accompaniment of flutes and drums. . . . An immense pile of logs had been collected before dark, and, as soon as the Indians were heard advancing,

The song was kept up till after mid-night; for long after we had retired to our tents, it frequently awoke us from our slumbers, or mingled in the phantasmagoria of our dreams.

[CHAPTER XLIX]

Separation from Party—Burning Prairie— Wolves—Journey

It was scarcely sunrise, before the dark grove echoed with preparations for our departure. The voice of our mongrel French boy, Joe, was heard, hailing the mules, which had strayed for pasturage, some distance down the bottom. The soldiers loaded the pack-horses; the Pawnees collected together their scanty stock of cooking utensils, and packed them upon the back of a lean, bony nag, whose evil destiny had made him drudge-horse to the Indian host; and the old Iotan saw his wife snugly tucked away in one of the dearborn wagons, and stationed himself as guide, at the border of the forest, waiting for the movements of the band.

It was a cold, blustering day, with a clear and cloudless sky. The wind swept in sudden gusts through the creaking trees, and the dead prairie grass waved and rustled as the gale brushed over it.

In a short time the party wound out of the grove, and struck

---

it was set on fire. As they arrived, they formed about it, in a large circle, with those who were to dance on the inside. . . . At a signal given by the Chief a song was commenced by a choir of a dozen or more warriors, accompanied in perfect time by four or five drums, and the wailing of some half dozen Indian flutes. This song had not continued over a minute, before first one warrior sprang into the area near the fire, and commenced his dance, brandishing his tomahawk and knife, and singing his war song, pausing every now and then to yell his unearthly and terrific battle cry—then another, and another, until the whole blazing fire was surrounded by these dancing savages—springing this way and that, as the song went on, and going through with all their movements of attack and defense with a fearful truth to nature" (*The Prairie Logbooks*, 101–102).

across the prairie, in the direction taken by the Iotan. He had been a bold marauder in his youth, and had traversed every woody nook, and every prairie swell which lay in this quarter. When standing upon some high bluff, he would call his young warriors round him, and point out the different scenes of his exploits. "There," said he, pointing to some clustering forest, "there have I scalped the Osages, and there," pointing in another direction, "have I stolen horses from the same nation. There is not a grove which has not echoed the screams of my enemies, or borne witness to my plunderings. There is not a bottom in which I have not encamped, nor a swell which I have not crossed, either in hunting, or when bound upon some war expedition." He loved in his old age to dwell upon the deeds of his youth, and when narrating them, his faded features would light up, and his eye would flash, "for then," said he, "my arm was heavy and my limbs were strong." Yet it seemed to me they could not have been much heavier, or stronger, unless they had been iron itself. Such was the Indian who acted as guide, and led the way in front of our party; nor could I see that age had impaired his vigour; for in traversing hills and ravines, forests and streams, I never knew his step to flag or falter, or his frame to show any symptoms of fatigue.

After following him for a short time, I turned off, in company with a strapping soldier named McClanahan,[1] to search for wild turkeys, which are abundant in the forests skirting the Nemahaw. We traversed several glades, opening in a thick growth of timber; but although we saw many, we were for a long time unable to get a shot at them.

In beating up the forest we separated, and I soon lost sight of my companion; though for nearly an hour I occasionally heard the report of his rifle, sometimes near, and sometimes far off. Gradually each discharge appeared to be more distant, and at

1 William McClenahan, private in Captain W. N. Wickliffe's Company F, Sixth Infantry. He had enlisted at Louisville, February 3, 1829, was in confinement in March and April, 1833, but had been returned to duty in May (Muster Rolls, February 30–April 30, April 30–June 30, 1833, Richard Graham Papers).

length they ceased altogether. I kept on after the turkeys without killing any. Sometimes I succeeded in *winging* one, and then followed a hot scrambling chase through bushes, briars, and underwood, which invariably terminated in the escape of the bird.

Several hours had passed in this way. I had strayed many miles through the bottom, when the height of the sun warned me that it was near mid-day, and time to think of rejoining my companions.

Leaving the woods I took to the prairie, and sought the trail of the party, and for several hours pursued my course, examining every hill and hollow, in hopes of finding it; but no trail could I see. As the day waned, I increased my speed; but still without success. The prairie was deserted. The long grass waved before the blast but not a living thing met my eye. I then feared that I might have crossed the trace without noticing it; but the more I thought of it, the more impossible did it seem, that the heavy track of so numerous a body of men, should have escaped my eye. I ascended a ridge which commanded a wide prospect. A wilderness of grass was before me, with small rolling hills extending in every direction; but there was no appearance of my companions; nothing to be seen, but the sky and the prairie. It was time to seek a resting place for the night. I looked round for some tree, but not one was in sight. Dead grass, wild weeds, and withered stalks, were the only covering of the hills. I was like a mariner alone in the midst of an ocean. I knew not which way to turn. If I travelled to the west I might be approaching my companions, or I might be going from them; and then too, I would be journeying away from the settlements. So I at length determined to take an easterly course, until I reached the Missouri, which I intended should be my guide to the abodes of the whites.

With a quick pace I pressed forward, anxious to find a sheltering place for the night. It was the end of October; the wind was chilling, and I was clad in a dress of drilling, such as is used only for summer wear. Just as the sun was sinking, I caught sight of a line of forest, at many miles' distance. This acted like a spur upon a jaded horse. With fresh spirits I bounded down the sides of the prairie swells, and forced my way through the tall, clogging grass. But at last the sun set, and as the twilight darkened, objects grew indistinct, and the forest which could not have been more than two miles off, was gradually lost in the obscurity. In front of me was a large hill; I ascended it, to wait on its summit until the moon rose; for I feared to lose my course in the darkness.

A feeling of very desolation came over me, as I sat there, with nothing but the dreary waste around me, and the blue, cold sky twinkling with stars, above. The wind had increased to a gale, and swept howling along, occasionally bearing with it the yell of some prowling wolf. For hours I sat shivering, with my eyes fixed upon the eastern horizon, watching eagerly for the moon; and never had I greeted her appearance, with such heartfelt pleasure, as when she emerged to view.

I resumed my journey, and after toiling for an hour, through a wide bottom of tall weeds and matted grass, I reached the grove—erected a small shed of boughs after the manner of the Indians, and lying down was soon asleep, before a huge fire, which I built against the trunk of a fallen tree.

I was awakened by the increasing violence of the gale. At times it sank into low wailings, and then would swell again howling and whistling through the trees. After sitting by the fire for a short time, I again threw myself upon my pallet of dried grass, but could not sleep. There was something dismal and thrilling in the sound of the wind. At times, wild voices seemed shrieking through the woodland. It was in vain that I closed my eyes; a kind of superstitious feeling came over me, and though I saw nothing, my ears drank in every sound. I gazed around in every direction, and sat with my hand on my gun-trigger, for my feelings were so wrought up, that I momentarily expected to see an armed Indian start from behind each bush. At last I rose up, and sat by the fire. Suddenly, a swift gust swept through the grove, and whirled off sparks and cinders in every direction. In an instant, fifty little fires, shot their forked tongues in the air, and seemed to flicker with a momentary struggle for existence. There was scarcely time to note their birth, before they were creeping up in a tall, tapering blaze and leaping lightly along the tops of the scattering clumps of dry grass. In another moment they leaped forward into the prairie, and a waving line of brilliant flame, quivered high up in the dark atmosphere.

Another gust came rushing along the ravine. It was announced by a distant moan; as it came nearer a cloud of dry leaves filled the air; the slender shrubs and saplings bent like weeds—dry branches snapped and crackled. The lofty forest trees writhed, and creaked, and groaned. The next instant the furious blast reached the flaming prairie. Myriads and myriads of bright embers were flung wildly up in the air: flakes of blazing grass, whirled like meteors through the sky. The flame spread into a vast sheet, that swept over the prairie, bending forward, illumining the black waste which it had passed, and shedding a red light far down the deep vistas of the forest; though all beyond the blaze was of a pitchy blackness. The roaring flames, drowned even the howling of the wind. At each succeeding blast, they threw long pyramidal streams upwards in the black sky, then flared horizontally, and seemed to bound forward, lighting at each bound, a new conflagration. Leap succeeded leap; the flames rushed onward with a race-horse speed. The noise sounded like the roar of a stormy ocean, and the wild, tumultuous billows of flame, were tossed about like a sea of fire. Directly in their course, and some distance out in the prairie, stood a large grove of oaks—the dry leaves still clinging to their branches. There was a red glare thrown upon them, from the blazing flood. A moment passed, and a black smoke oozed from the nearest tree—the blaze roared among their branches, and shot up for a hundred feet in the air—waving as if in triumph. The effect was transient. In a moment had the fire swept through a grove covering several acres. It sank again into the prairie, leaving the limbs of every tree scathed and scorched to an inky black-ness; and shining with a bright crimson light, between their branches. In this way the light conflagration swept over the landscape: every hill seemed to burn its own funeral pyre, and the scorching heat licked up every blade in the hollows. A dark cloud of gray smoke, filled with burning embers, spread over the course of the flames, occasionally forming not ungraceful columns, which were almost instantly shattered by the wind, and driven in a thousand different directions.

For several hours the blaze continued to rage, and the whole horizon became girdled with a belt of living fire. As the circle extended, the flames appeared smaller and smaller: until they looked like a slight golden thread drawn around the hills. They then must have been nearly ten miles distant. At length the blaze disappeared, although the purple light, that for hours illumined the night sky, told that the element was extending into other regions of the prairie.

It was sunrise when I rose from my resting place and resumed my journey. What a change! All was waste. The sun had set upon a prairie still clothed in its natural garb of herbage. It rose upon a scene of desolation. Not a single weed—not a blade of grass, was left. The tall grove, which at sunset was covered with with-ered foliage, now spread a labyrinth of scorched and naked branches—the very type of ruin. A thin covering of gray ashes was sprinkled upon the ground beneath, and several large, dead trees, whose dried branches had caught and nourished the flame, were still blazing or sending up long spires of smoke. In every direction, barrenness marked the track of the flames. It had even worked its course against the blast, hugging to the roots of the tall grass.

The wind was still raging; cinders and ashes were drifting, and whirling about, in almost suffocating clouds, sometimes rendering it impossible to see for more than one or two hun-dred yards.

In surveying the dreary landscape, I caught sight of a gaunt, gray prairie wolf, stealing with a thief-like step down one of the hollows, as if his spirits were cowed by the scene. He was the only living thing to be seen. He saw his fellow-wanderer, but he did not fly. The very desolation around, appeared to have brought him a link nearer to man, for he had lost his terrors of him. He paused as he reached the foot of the hill. Here he uttered a low, querulous howl, which was answered from the woods, and three others emerged from the timber, and joined him.

They stood for a few moments gazing at me, and then commenced slowly to approach. I knew that there was not a more cowardly beast upon the prairie, than the wolf; but a chill shot over me, as I saw them advance. It seemed as if they regarded me, as the cause of their desolation, that had swept over their homes; and I felt guilty and lonely.

But even amid this want of companionship, I had no relish for that of wolves: so I raised my rifle, and sent a bullet among them. A loud howl answered its report; and the limping step of one of them, as the gang fled for the woods, convinced me, that my messenger had performed its errand.

I now gave up the hopeless task of searching for my fellow travellers; and as the Iotan had mentioned, that they were but a few days' journey from the settlements, I shouldered my rifle, and taking an easterly course, by aid of the sun started forward, trusting to make my way to the abodes of white men. It was weary wandering. Hill succeeded hill, and one valley swept off into another. The faint tracery of distant trees, disappeared as I journeyed onward, and soon there was nothing to be seen but the cold, unspecked blue of the sky, and the boundless black of the ravaged prairie.

CHAPTER L

A Hunted Deer—Deserted Encampment—Distant Indians—Night Camp—Owls—Burning Sycamore

For hours I continued my course, pausing upon the summit of every hill, in a faint, but vain hope of seeing my comrades. At last, at a distance, I saw a deer scouring over the top of a ridge, and making directly towards me. I crouched upon the burnt sod, cocked my rifle, and waited for him. I wondered at his speed, for there was no hunter in sight; but it was soon explained. As he descended into a hollow, three wolves came following at full speed, over the hill. The deer soon rose out of the bend, and kept on towards me. Almost without breathing, I watched him. I had eaten nothing since the morning of the preceding day, and there was something of ferocity in my feelings, as I gazed at him. I gathered my feet under me, and slowly raised my rifle. The animal still approached. I should have waited; but a burning feverishness rendered me impatient, and while he was at least a hundred and fifty yards distant, I rose and took aim. He stopped short, and gazed steadily at me, with his head raised high in the air, and presenting only his front. I pulled the trigger; the bullet might have grazed him, but did him no injury. He did not wait for a second shot, but darted like an arrow across the prairie. I watched him until he faded from my sight, and then re-loaded my rifle.

This incident, which for an instant had diverted the current of my thoughts, now served only to render them more heavy. At the sound of my rifle, the wolves in pursuit, had scampered off as hastily in one direction, as the deer had gone in the other; and I felt a kind of selfish satisfaction in knowing, that if I had not been able to obtain a meal from his ribs, this gang of vagabonds was equally disappointed.

Once more I proceeded on my journey, directing my course

by the sun. I had hunted much on foot, and my limbs had become hardened by toil; so that I could journey long without sinking, though not without feeling fatigue. It was about an hour after mid-day when I again came in sight of a forest. There was a golden mark upon the prairie. The blackness stopped abruptly, and pointed out the spot where the fire, from some cause or other, had ceased its course in this direction. A lowering column of smoke, however, hanging like a sullen pall, in another quarter, showed that the element was still at work.

Within half an hour, I reached the wood, and striking an Indian trail, entered it. It was a grove of tall, and beautiful hickories; and in the centre were the remains of an Indian hunting-camp. It had been occupied for some time, as the frames of the wigwams were more strong and durable in their structure, than those usually erected for transient purposes. They could have been abandoned but lately; for the bark was still green on the boughs composing them, and there were the recent footprints of horses. The dead pea-vines were trampled down by hoofs: and there was one rock, jutting out in the small stream meandering through the grove, which was covered with racoon fur, and here and there sprinkled with drops of blood. I sat down upon the rock, watched the waters, and thought of the former occupants of the grove. Had I been a day sooner, I might have met them; but then they might have been enemies. So I began to think that things were better as they were; for even the most friendly tribes, are apt to lose their good will towards the whites, when a single one falls into their power. Desolate as I was, I could not but be sensible of the beauty of the grove. I could see far down deep vistas, gilded here and there by the sun-beams. The wind had gradually died away. The stream glided murmuring over a rocky bottom, and here and there glittered like silver in the beams of the sun. The wild cry of the blue-jay was heard, hailing some noisy comrade in a distant tree-top. As I sat looking upon the water, I heard a slight noise in the stream, above me, and caught sight of a number of wood-ducks, borne on by the current. They are a beautiful bird. Now they glided beneath the shade of some plant that drooped over the water's edge; now they whirled easily round, as some changeful current caught them in its lilliputian whirlpool. They chased each other sportively across the water, sometimes scouring up the stream, then again relinquishing themselves to its course. They were small game, but I was famished, and had my rifle in readiness. I waited until I got two of them in a range, and then fired. My bullet struck off the head of the first, and considerably confused the ideas of the second; but after splashing about, bottom upwards, and trying several other novel modes of navigation, he recovered himself, and flew after his companions.

Having secured my prize, I crossed the brook, struck into a winding pathway, which led up the steep bank opposite.

I had scarcely left the grove, when upon looking round, I caught sight of a train of figures moving along the top of a ridge, far away to the westward. There were six in it, and they must have been many miles distant. So faint was their outline, and so small did they appear in the vast space that lay open in that direction, that they reminded me of the dim, spectre-like forms of a phantasmagoria. At first I felt a start of joy, for I thought that they might be my companions: but a second reflection convinced me that I was mistaken, for the train was moving along to the northwest—the very reverse of the route to the settlements. Then too the idea flashed across me, that they must be Indians—perhaps hostile ones. Although so distant that there was scarcely a probability of their seeing me, I returned to the grove, where I watched their gliding forms, until they at last sunk behind one of the ridges, and then I pursued my course. In front of me again, was a prairie which had escaped the flame, and was covered with herbage. But though it was pleasing to the eye, I soon began to wish for the black waste; for the tangled grass impeded my steps, and rendered my journey extremely toilsome. I had not accomplished many miles before the sun began to sink in the west. I then determined to travel no farther that night, but take up my quarters in a small clump of trees, which clustered like an island upon the borders of a brook. I collected a pile of dry wood; kindled a fire; made a spit of a green twig, on which I impaled my duck, and stuck it upright in the ground in front of the fire; then stretching myself upon a bed of dry grass, I watched the roasting of my supper with a hungry eye. When I had made a meal with the relish of a half-famished man, I turned upon my bed and fell asleep. After a time I awoke; added fresh fuel to the fire, and stretched myself upon my pallet, again to sleep.

It was a bright and beautiful night; the moon was shining amidst myriads of stars, veiled now and then by a light, fleecy cloud, from which she seemed to emerge with increased splendour. I lay gazing at her as she moved along like a queen surrounded by her maids of honour.

"Whoop! whoop! whoo!" sounded a loud voice near me.

I started to my feet: for I thought that I had heard a human cry; perhaps one of my party, and with a loud hail I answered the sound.

"Whoop! whoo! whoo!" again repeated the voice. A gigantic sycamore reared its naked and scathed trunk in the moonlight. At the extremity of a single dry limb, which stretched out from nearly the top of the tree, was seated an owl of the largest species.

He repeated the cry which had started me. "Whoop! whoo! whoo!"

"Whoop! whoo! whoo!" responded another from a different quarter, and a dusky bird flitted by, and perched on the long limb beside his companion. I again stretched myself upon my couch and watched them, as they sat between me and the moon. There was a confused jabbering carried on between them: they probably had charge of the grove, and were puzzled, at the intrusion of a stranger. After debating for some time, they concluded to take a nearer view of the intruder, and descended to a lower branch. Here they carried on the debate; apparently wondering who I was, and what I wanted. They rubbed their huge heads together with an air of vast perplexity: they rocked and fluttered on their perch. Occasionally one of them threw his head on one side, and cast a very inquisitive look down upon me; and then a fresh jabbering went on. After about fifteen minutes spent in this way, the two dignitaries giving a farewell "whoop! whoop! whoo!" flapped off and disappeared.

Again I turned and fixed my gaze upon the moon. There was a feeling of fellowship connected with it. I knew that other eyes were resting upon her pale orb, and I knew that while she was shining upon my solitary couch, she was at the same time pouring her mellow light, upon the abodes of my friends, far away and unconscious of my situation.

Chilled by the night air, I turned away and looked into the fire—forming palaces, groves, and arcades, amid its glowing embers, until gradually my eyes closed, and I slept.

When I awoke the sun was shining, and I resumed my solitary journey. I continued on foot from sunrise till sunset, without seeing a living thing, unless, perhaps, a distant deer; and halted for the night, in a forest of thick timber. I found a large, dead sycamore standing upright, with a complete chamber formed in its trunk by decay. I kindled a fire in front of it, and filled the empty trunk with dried grass, and pea-vines for a couch. I was wearied and slept soundly, until near mid-night, when I was awakened by the intense heat. The fire had by some means communicated to a pile of fuel, which I had collected to sustain it during the night. This was in a furious blaze, causing the old tree to smoke with the heat. The hollow trunk was no place for me, unless I chose to be roasted. I pulled my cap from my head, and wrapped it round my powder-horn—seized my rifle, and sprang through the fire. The next instant, the flame leaped upon my bed of dried vines, and the whole interior of the dead tree, was in a blaze, that lasted for an instant and then expired. As it was no longer possible to return to it, I seated myself upon a stump, and remained half shivering, half dozing, until morning.

CHAPTER LI

Wild Turkey—Squirrel—Parroquets—Trail—Konza Indian—Night Camp—Deserted House—Konza Agency—Reaching Leavenworth

Before the sun had risen, I was on my way, directing my course by the purple streak in the east, which announced his approach. This was the morning of the fourth day since I had parted from my companions. I had made but one meal, and the cravings of hunger were becoming excessive. I looked round, when I reached the edge of the prairie, but saw nothing; I looked through the bottom of forest, but no game was visible. I stretched out my leg, looking at the leather legging which covered it, and considered whether it was easy of digestion. I felt it; it *was* rather tough; so I determined to keep on, and wait till night, before I proceeded to extremities.

Just then, I caught sight of a turkey, leading a troop to take an airing in the prairie. I whizzed a bullet after him; his wing dropped and dragged, and I commenced a hot pursuit. But though I had injured his wing, I had not damaged his legs, and after following him for nearly fifteen minutes, I threw myself down completely exhausted. The rest of the *gang*, taking advantage of the diversion created in their favour, had disappeared among the trees. I gave up all hopes of again finding them, and wandered slowly along the edge of the woods. As I was winding my way through the trees, I heard a loud *click* above me, and observed a large red squirrel springing from one limb to another, of a bur-oak. As he caught sight of me, he darted round the trunk and peered out, with about an inch of his head, to take an observation. I was hungry, and this cowardly manoeuvre made me angry. I determined, that *have* that squirrel I *would,* if I spent the whole day in shooting at him. I rested my rifle against the trunk of a tree, and after a long aim, fired; the bullet dashed

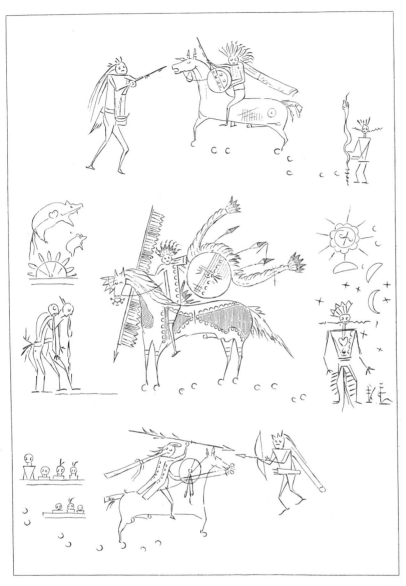

A facsimile copy of the paintings on a Pawnee robe
belonging to a medicine man and showing him to be
a distinguished doctor and warrior.

the head of the little animal to pieces, and whirled him some twenty feet off in the air.

I had lost my knife on the day previous, but with the assistance of a nail which I found in my pouch, I skinned my prize, and impaling him upon the point of a spit made of a dry stick, stuck it in the ground before the fire to roast. While the process of cooking was going forward, a flock of screaming parroquets came whirling through the trees; but upon catching sight of me, they determined to stop and see what I was about. They accordingly alighted upon a dead tree directly above me, casting side-looks down upon my roast, and from the joyous chattering that they kept up, no doubt were congratulating each other, upon having called, just in time to be invited to breakfast. But I had a meal in store for them, of a very different description; for after hovering round under the tree, for some time, I contrived to get three of them in a range, and fired. My bullet missed, and the flock whirled off, though I could hear their voices raised in a clamorous outcry, at my want of civility, long after they had disappeared among the trees.

I despatched my breakfast with a ravenous appetite, and taking with me the skin of the animal, to serve as a future meal in case of extremity, I continued my course until it was afternoon. However, I was now becoming perplexed. I thought to have reached the settlements before this. Still I saw no signs of human habitation, and I began to yield to the idea, which, strange as it may seem, invariably fastens itself upon persons, when wandering, bewildered through these regions. I thought *that the sun had got turned and was setting in the east.* For some time this idea was strong; but I remembered the almost parting words of an old hunter, who accompanied our party. "Look ye," said he, "you straggle so much from the party, that some day or other you will not be able to find it again. Then, all you have to do, is to keep straight away for the east. It will be sure to bring you right in the end. But remember one thing—never get bothered. When the sun rises, strike to the east, and don't *do*, as many have done when puzzled; don't think that the sun rises or sets wrong: for if you do, you will go to the d——l." I was becoming bewildered, and I remembered this advice, just at the time when it was most needful. So I turned my back towards what I had been positive was the east, and travelled in the direction, which I was equally positive was the west.

I had continued along the prairie for some hours, when suddenly I struck into a wide trail. There were four paths running along side by side, all evidently much travelled, and bearing prints of recent hoofs. While I was examining them narrowly, I caught the race of a wagon wheel. New strength seemed to course through my limbs at this discovery, and I bounded along the path, as swiftly as if I had just started, upon a fresh and joyous journey. I continued in the trail for several hours. On my right, was a tall, dense bottom of timber; and here and there, through the branches, I could perceive the waters of a mighty river. I instantly supposed this to be the Missouri; that I had struck the trail which led to Leavenworth, and that by continuing in this direction, I would be able to reach it before nightfall. I walked swiftly forward for some time; but still I could see nothing that I recognized. If it was the road to Leavenworth I had passed it before, and ought to recall the landmarks: but here all was new. As I was looking around I caught sight of a black speck moving over the distant path, which I had already passed. It came nearer and nearer. I could discern that it was a horseman. It might be one of the officers from the garrison, and I slackened my pace for him to come up; but as he came nearer I discovered that he was an Indian. I was then certain that I must be on the banks of the Konzas; that I had struck too far to the south, and had reached it before its junction with the Missouri.[1] I had been longing feverishly for the sight of a human being; yet no sooner did I behold one, than my first movement was to await his ap-

[1] Irving must have struck the Kansas River somewhere near the eastern limits of the Kansas Reservation, i.e., near Topeka, and was therefore some sixty miles from the Missouri.

proach, with my finger upon my trigger. When he drew near, he held up the palm of his hand, in token of friendship, and galloped directly up to me. He was a fine-looking man of the Konza tribe, apparently not above thirty—wrapped in a blue blanket, armed with a rifle, and mounted upon a black pony. From that moment we were friends. I learned from him, that the river near, was the Konzas, and that it would be daylight before I could reach the nearest abode of a white man. As soon as our truce was settled, my Indian friend mounted, and left me to follow on foot as well as I was able. I was wearied and hungry, and this want of civility did not increase the mildness of my disposition. I trudged after him; while he occasionally thumped his little nag into a trot, casting a look behind, to see whether I could contrive to keep up with him. This vexed me, and I began to cast around, for the means of paying the fellow for his ill breeding. He at last checked his horse—reached out his rifle with the lock broken, and wished me to mend it. He then handed me a horn, without a grain of powder in it, and wished me to fill it. I took the gun, and blew into the muzzle; and air passed freely through the touch-hole. "Ha!" thought I, "it is not charged; so Mr. Indian I have you on the hip." I quietly reached it to him, and he, seeing that I was not disposed to put it in order, took it and said nothing more about the matter.

We proceeded in silence until we reached the edge of a narrow stream, about two feet in depth, which ran across the route. Here the Indian paused, by which means I came up with him, and signified my wish to mount his horse to cross the water. He demurred at first, but I persisted; I had a loaded rifle; his was empty: so I gave myself airs, and "spoke as one having authority." At last, though with evident reluctance, he acceded to my request, and in another moment I was behind him on the horse, and upon the opposite side of the brook. I had been mounted only for a few moments; but I found the transition far from disagreeable. I was wearied with walking, and there was some-

thing highly pleasing in travelling upon other legs than my own.
I therefore quietly retained my seat; and though my companion
halted the horse, for the purpose of my dismounting, I was so
satisfied with my situation, that I pretended not to understand
his meaning, and listened to his words, and viewed his gestures
with an appearance of the greatest stolidity. At length, he determined to endeavour to shake me off. For this purpose he
wriggled and twisted in his seat. I, however, clung still more
closely to him; and the only one that appeared annoyed by the
action, was the horse, who expressed his displeasure by kicking up.

The Indian finding this unsuccessful, increased the speed
of his nag to a gallop—but in vain; I was as securely fixed behind,
as the Old Man of the Sea, to the shoulders of Sinbad. At length
he gave up, and checking his horse sprang off. As he did this I
slid forward into his seat. I felt some twinges respecting my un-
grateful conduct, but my weariness overcame them.

My next object was to gain something to eat; for notwithstanding the squirrel, I felt a vacuum within, that required filling. I observed that my fellow traveller carried a bundle of dried
venison, slung from his shoulder. I accordingly signified to him
that I had eaten nothing for two days—at the same time pointing
to the venison: but the fellow was obstinate; he shook his head,
and afterwards whenever I started the subject, he looked in a
different direction. Finding that fair means were of no avail, I
determined to try what foul could do. As I was mounted, I resolved that he should think I intended to scamper off with his
horse: so I thumped my rifle against his ribs, and scoured along
the trail at full gallop.

The moment I started, the Indian followed, with a speed that
almost equalled that of the pony; but unfortunately for himself,
his wind was soon exhausted. He then began to think of a compromise, and at last with much reluctance, loosed a piece of
the deer's flesh, and held it up towards me, at the same time
signifying by his gestures, that if I would stop, he would give

me a portion. This was all that I desired; and pulling in the horse, I received the venison, and dismounted—relinquishing the nag to his owner. He, however, thinking the treaty between us, not yet sufficiently ratified, immediately lit his pipe, and passed it to me for a second smoke. We then set out, and at dusk reached a small wood: here the Indian hobbled his horse, and throwing a few sticks together, he kindled a fire. He then offered me a small piece of venison, which he had broiled upon the coals; after which he drew his blanket round him, and stretched himself at full length on one side of the fire, while I threw myself across my rifle, on the other side. I must have slept for an hour. When I awoke it was intensely cold, the fire having burnt very low. My companion lay exactly as I left him when going to sleep; he did not seem to notice that the fire was expiring, nor did the cold seem to affect him.

I rose and stood over him; but he did not move. I then stirred him with my foot, and shouted to him—at the same time motioning to him, to assist in collecting wood to keep alive the fire. He apparently was [not] aware of my object, for all I could elicit, was a grunt; nor would he even open his eyes to look at me. So in no very pleasant humour, I went in search of fuel, taking my rifle with me.

I had not gone far, before I came upon his little devil of a horse. I was so much vexed with the master, that I could not help bestowing a thwack upon the animal, who came smelling up to me, with the air of an old acquaintance. With a loud snort, and a half attempt at a kick, he hobbled off, as well as the confined state of his legs would let him.

Hard of hearing, and difficult to rouse, as the Indian had been, when I attempted it, no sooner was the tramping sound of the horse's hoofs heard, as he crashed over the dead brushwood, than he sprang to his feet and came flying towards me with the swiftness of a deer.

I have but little doubt, that he thought I had served him an Indian trick, and was scouring off through the bushes with his nag. As it was, when he found him safe, he was for returning to stretch himself before the fire. I however arrested him, and motioned to him to assist in carrying a large limb to our sleeping place; which he did with evident reluctance; for he seemed to possess in a high degree the Indian aversion to labour.

About midnight he awakened me, and signified that it was time to be on the move. He first unhobbled his horse, and led him to the bank of the river, which was clayey and very steep, for the purpose of watering him. Here a violent contest took place between the nag and the Indian: the first being afraid to venture down the slippery descent, and the master endeavouring by coaxing and kicking to induce him to advance. He had planted his feet in the very edge of the bank, and although his nose and head were pulled out to a horizontal line, by the efforts of the Indian, the rest of his body was immoveable, as one of the trees around. The Indian then made signs to me to assist him, for he seemed determined that the horse should drink, whether thirsty or not. I did not feel in a very good humour with him, but as he seemed to wish it, I bestowed a few hearty thwacks upon the hinder parts of the animal, which seemed only to increase his desire to retrograde, instead of advancing. Finding this of no avail, I seized a small sapling, and placing it under his belly, made use of it as a lever, to press him sidewise over the bank. The pressure against his ribs, drove him within a foot of the edge. I placed the pole beyond the verge of the bank, and again made use of it as a lever; it pushed him still nearer. He made a violent effort to resist; but just then the Indian jerked his little halter violently, and over the horse went, treading upon the toes of his master, and sousing heels over head in the river, where he swam up and down, puffing and snorting. Several times he attempted to climb the bank; but rolled back, and floundered in the water. The Indian was now alarmed lest he should be drowned. But he at last succeeded in helping him up the steep, and being satisfied that his thirst was completely quenched, he once more hobbled him, and then signified that we should move forward. Before starting, however, he took from his shoulders his load of venison, and hung it upon a tree. I then followed him silently, though I could not imagine why he had left his venison, or why he travelled on foot, when he had a horse to carry him. We soon came to a river, across which, though full of ice, we waded,[2] and then started forward on a trail which led through a wood. Occasionally I took the lead; but the trail grew so indistinct, that I was obliged to give place to my companion, who always kept on without hesitation.

We had travelled about twelve miles, making many circuits and windings, and striking from one trail to another, until we emerged from the wood, and I found myself again near the bank of the Konzas river. Before me was a large house, with a court-yard in front. I sprang with joy through the unhung gate, and ran to the door. It was open; I shouted; my voice echoed through the rooms: but there was no answer. I walked in. The doors of the inner chambers were swinging from their hinges, and long grass was growing through the crevices of the floor. While I stood gazing around, an owl flitted by, and dashed out of an unglazed window. Again I shouted; but there was no answer: the place was desolate and deserted. I afterwards learned that this house had been built for the residence of the chief of the Konza tribe, but that the ground upon which it was situated, having been discovered to be within a tract, granted to some other tribe, the chief had deserted it, and it had been allowed to fall to ruin.[3]

My guide waited patiently until I finished my examination, and then again we pressed forward. Several times I was deceived by the howling of wolves, which I mistook for the baying of

2 Almost certainly the Sauterelle (Grasshopper), now the Delaware River.

3 According to John McCoy, writing in 1879, this stone building was about two miles northwest of the Kansas Agency. It had been built for White Plume, the Kansas chief, in 1827 or 1828 (J. J. Lutz, "Methodist Missions in Kansas," *Kansas Historical Society Collections*, Vol. IX [1905–1906], 195). In his 1830 journal, Isaac McCoy described it as being three miles from the agency (Barnes, "Journal of Isaac McCoy for the Exploring Expedition of 1830," *Kansas Historical Quarterly*, Vol. V [November, 1936], 352).

house-dogs; and when I was passing through some dark skirt of timber, and expected to come upon a human habitation, I would be disappointed, by seeing my guide once more launch out into the open prairie. Several times too, my hopes were excited by a light, glimmering in the darkness, which upon coming up, I would discover to proceed from the trunk of a tree, which had caught fire from the burning of the prairies.

Thus we kept on until near daylight, when we emerged from a thick forest, and came suddenly upon a small hamlet.[4] The barking of several dogs, who came flying out to meet us, convinced me that this time I was not mistaken. A light was shining through the crevices of a log cabin; I knocked at the door with a violence, that might have awakened one of the seven sleepers.

"Who dere—and vot de devil you vant?" screamed a little cracked voice from within.

It sounded like music to me. I stated my troubles. The door was opened; a head, garnished with a red night-cap, was thrust out, and after a little parley, I was admitted into the bed-room of the man, his Indian squaw, and a host of children. As, however, it was the only room in the house, it was also the kitchen. I had gone so long without food, that notwithstanding what I had eaten, the gnawings of hunger were excessive, and I had no

4 John McCoy (1879) located this settlement on the north bank of the Kansas River about seven or eight miles above Lawrence. In 1830, besides the houses of the agent and the blacksmith, there were those of Daniel Morgan Boone, the government farmer, and his family; of Clement Lessert, the interpreter, and his family; and of several half-blood families: Joe Jim, Gonvil, and others (Lutz, "Methodist Missions in Kansas," *Kansas Historical Society Collections*, Vol. IX [1905–1906], 195). In *The Hunters of the Prairie*, (I, 77–79) Irving described the hamlet in more detail: "It was a half savage white settlement. . . . Three cabins built of unbarked logs, and thrown together in the rudest style of architecture, composed the dwellings of the workmen belonging to the agency. A little apart from the rest stood a house of larger dimensions, but scarcely more finished in its construction. This was the dwelling of the agent. Attached to it was a large field of Indian corn, almost the only grain raised by a backwoodsman; and in front was a small yard, surrounded by a slender white railing. Not only the corn-field, but a large space around the hamlet was filled with burnt and scathed trunks, giving intimation that a luxuriant growth of giant forest-trees had once covered the spot, but had yielded to the unsparing inroads of man."

sooner mentioned my wants, than a fire was kindled, and in ten minutes a meal (I don't exactly know whether to call it breakfast, dinner, or supper) of hot cakes, venison, honey, and coffee, was placed before me, and disappeared with the rapidity of lightning. The squaw having seen me fairly started, returned to her couch. From the owner of the cabin, I learned that I was now at the Konza Agency, and that he was the blacksmith of the place.[5]

About sunrise I was awakened from a sound sleep, upon a bear-skin, by a violent knocking at the door. It was my Indian guide. He threw out broad hints respecting the service he had rendered me, and the presents he deserved. This I could not deny; but I had nothing to give. I soon found out, however, that his wants were moderate, and that a small present of powder would satisfy him; so I filled his horn, and he left the cabin apparently well pleased.

In a short time I left the house, and met the Konza Agent, General Clark, a tall, thin, soldier-like man, arrayed in an Indian hunting shirt, and an old fox-skin cap.[6]

[5] Gabriel Phillibert. John McCoy recorded his family as whites (Lutz, "Methodist Missions in Kansas," *Kansas Historical Society Collections*, Vol. IX [1905–1906], 195).

[6] In the 1888 edition (p. 337) Irving said that he had first met Marston G. Clark at Fort Leavenworth before setting out on the Pawnee expedition. The description of this agent in *The Hunters of the Prairie* (I, 80–81) is more detailed than in the *Indian Sketches*: "He was a tall thin man, of that hardened appearance which rather denotes extreme toughness, than great muscular strength. His hair was snowy white. His forehead was high and narrow, and his nose aquiline. His light blue eyes, half extinguished by two heavy lids, betokened calm reflection. His mouth was large, firmly set, and surmounted by two or three deeply-furrowed wrinkles. There was something in his look that betokened a man of resolution, bordering on obstinacy. He was dressed in a deer-skin hunting-shirt, trimmed, after the Indian fashion, with a border of bear's hair, and ornamented with porcupine quills. His pantaloons were of coarse cloth, such as is universally worn by frontier men. In his hand he held a large cap of fox-skin, so constructed that the snarling head of the animal was preserved, and appeared to be keeping guard over the cranium of the wearer." Since Irving was now writing a novel, it is uncertain how much of this description was fact, how much fancy.

General Clark and the missionaries did not much like each other. The Presbyterian W. D. Smith, discussing the prospects of a mission among the Kansas, wrote: "He is an open and avowed infidel, and I may add, 'foul mouthed'—a man

He received me cordially, and I remained with him all day, during which time he talked upon metaphysics; discussed politics, and fed me upon sweet potatoes. In speaking of my guide, I found that he had departed after receiving a large present from the Agent, to whom he stated that he had eaten nothing for twenty-four hours. I spoke of the deer's-flesh he had left behind.

"The lying rascal!" said the General, "he said he was starving."

I spoke of the Indian pony.

"What colour was he?" asked the General.

"Black; with short mane, and crop ears."

"My God! that's my horse," exclaimed he, "stolen four days ago. What a d——d villain that Konza is!"

At night the General furnished me with a mule, and kindly accompanied me to the garrison, which was forty miles distant, and which we reached on the following morning a little before daylight.

As I passed one of the out-houses in riding up to the cantonment, I perceived an Indian leaning against one of the door-posts. "Ugh!" exclaimed he, starting forward; and the next moment my hand was grasped in the cordial, but iron gripe of the Iotan chief.

The party had reached the garrison on the evening previous; and the whole wild band, both Pawnees and Otoes, were now under the protection of the whites.[7]

---

of inordinate self conceit, and (of course) of a very little mind. As might be expected of such a man, he is in heart opposed to all religious instruction and expresses himself as having no confidence in schools or any attempt to civilize the Indians. He says however he will do what he can in favour of an establishment, and I am led to believe he would not secretly oppose missionary operations, if the missionary should be so fortunate as to get into his favour, which I did not find very difficult . . ." (Smith to Swift, Shawanoe Villages, Kanzas River, July 29th, 1833). Washington Irving, who met him a year earlier at Independence, Missouri, noted in his journals that Clark "thinks the clergymen the only class of people on earth that he hates—thinks we ought not to set our faces ag[ain]st Indians stealing horses—must not shut up only road left them to honour & promotion" (McDermott [ed.], *Western Journals of Washington Irving*, 90).

7 At this point in the 1888 edition (pp. 340–49) Irving added a chapter:

[CHAPTER LII]

Assembling of Council—Council

Messengers had been sent in every direction, to summon the neighbouring tribes, to meet their ancient enemy, the Pawnees, in council;[1] and the day arrived upon which these rival nations, who had never before met except in deadly hostility, were to mingle in peaceful ceremonial.

The different tribes had been for several days collecting round the garrison, and had pitched their wild camps in the adjacent groves. There had always existed a bitter hostility, between many of the civilized and savage tribes. For this reason, especial care had been taken, to keep them separate, until by the influence of the council, this cessation of hostilities, should be converted into a permanent peace.

Early in the morning, the loud report of a piece of artillery bellowed through the woods, echoing in the deep forest upon the opposite side of the Missouri. This was the signal for the assembling of the council.[2] In a few moments the warriors of the different tribes, were seen leaving their camps, and moving for the place appointed, beneath several of the large trees, in front of the quarters of the officers.

First came the Delawares, dressed for the occasion, glittering

On reaching the fort he found that Ellsworth, in haste to meet the Indians gathering for the peace council, had pushed rapidly on with the best horses and that Dunlop had remained some fifty miles behind to come on as soon as the strength of the remaining horses would permit. Irving then accompanied two soldiers carrying supplies to Dunlop and returned with his friend to the fort.

1 That is, Ellsworth had sent his summons out before leaving for the Pawnee country.

2 Date of the council opening is unknown. On November 6 Ellsworth wrote Herring that "the hostile tribes are fast assembling here to make peace." Two days later: "Peace will be concluded at this council between the hostile Indians upon terms highly satisfactory; the wampum has been exchanged, but the speeches not finished." The articles of peace were signed by most of the tribes on November 12 (*Sen. Doc. 512,* IV, 654, 659, 728).

with trinkets; their silver ornaments glistening in the sunshine, and their gay ribands fluttering in the wind. They were a gaudy, effeminate-looking race. Yet beneath all their frippery of dress, lurked that indomitable courage, and that thirst for glory, which not even intemperance, and their intercourse with the whites could destroy. Behind the band, followed the proud Delaware warrior Sou-wah-nock. It was he that first kindled the torch of war, between his own tribe and the Pawnees, and led the expedition that sacked the Pawnee village. He was without ornament, except a heavy silver plate, resting upon his calico hunting-shirt. He was not tall, but muscular, and his eye was as searching as an eagle's. There was a proud curl upon his lip; and withal, an iron firmness marked his whole deportment. He seemed to think that the whole weight of anger of the Pawnee nation, was about to descend upon himself, but was ready to meet it. He did not deny that he had incited his nation to the outrage, upon the Pawnee town. Nay, he gloried in it; and was now ready to meet them in friendship, or as enemies. He knew that his nation looked up to him, and determined that no act of his should ever sink him in their opinion.[3]

After the Delawares, followed the Shawanese, headed by the same portly personage who had greeted us when we entered as strangers, into the Indian country. The same enormous pair of black spectacles were seated astride of his nose, and from his

[3] The trouble had begun somewhat earlier than these remarks indicate. On April 24, 1832, William Clark wrote to the Secretary of War, on information from Richard M. Cummins, Delaware agent, that "the Panis [had] attacked a hunting party of Delawares, accompanied by Shawanock and Ponshees, (two of their chiefs,) the latter of whom, and two others, were reported to have been killed. . . . Shawanock has returned with the party, bringing in one wounded man. This party was warned by the agent against hunting in the Panis country, notwithstanding which, they went in October last" (*Sen. Doc. 512*, III, 306). Having waited for redress until the summer of 1833 (see n. 1, p. 6), Souwahnock led a party of twenty warriors to the Grand Pawnee village, burnt the lodges, and destroyed the corn. Souwahnock (The White Man) and Pooshies (The Cat) had both signed the Delaware Treaty of September 24, 1829 (Kappler, *Indian Affairs, Laws and Treaties*, II, 305). Souwahnock was not the chief of the tribe. Nine other Delawares were present at the council (*Sen. Doc. 512*, IV, 728).

whole appearance, it is probable that he had not undressed from the time that we had last saw him, some four months previous. At his heels followed the same little potatoe-headed Indian, who had also met us on the same occasion.[4] Behind them, came the gaudy warriors of the tribe, reeking with paint, shining with tin ornaments, and flaunting with ribands. These seated themselves beside the Delawares.

Then followed the rest of the migrating tribes; the Peorias, the Piankashaws, the ragged Pottawattomies, and the lazy Kickapoos, who all in turn seated themselves, among their civilized brethren.[5]

They had scarcely become stationary, when the Otoes made their appearance. They moved in Indian-file over the green, headed by their sagacious old chief the Iotan. They walked swiftly and silently, and ranged themselves at a little distance from the more civilized, though less noble band, which had already collected. A few moments more, and the wild troop of Pawnees were seen approaching. They were muffled in their shaggy robes, and marched forward with a heavy though smothered tread. In front of them strode the giant form of the Wild Horse; his savage features not rendered any the less hideous by a drunken frolic, in which he had been engaged on the day previous. His long hair hung tangled round his head and shoulders. He wore no ornaments, and his body as usual was smeared with red ochre.

4 Chap. III. Eight Shawnees signed the articles of peace (*Sen. Doc. 512*, IV, 728). Lah-to-wah (John Perry) and Pew-sah-tah (William Perry) were the principal chiefs. Much about this tribe will be found in Joab Spencer, "The Shawnee Indians: Their Customs, Traditions and Folk-Lore," *Kansas Historical Society Collections*, Vol. X (1907–1908), 382–96. At this time they numbered 1,250 (*H. Rep. 474*, p. 87).

5 The peace treaty signers on November 12 included, in addition to the Delawares and Shawnees, two Kickapoos (Pat-sa-che-haw, the chief, and Kan-ne-kuh-kah, the prophet), two Potawatomi, two Ottawas, four Peorias and Kaskaskias, five Weas, four Otoes (She-moh-ne-kah-say or Iotan, Ah-che-kah-sucker or He That Strikes the Osages, Keh-gah-ne-gah-rah or He That Judges for Himself, and Chak-wong-guh-he-gah or Buffalo Chief), one Omaha, and four from each of the four Pawnee tribes (whose names have already been given in n. 2, p. 194). Since the Piankashaws signed at the Shawnee Agency on November 21, it is unlikely that they were present at the council (*Sen. Doc. 512*, IV, 728–30).

The whole of his enormous chest was bared, and exposed to the cold chilling air of a frosty November morning. Behind him followed the graceful, though stern form of the Long Hair. He walked to his allotted place, without appearing to notice the congregated band of civilized Indians. There were several other chiefs in the train, and after them followed the whole savage herd, from the four Pawnee villages.

These stationed themselves directly opposite the Delawares. Stern looks passed between them, and burning feelings were at work in their hearts. There they sat brooding over past wrongs. Enemies from the time that the Delawares had left the eastern states, they were now assembled to crush their bitter feelings, to put an end to that dark hatred which had hitherto existed between them, and to view each other, in a strange and novel light—that of friends. A total revulsion was to take place in their feelings. Old habits, old associations, were to be blotted out; deep-rooted prejudices were to be removed, and hands which before had clenched each other, only in the death-grapple, were now to be clasped in the warm pressure of friendship.

Several days before the commencement of the meeting, a trifling incident was near putting an end to the incipient peace.

The little tribe of Delawares, who muster but a hundred and fifty warriors at most,[6] had always considered themselves the source from whence sprang the numerous and powerful tribes scattered throughout the whole of North America. It is probable that this opinion is founded upon some tradition still current among them, respecting the power and antiquity of their fore-fathers. These, were the Lenni Lenape, who, coming up from the south, seated themselves upon the eastern shores, and were afterwards known to the whites by the name of Delawares. They are among the oldest of the tribes of which tradition speaks. The remnant of this race, in pursuance of their fatherly dogma, had now appropriated to themselves the title of great grand-

6 The Delawares numbered at this time 835; the Pawnees 10,000 to 12,000 (*H. Rep. 474*, pp. 87, 131).

fathers to the whole Indian race.[7] Among the host of their descendants were numbered those most unfilial of all great grandchildren, the rebellious Pawnees. Notwithstanding the injunctions of obedience to parents, which have been laid down in all quarters of the globe, this nation had been unwilling to submit to the fatherly corrections, bestowed upon their tribe by their great ancestors. Nor is it to be wondered at; for they consisted, in quietly killing and scalping, all who fell in their way, and helping them forward in their journey towards the bright hunting grounds—a theme upon which an Indian is for ever harping, during the whole period of his probation here. In addition to the bitter feelings created by these hostilities, the Pawnees, looked upon this little handful of warriors with the most sovereign contempt. Like many other undutiful children, they were ashamed of their great grandparents, and denied that they had ever sprung from the "Delaware dogs," or that a drop of Delaware blood was mingled with that which coursed through their veins. They concluded their expression of ill will, by refusing to commence the council, if they were to be looked upon as the descendants of that race. The Delawares, on the other hand, were equally obstinate. They insisted on adopting the refractory Pawnees as their great grandchildren, and that the latter should acknowledge them as their great grandparents.[8]

[7] Back home in the East, the Delawares were accustomed to being addressed as "grandfather" by all the other Algonquian tribes (Hodge [ed.], *Handbook of American Indians*, I, 385). Washington Irving, the year before, had noted: "The various western tribes call the Delaware their grandfather & mediator. If one kills another, a friend, relative of the murderer, hastens to the Delaware who interposes & prescribes the quantity of wampum to cover the deceased. . . . The bravest and finest race is the Delawares. They are called the *fathers*—all the others give them preference. . . . all their equipments of the best—their camp kettles of brass. They are clean, neat, civil, generously obliging, light hearted, gay, fearless —go to the Rocky Mountains in bands of 20 men—have frequent skirmishes. Excellent hunters—when they go out to kill a deer you may be sure of their succeeding" (McDermott [ed.], *Western Journals of Washington Irving*, 87, 164).

[8] "The Delawares claim to be the grand fathers of all the tribes around here; a brave of the Delawares has been slain by the Pawnees, and it has hitherto been impossible to assuage the grief of the friends of the deceased. The Delawares demanded of me, in private council, $1,000 for each scalp taken from their nation

For a short time the commissioner was perplexed. But at length, privately assembling the chiefs of the Pawnees, he endeavoured to overcome their prejudices by means of fair words, and finally succeeded in satisfying their scrupulous pride. He begged that for the sake of peace, the Delawares should be humoured, although he acknowledged to the Pawnees, that he knew there was no ground for their claim of relationship. At the same time, he added, it was so absurd in itself that no person would for a moment credit, that so brave and powerful a people as the Pawnees, should have sprung from so paltry a stock as the Delawares. The chiefs smiled grimly as they received the pleasing unction of flattery, and at length consented, though with wry faces, to submit to the degrading appellation until the council should be ended, and the treaty ratified. They then threw out sage hints, which if translated literally, would amount nearly to the same thing, as sending the Delawares to the devil.

These preliminaries had been settled before the day of council. The great grandchildren, reversing the usual order of things, no longer disowned their great grandfathers; though farther than the mere title, there was no display of kindly feeling. The two bands sat opposite each other, with the same grim expression of countenances, that might have been expected from so many wild cats. Each seemed fearful to make a single friendly step in advance, lest he should compromise the dignity of his tribe. After a short time the commissioner rose up, and stated the object of the meeting:—that war had long enough, been raging among them; and that the different tribes had now assembled for the purpose of uniting themselves in the bonds of friendship. He then entered explicitly, into the conditions of the intended peace.[9]

---

before a treaty could be made. I have tried to show them the impropriety of the demand; the great sufferings of one village of the Pawnees; the cession of the Pawnees of the land in dispute; and, also, the provision for a large common hunting ground south of the Platte river. I now believe that by to-morrow noon the Pawnees and Delawares will shake hands" (Ellsworth to Herring, Fort Leavenworth, November 6, 1833, *Sen. Doc. 512*, IV, 654).

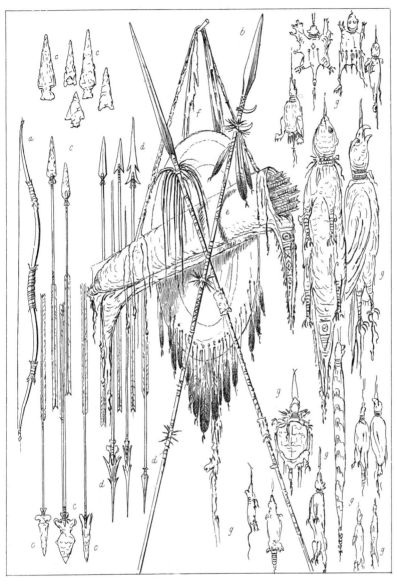

From George Catlin, North American Indians, i, *Plate* 18.

Indian War Equipment and Medicine Bags

When he had ended, different warriors of each tribe addressed the council. They all professed the greatest friendship for their enemies, and poured out very penitential speeches, bewailing their past transgressions, and winding up, by throwing the whole blame, upon the shoulders of some neighbouring tribe.

For a short time the potentates of several little nations, which had barely inhabitants enough to hang a name upon, eased their own importance by speaking.[10] The Delaware warrior Sou-wah-nock then rose. He spoke of the destruction of the Grand Pawnee village. He did not deny his agency in the deed. "The Pawnees," said he, "met my young men upon the hunt, and slew them. I have had my revenge. Let them look at their town. I found it filled with lodges: I left it a heap of ashes." The whole of his speech was of the same bold, unflinching character, and was closed in true Indian style. "I am satisfied," said he, "I am not afraid to avow the deeds that I have done, for I am Sou-wah-nock, a Delaware warrior." When he had finished, he presented a string of wampum to the Wild Horse, as being the most distinguished warrior of the Pawnee nation. When the slight bustle of giving, and receiving the present, had been finished, the chief of the Republican village rose to answer his warrior enemy.[11]

His speech abounded with those wild bursts of eloquence, which peculiarly mark the savages of North America, and concluded in a manner, which spoke highly of his opinion of what a warrior should be. "I have promised to the Delawares," said he, "the friendship of my tribe. I respect my promise, and I cannot lie, for I am a Pawnee chief."

When the Delawares had spoken, our little fat friend from the Shawnee village rose. After frequent expectorations, he at

9 This was a peace treaty between the tribes, not between them and the United States. The terms are recorded in *Sen. Doc. 512*, IV, 727–28.

10 No speeches at nor minutes of this council were published in *Sen. Doc. 512* nor found in the records of the Office of Indian Affairs in the National Archives.

11 Irving seems to have slipped here. Why the Republican village when the attack had been made on the Grand, and why imply that Wild Horse is a Republican?

length succeeded in clearing a passage for the escape of his voice. He contrived with great difficulty to wheeze through a speech of about ten minutes in length. There appeared to be but two ideas in the whole of the address; and when he had thoroughly belaboured one, he most assiduously returned to the other. After repeating them again and again, with the addition of a new dress for each time, he seated himself, perfectly convinced that he had thrown a great deal of light upon the subject.

There was a strange contrast between the deportment of the civilized, and savage Indians. The first, from long intercourse with the whites, had acquired many of their habits. Their iron gravity had yielded to a more mercurial temperament. Even in the midst of the council they gave free vent to their merriment, and uttered their gibes and jests. They were constantly on the move, coming and going to and from the place of assembly, and paying but little heed to the deliberations.

The Pawnees sat unmoved, listening in silence and with profound attention, to the addresses of those who spoke. They rarely uttered a word, and the only smile which curled their lips, was one of scorn at the frivolous deportment of their enemies.

From early in the morning, till near sunset, the council continued. They then adjourned until the following day; in order that a few little potentates, who considered themselves the luminaries of their respective villages, might receive an opportunity to display their eloquence.

[CHAPTER LIII]

Pawnee Dance—Delaware Visitors

In the evening it was determined, to bring the Delawares and the Pawnees together as friends, for as yet they had held no intercourse. A large fire was accordingly built before the outhouses in which the Pawnees had taken up their quarters, and the wild troop sallied forth, prepared to commence one of their national dances, round the flame. A group of eight or ten savage looking fellows, seated themselves a little distance off, furnished with a drum and rattle. They commenced a song, accompanied by their rude instruments. For a time there was no movement among the Pawnees, who stood huddled in a large, condensed crowd. Suddenly one of them, a tall muscular savage, sprang into the middle of the circle, and gazed around with a hurried air, then with a loud yell he commenced his dance. He jumped slowly round the fire, with a kind of zig-zag step: at every leap uttering a deep guttural "Ugh!" occasionally accompanied with a rattling sound, from the very bottom of his lungs. His comrades looked on silently, but with intense interest. They were a savage group; face and body begrimed with paint; their fierce features reflecting the flame, their teeth bared, and every brow knotted into a frown. Head rose behind head, and gleaming eyes were seen peering through the living mass, until those farthest off were hid by the darkness.

When the first warrior had made two or three circles about the fire, a second left the crowd and sprang forward in the dance; a third followed, and a fourth, until about twenty were flitting swiftly round, and joining in the song. Occasionally they stopped short in their course, and uttered a loud shrill yell, which was taken up by the whole surrounding horde, until the very trees echoed to the sound. At one moment they moved swiftly forward, and at another their steps were slow and wearied. As we watched their fierce, earnest faces, the forms of some wrapped in shaggy robes, the painted bodies of others, writhing in the dance, and then turned to the silent, and equally savage group of lookers on, it required no great stretch of the imagination, to fancy them a host of evil spirits, busied in fiendish revel.

While they were thus engaged, the crowd separated and revealed a Delaware watching their movements. Behind him were about twenty more of the same tribe. No sooner had the Pawnees caught sight of them, than they retired. Old prejudices could not be rooted out at once, and though the dancers remained at their employment, the rest of the tribe drew off in a sullen and haughty group, and stood watching the countenances of their *quondam* enemies.

This continued during the whole evening. As it grew late, group after group of the Pawnees left the fire, and retired into their dwelling. The Delawares soon followed their example, and although their visit had continued for several hours, I fear it did but little towards removing that ancient venom, which, in spite of their apparent friendship, was rankling in their hearts.

[CHAPTER LIV]

Konza Council—White Plume—Tappage Chief— Treaty—Interpreter—Departure

On the following morning, the loud report of a piece of artillery announced the hour of council. Once more the different tribes left their respective encampments, and assembled at the place of meeting. Scarcely, however, had they collected, before a long train of warriors were seen stringing over the distant prairie— making for the cantonment. They approached swiftly until they reached the quarters of the officers. They were clothed in white blankets; each man carried a rifle. They were a band from the Konza nation, come to attend the council and settle the terms of peace.[1] In front of the troop was the White Plume, enveloped in a large drab-coloured over coat. This piece of dress deprived him altogether of that dignity of appearance which had marked

[1] Irving has taken liberty with facts to make his narrative more compact. On November 14 Ellsworth wrote to Herring: "All the neighboring tribes have made peace and returned home, except the Kansas and Ioways. It was too expensive to detain them; those who yet come in and sign the articles are equally parties. The Kansas have just arrived. . . . The Ioways are expected to-morrow. A limited delegation of Pawnees, Ottoes, and Omahaws accompany me to Fort Gibson, to make peace with the Osages, Creeks, Cherokees, &c." (*Sen. Doc. 512*, IV, 702–703).

him upon our first meeting. He now bore a strong resemblance in form and gracefulness, to a walking hogshead. However, he seemed perfectly satisfied with his attire: and in truth, I believe there was scarcely a Pawnee who did not envy him the possession of this cumbersome article of apparel.

The appearance of this chief, and of a delegation from his tribe, had been anxiously expected.[2] They were more venomous in their hate against the Pawnees, than any other of the neighbouring Indians, and their hostility had been marked by deeds of a more bloody character. The Pawnees sat in silence, but with looks of smothered ferocity, as they saw them approach. However, they evinced no hostile feelings, other than those conveyed by their glances.

After a short conference with their agent, the Konzas withdrew from the green, and encamped in the prairie, at a few hundred yards' distance. The council then proceeded. The different chiefs and warriors of the small tribes of the vicinity, addressed the Pawnees—all agreeing to bury their hostility, and regard them as friends. These offers were most thankfully received by the Pawnees, though one of them afterwards remarked to the interpreter, "that they had now made peace with several nations with whom they had never been at war, and of whom they had never heard, until they rose to address them in council." This was little to be wondered at; as many of them were most pitifully represented; and two or three little, pursy, short-winded fellows, dressed in dirty calico, and bedraggled ribands, composed the whole of their delegation, and probably the whole of their tribe.

The deliberations lasted during the whole day: for as these Indians had no particular injuries to dwell upon, they confined themselves to things in general; and as this was a subject that would bear to be expatiated upon, every man continued his address until he had exhausted his wind. The Pawnees listened

2 White Plume and ten other Kansas signed the treaty on November 16 (*Sen. Doc. 512*, IV, 731).

with exemplary patience; though I doubt if there was one who regretted when the last speaker had finished.

The morning following, the Pawnees and Konzas had a meeting to settle their difficulties. A large chamber in the garrison had been selected for the purpose. About ten o'clock in the forenoon they assembled. The two bands seated themselves upon long wooden benches, on opposite sides of the room. There was a strong contrast between them. The Konzas had a proud, noble air, and their white blankets as they hung in loose and graceful folds around them, had the effect of classic drapery.

The Pawnees had no pride of dress. They were wrapped in shaggy robes, and sat in silence—wild and uncouth in their appearance, with scowling brows, and close pressed mouths.

At length the speaking commenced. First rose the White Plume. He had boasted to his tribe, that he would relate such things, in his speech, as should cause the Pawnees to wince. With true Indian cunning, at first, in order that he might conciliate the favourable opinion of those present, he spoke in praise of the whites—expressing his high opinion of them. After this, he gradually edged off, into a philippic against the Pawnee nation, representing them as a mean and miserly race—perfidious, and revengeful. There was a hushed silence among his own people as he spoke, and every eye was fastened upon the grim group opposite. The White Plume went on; and still the deepest silence reigned through the room: that of the Konzas arose from apprehension: the silence of the Pawnees was the hushed brooding of fury.

The chief of the Tappage village was sitting directly opposite the speaker; his eye was dark as midnight: his teeth were bared, and both hands were tightly grasped round his own throat; but he remained silent until the speech had finished. When the White Plume had taken his seat, half a dozen Pawnees sprang to their feet; but the Tappage chief waved them down: three times did he essay to speak, and as often, did he fail. He rubbed his hands across his throat, to keep down his anger; then stepping out, and fixing his eye on that of the Konza chief—in the calm, quiet voice of smothered rage, he commenced his answer: he proceeded; he grew more and more excited—indulging in a vein of biting irony. The White Plume quailed, and his eye drooped, beneath the searching, scornful glance of his wild enemy. Still the Pawnee went on: he represented the injury which first kindled the war between the two nations. "My young men," said he, "visited the Konzas as friends: the Konzas treated them as enemies. They were strangers in the Konza tribe, and the Konzas fell upon them, and slew them—and concealed their death." He then entered into the particulars of the quarrel, which unfortunately for the Konzas, were strongly against them. The chief of the latter tribe, received the answer with great philosophy; nor did he attempt to utter any thing in reply. Perhaps, too, he did not wish to invite a second attack, from so rough a quarter. When the Pawnee had finished, the commissioner interposed, and after a short time, harmony was restored, and several of the inferior chiefs made their harangues. They were of a more calm and conciliating nature, and gradually tended to soothe the inflamed feelings of their foes. The council lasted until sunset, when the terms of the treaty were finally adjusted.

On this occasion I was made sensible of the justice of the complaint generally made, by those who have had public negotiations with the savage tribes, of the insufficiency of the interpreters through whom they are obliged to receive the sentiments and language of the Indians. They are with few exceptions, ignorant and illiterate. Those we employed, spoke a wretched French patois, and a still more wretched English.[3] On such, even the high imaginative vein, the poetical thought, which run through Indian eloquence, is entirely lost. There was not a savage who addressed us, who did not at times, clothe his ideas in

[3] The interpreters were A. Shane (Shawnees), James Connor (Delawares), Baptiste Peoria (Peorias, Kaskaskias, and Weas), Peter Cadue (Kickapoos, Ottawas, and Potawatomi), Louis La Chapelle (Pawnees), Clement Lessert (Kansas) (*Sen. Doc. 512*, IV, 728-31).

beautiful attire, and make use of wild and striking similes, drawn from the stores of his only instructress, nature. This we ascertained from some persons present of cultivated minds, and who were well versed in the Indian tongues. As to the interpreters, they reduced every thing to a bald, disjointed jargon.[4]

On the day following the council, the articles of peace were signed, and most of the tribes departed for their respective homes.[5] A few of the Pawnees and Otoes remained to accompany the Commissioner to the village of the Osages, for the purpose of negotiating a peace with that tribe; with whom they had long been at deadly enmity.

Here then I will conclude this series of Indian Sketches; for the council being ended and my curiosity satisfied, I determined to return homeward on the following day. A feeling of sadness came over me as I prepared to leave those, with whom I had for months associated.[6] However different in dispositions and feelings, we had until then, been united by a link of sympathy. We had led the same life; viewed the same scenes, and undergone the same privations. For months together one tent had sheltered us, and we had eaten from the same board. A rough, untrammeled friendship had sprung up between us, increasing with the distance between ourselves and our homes, and strengthening as we retired farther from the abode of civilized man.

But now we had returned from our wanderings, and were once more in the circle of our fellows. Still old recollections bound us together by a golden tie, that was painful to sever; and although my home with all its attractions rose in my fancy,

---

4 "To give an instance of this—One of the chiefs, in speaking of their treaty, said he was so much pleased at meeting his old foes as friends, 'That it made his bosom glow with warmth.' Interpreter's version: 'He say, "he so glad, he sweat a heap." ' " (Irving, *Indian Sketches*, 1888, p. 364).

5 See n. 1, p. 250. It is possible that Irving meant November 16, not November 12.

6 Irving may have left on November 17. At least he was not present at the Shawnee Agency to witness the signatures of the Piankashaws on November 21, though he had witnessed the main treaty on November 12 and the Kansas signatures on November 16 (*Sen. Doc. 512*, IV, 729, 731, 732).

yet I felt sad, when one of the orderlies informed me that all was ready.

I shook hands with my friends and comrades of the wilderness, and mounting my mule, with a heavy heart, turned my back upon Leavenworth.

THE END

Sources Consulted

MANUSCRIPTS

Chouteau-Papin Collection. Missouri Historical Society, St. Louis.

Ellsworth, Edward A., to Chauncey Goodrich, Jr., Fort Leavenworth, August 8, 1833. Goodrich Collection, Yale University Library.

———, to Chauncey Goodrich, Fort Leavenworth, August 28, 1833. Goodrich Collection, Yale University Library.

———, to John Treat Irving, Jr., Fort Gibson, Arkansaw, January 7, 1833 [i.e., 1834]. Collection of Harold Irving.

———, to John Treat Irving, Jr., Fayetteville, Ark. Terr., May 22, 1835. Collection of Harold Irving.

Ellsworth, Henry L. Documents relating to the visit of H. L. Ellsworth to the Pawnee and other Tribes in 1833 from Western Superintendency, Upper Missouri, and Treaty Files. Office of Indian Affairs, The National Archives. (Some of these letters were printed in *Sen. Doc. 512*, Vol. IV.)

Graham, Richard. Papers. Missouri Historical Society, St. Louis.

Irving, Washington, to Col. Thomas Aspinwall, New York, May 31, 1835. Henry E. Huntington Library and Art Gallery, San Marino.

McCoy, Isaac. Journals and Letters. Kansas Historical Society, Topeka.

Smith, Rev. W. D. Letters from the Shawnee Village, 1833. Presbyterian Historical Society, Philadelphia.

CONGRESSIONAL DOCUMENTS

Correspondence on the Subject of the Emigration of Indians, between the 30th November, 1831, and 27th December, 1833. 23 Cong., 1 sess., *Sen. Doc. 512*. 5 vols. Serial Nos. 244–48.

Regulating the Indian Department, May 20, 1834. 23 Cong., 1 sess., *H. Rep. 474*. Serial No. 263.

PRINTED

Allis, Samuel. "Forty Years among the Indians and on the Eastern Borders of Nebraska," *Nebraska Historical Society Transactions and Reports,* Vol. II (1887), 133–66. See also "Letters Concerning the Presbyterian Mission in the Pawnee Country."

Atkinson's Casket (Philadelphia), Vol. I (October, 1827), 392–93.

Barnes, Lela. "Journal of Isaac McCoy for the Exploring Expedition of 1830," *Kansas Historical Quarterly,* Vol. V (November, 1936), 339–77.

Beers, Henry P. *The Western Military Frontier, 1815–1846.* Philadelphia, University of Pennsylvania Press, 1935.

Berryman, Jerome C. "A Circuit Rider's Frontier Experiences," *Kansas Historical Society Collections,* Vol. XVI (1923–25), 177–226.

Carleton, J. Henry. *The Prairie Logbooks: Dragoon Campaigns to the Pawnee Villages in 1844, and to the Rocky Mountains in 1845* (ed. by Louis Pelzer). Chicago, The Caxton Club, 1943.

Catlin, George. *Illustrations of the Manners, Customs, and Condition of the North American Indians: in a Series of Letters and Notes Written during Eight Years of Travel and Adventure among the Wildest and Most Remarkable Tribes Now Existing* (7th ed.). 2 vols. London, H. G. Bohn, 1848.

Chittenden, Hiram Martin, and Alfred Talbot Richardson. *Life, Letters and Travels of Father Pierre-Jean De Smet, S. J., 1841–1873.* 4 vols. New York, Francis P. Harper, 1905.

"Cholera Epidemics in St. Louis," *Glimpses of the Past* (Missouri Historical Society), Vol. III (March, 1936), 45–76.

Cooke, Philip St. George. *Scenes and Adventures in the Army.* Philadelphia, Lindsay & Blakiston, 1857.

Culin, Stewart. *Games of the North American Indians* (Bureau of American Ethnology *24th Annual Report* [1902–1903]). Washington, D. C., 1907.

Cullum, George W. *Biographical Register of the Officers and Graduates of the U. S. Military Academy at West Point.* 2 vols. New York, D. Van Nostrand, 1868.

Densmore, Frances. *Pawnee Music* (Bureau of American Ethnology *Bulletin 93*). Washington, D. C., 1927.

DeZurko, Edward R. "A Report and Remarks on Cantonment Leavenworth," *Kansas Historical Quarterly,* Vol. XV (November, 1947), 353–59.

Dictionary of American Biography (DAB). 20 vols. New York, Charles Scribner's Sons, 1928–36.

Dictionary of American English (DAE). 4 vols. Chicago, University of Chicago Press, 1938–43.

Donaldson, Thomas. *The George Catlin Indian Gallery in the U. S. National Museum (Smithsonian Institution), with Memoir and Statistics* (Smithsonian Institution *Annual Report for 1885*). Washington, D. C., 1886.

Dorsey, George A. *Traditions of the Skidi Pawnee (Memoirs of the American Folklore Society,* VIII). Boston and New York, Houghton, Mifflin and Co., 1904.

Dunbar, John. See "Letters Concerning the Presbyterian Mission in the Pawnee Country."

Dunbar, John B. "The Pawnee Indians: Their History and Ethnology, Their Habits and Customs," *Magazine of American History,* Vol. IV (April, 1880), 241–81; Vol. V (November, 1880), 321–42; Vol. VIII (November, 1882), 734–54.

Fletcher, Alice C., and Francis La Flesche. *The Omaha Tribe* (Bureau of American Ethnology *27th Annual Report* [1905–1906]). Washington, D. C., 1911.

Ford, Lemuel. "Journal [of Dodge's Dragoon Expedition, 1835]" (ed. by Louis Pelzer), *Mississippi Valley Historical Review,* Vol. XII (1925–26), 550–79.

———. "A Summer on the Prairie," *Army and Navy Chronicle,* Vol. II (May and June, 1836), 277–78, 292–93, 311–12, 321–22, 337–38, 363–64, 369–70, 385–86; Vol. III (July, 1836), 1–2, 17–18, 30–31.

Foreman, Carolyn Thomas. "General Bennet Riley," *Chronicles of Oklahoma,* Vol. XIX (September, 1941), 225–44.

Foreman, Grant. "The Life of Montfort Stokes in the Indian Territory," *North Carolina Historical Review,* Vol. XVI (October, 1939), 373–403.

Foster, William Omer. "The Career of Montfort Stokes in North Carolina," *North Carolina Historical Review,* Vol. XVI (October, 1939), 237–72.

———. "The Career of Montfort Stokes in Oklahoma," *Chronicles of Oklahoma,* Vol. XVIII (March, 1940), 35–52.

Garraghan, Gilbert J. *Catholic Beginnings in Kansas City, Missouri.* Chicago, Loyola University Press, 1920.

Grinnell, George Bird. *Pawnee Hero Stories and Folk-Tales, with*

Notes on the Origin, Customs and Character of the Pawnee People. New York, Forest and Stream Publishing Co., 1889.

Heitman, Francis B. *Historical Register and Dictionary of the United States Army.* 2 vols. Washington, D. C., Government Printing Office, 1903.

Hodge, Frederick Webb (ed.). *Handbook of American Indians North of Mexico* (Bureau of American Ethnology *Bulletin 30*). 2 vols. Washington, D. C., 1907–10.

Hunt, Elvid. *History of Fort Leavenworth, 1827–1927.* Fort Leavenworth, Kansas, The General Service Schools Press, 1926 [*sic*].

Hyde, George E. *The Pawnee Indians.* Denver, University of Denver Press, 1951.

Irving, John Treat, Jr. *The Hunters of the Prairie, or The Hawk Chief, A Tale of the Indian Country.* 2 vols. London, Richard Bentley, 1837.

———. *Indian Sketches, Taken during an Expedition to the Pawnee Tribes.* 2 vols. Philadelphia, Carey, Lea and Blanchard, 1835.

———. *Indian Sketches, Taken during an Expedition to the Pawnee and Other Tribes of American Indians.* 2 vols. London, John Murray, 1835.

———. *Indian Sketches Taken during a U. S. Expedition to Make Treaties with the Pawnee and Other Tribes of Indians in 1833.* New York, G. P. Putnam's Sons, 1888.

Irving, Pierre M. *The Life and Letters of Washington Irving.* 4 vols. London, Richard Bentley, 1852–64.

James, Edwin. *Account of an Expedition from Pittsburgh to the Rocky Mountains Performed in the Years 1819, 1820 . . . under the Command of Major S. H. Long* (Vols. XIV–XVII in Reuben Gold Thwaites [ed.], *Early Western Travels, 1748–1846* [*q.v.*]).

Kappler, Charles J. *Indian Affairs, Laws and Treaties.* 4 vols. Washington, D. C., Government Printing Office, 1903.

Kingsbury, G. P. "Journal of the March of a Detachment of Dragoons, under the Command of Colonel Dodge, during the Summer of 1835," *American State Papers, Military Affairs,* Vol. VI, 130–144.

Latrobe, Charles Joseph. *The Rambler in North America* (2nd ed.) 2 vols. London, R. B. Seeley and W. Burnside, 1836.

"Letters Concerning the Presbyterian Mission in the Pawnee Country, near Bellevue, Neb., 1831–1849," *Kansas Historical Society*

Collections, Vol. XIV (1915–16), 570–784. (Letters and Journals of John Dunbar, Samuel Allis, and others.)

Lutz, J. J. "The Methodist Missions among the Indian Tribes in Kansas," *Kansas Historical Society Collections,* Vol. IX (1905–1906), 160–235.

McCoy, Isaac. *The Annual Register of Indian Affairs within the Indian (or Western) Territory, No. 1.* Shawanoe Mission, J. Meeker, 1835.

———. *History of Baptist Indian Missions: Embracing Remarks on the Former and Present Condition of the Aboriginal Tribes; Their Settlement within the Indian Territory, and Their Future Prospects.* Washington, D. C., W. M. Morrison; and New York, H. and S. Raynor, 1840.

McDermott, John Francis. *A Glossary of Mississippi Valley French* (Washington University Studies, New Series, Language and Literature, *No. 12*). St. Louis, 1941.

———. (ed.). *Tixier's Travels on the Osage Prairies* (translated by Albert J. Salvan). Norman, University of Oklahoma Press, 1940.

———. (ed.). *The Western Journals of Washington Irving.* Norman, University of Oklahoma Press, 1944.

McKenney, Thomas L., and James Hall. *The Indian Tribes of North America* (ed. by Frederick Webb Hodge). 3 vols. Edinburgh, John Grant, 1933.

Maximilian, Prince of Wied. *Travels in the Interior of North America.* (Vols. XXII–XXV in Reuben Gold Thwaites [ed.], *Early Western Travels, 1748–1846 [q.v.]*).

Merrill, Moses. "Extracts from the Diary of Rev. Moses Merrill, a Missionary to the Otoe Indians from 1832 to 1840," *Nebraska Historical Society Transactions,* Vol. IV (1892), 160–91.

Missouri Republican (St. Louis), 1833.

Mooney, James. *The Ghost-Dance Religion* (Bureau of American Ethnology *14th Annual Report* [1892–93]). Washington, D. C., 1896.

Morehouse, George P. "History of the Kansa or Kaw Indians," *Kansas Historical Society Collections,* Vol. X (1907–1908), 327–68.

Morse, Jedidiah. *A Report to the Secretary of War . . . on Indian Affairs, Comprising a Narrative of a Tour Performed in the Summer of 1820.* New Haven, 1822.

Murray, Charles Augustus. *Travels in North America During the Years 1834, 1835, & 1836. Including a Summer Residence with* the Pawnee Tribe of Indians in the Remote Prairies of the Missouri . . . (2nd ed.). 2 vols. London, R. Bentley, 1841.

Paul Wilhelm, Duke of Württemberg. *First Journey to North America in the Years 1822 to 1824* (translated by William G. Bek), *South Dakota Historical Collections,* Vol. XIX (1938), 7–462.

Pelzer, Louis. *Henry Dodge.* Iowa City, State Historical Society of Iowa, 1911.

———. *Marches of the Dragoons in the Mississippi Valley . . . between the Years 1833 and 1850.* Iowa City, State Historical Society of Iowa, 1917.

Perrine, Fred S. "Military Escorts on the Santa Fé Trail," *New Mexico Historical Review,* Vol. II (1927), 175–93, 269–304; Vol. III (1928), 265–300.

Spencer, Joab. "The Shawnee Indians: Their Customs, Traditions and Folk-Lore," *Kansas Historical Society Collections,* Vol. X (1907–1908), 382–96.

Stanley, John Mix. *Portraits of North American Indians Painted by John Mix Stanley. Deposited with the Smithsonian Institution.* Washington, D. C., Smithsonian Institution, 1852. (Bound in *Smithsonian Miscellaneous Collections,* Vol. II.)

Stauf, Margaret. "John Dougherty, Indian Agent," *Mid-America,* Vol. XVI (January, 1934), 135–46.

Thwaites, Reuben Gold. *How George Rogers Clark Won the Northwest and Other Essays in Western History.* Chicago, McClurg, 1903.

———. (ed.). *Early Western Travels, 1748–1846.* 32 vols. Cleveland, Arthur H. Clark Co., 1904–1907.

"United States Indian Agencies Affecting Kansas," *Kansas Historical Society Collections,* Vol. XVI (1923–25), 722–45.

Wedel, Waldo Rudolph. *An Introduction to Pawnee Archaeology* (Bureau of American Ethnology *Bulletin 112*). Washington, D. C., 1936.

———. "The Kansa Indians," *Kansas Academy of Science Transactions,* Vol. XLIX (June, 1946), 1–35.

Wetmore, Alphonso. *Gazetteer of the State of Missouri [with] an Appendix Containing Frontier Sketches, and Illustrations of Indian Character.* St. Louis, C. Keemle, 1837.

Wharton, Clifton. "Journal of the Expedition of Major Clifton Wharton in 1844," *Kansas Historical Society Collections,* Vol. XVI (1923–25), 272–305.

Williams, Stanley T. *The Life of Washington Irving.* 2 vols. New York, Oxford University Press, 1935.

———, and Nelson F. Adkins. "John Treat Irving," *Dictionary of American Biography* (*q.v.*), IX, 503.

———, and Barbara D. Simison (eds.). *Washington Irving on the Prairie; or, a Narrative of a Tour of the Southwest in the Year 1832, by Henry Leavitt Ellsworth.* New York, American Book Company, 1937.

Index

Indian Sketches

has been composed in Linotype Baskerville, a faithful copy of a type produced in the mid-eighteenth century by John Baskerville of Birmingham, England. Daniel Berkeley Updike says of him that "he made not merely his own types (cut for him by a certain John Handy), but also his ink, and if he did not make his own paper, he superintended its manufacture." In addition to the care devoted to these details of printing, Baskerville also inserted each wet sheet, as it came from the press, between hot copper plates. This endowed the printed sheets with what his contemporaries considered a high gloss. No such technique has been used in the production of this book, but the selection of a paper with a hard, smooth surface suggests the result Baskerville achieved. The illustrations have been printed separately by offset lithography on the same stock, and have been made (so far as possible) directly from the original sources.

UNIVERSITY OF OKLAHOMA PRESS
Norman